IAN HOGG

GREAT LAND BATTLES
OF WORLD WAR II

Doubleday & Company, Inc.

Garden City, New York
1987

Great Land Battles of World War II was edited, designed
and produced by Grub Street, London

Line illustrations by Mark Stiling
Map artwork by Graeme Andrew
All photographs were supplied by Ian Hogg and
The Research House

Library of Congress Cataloging in Publication Data

Hogg, Ian V., 1926 —
    Great land battles of World War II
    Includes Index
    1. World War, 1939-1945—Campaigns
    2. Battles
    I. Title
    D 743. H64   1987   940.54'1   86-32973

    ISBN 0-385-24240-9

Printed in Great Britain by
Blantyre Printing & Binding Ltd.,
London and Glasgow.

CONTENTS

INTRODUCTION
6

INTRODUCTION

No two battles are ever alike, even if fought over the same ground, as studies of the various wars across the Low Countries will show. But there are significant differences between *types* of battle, and in this book are ten examples of different kinds of battle to show the variety of problems, solutions and lessons to be learned. Each one chosen is great in its own way. The choice has been fairly arbitrary, however; there are, for example, no Russian battles mentioned, simply because it was possible to find the ten desired categories outside Russia where information is much easier to come by. Another hand could have chosen ten different battles to illustrate the same ten types, and doubtless those who fought on their feet or in tanks in the Reichswald may consider it strange to see it classified as an 'artillery' battle, just as those in the armor and artillery in Normandy might quibble at calling that an 'infantry' battle. But, as I have pointed out elsewhere, all battles are fought by combinations of arms, and it is almost impossible to find a modern battle in which armor, artillery and infantry are not all engaged. The classification, therefore, has been focussed on the principal protagonist, having regard to the particular tactical situation.

Inevitably, for reasons of space, the narrative of the battles has had to be condensed; all are, though, amply covered in more specialized books, and if these brief descriptions arouse the reader's interest, then reference to more detailed volumes will give all the information desired. My object has been to introduce the novice or enthusiast to the problems which stem from specific types of warfare and to describe how these particular situations have been dealt with in the course of a major war.

THE CULMINATING MOMENT: ALTHOUGH PATTON WAS FIRST OVER THE RHINE, IT FELL TO MONTGOMERY TO BE THE FIRST TO ACCEPT THE GERMAN SURRENDER FROM THE DELEGATION LED BY ADMIRAL FRIEDEBURG. THE TIME WAS 6.30 PM, MAY 4, 1945 AND THE SCENE IS CAPTURED HERE BY TERENCE CUNEO, OBE.

NOTE ON WEAPON MEASUREMENTS:

Throughout this book weapons have been referred to in the terminology current at the time. For those unfamiliar with it, conversions into metric caliber equivalents are shown below:

2-pounder gun	40mm
3.7in howitzer/gun	94mm
25-pounder gun	87mm
4.5in gun	114mm
5.5in gun	140mm
7.2in howitzer	183mm
8in howitzer/gun	203mm

Other useful conversions for this book are:

1 lb	0.453 kg		
1 gall	4 quarts	3.785 liters	
1 mile	5280 ft	1760 yards	1.609 km
1 yard	3 ft	0.91 meters	
1 ft	12 in	0.304 m	30.48 cm
1 in	2.54 cm	25.4 mm	
1 sq yard	1296 sq in	9 sq ft	0.836 sq m

THE TAKING OF CRETE

AIRBORNE ASSAULT
MAY 1941

Overleaf

The morning landing of the 3rd German Parachute Battalion which fell
into an area held by the 5th New Zealand Brigade and resulted in the German force being decimated.
(*Parachute Invasion of Crete* by T Cuneo, OBE)

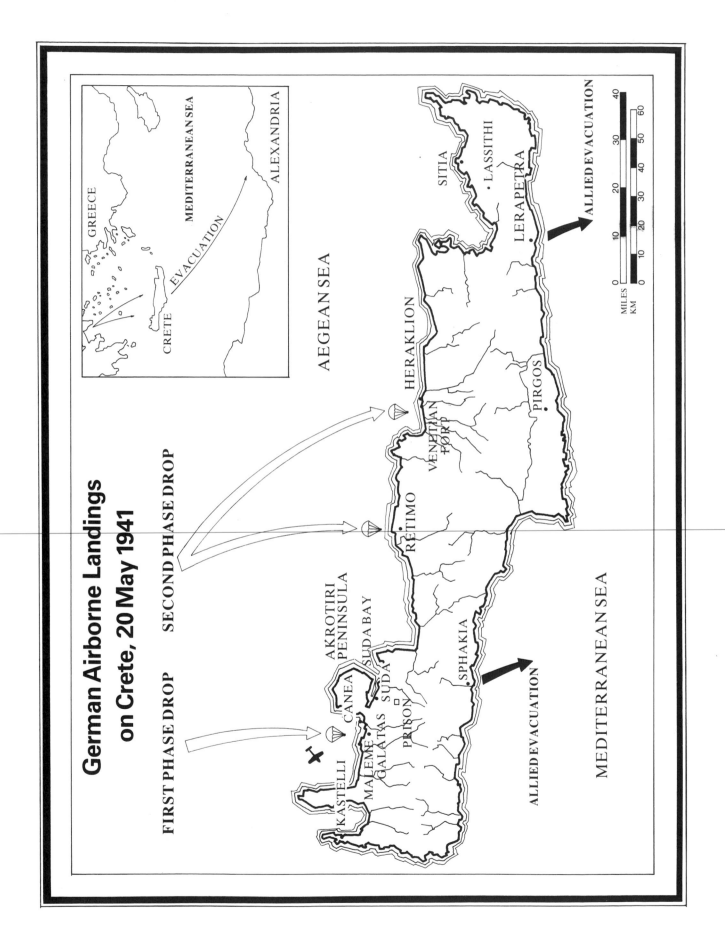

German Airborne Landings on Crete, 20 May 1941

FIRST PHASE DROP SECOND PHASE DROP

GREECE

MEDITERRANEAN SEA

EVACUATION

ALEXANDRIA

CRETE

AEGEAN SEA

ALLIED EVACUATION

SITIA

LASSITHI

LERAPETRA

HERAKLION

VENETIAN PORT

PIRGOS

RETIMO

AKROTIRI PENINSULA

SUDA BAY

CANEA

SUDA

GALATAS

PRISON

KASTELLI

MALEME

SPHAKIA

ALLIED EVACUATION

MEDITERRANEAN SEA

MILES
KM

The utility of airborne forces is, and has always been, open to debate. On the face of it — and this was the general wartime view — the attraction of being able to throw a powerful force down at any point on or behind the enemy's front is considerable. But when the proposition is examined in greater detail there are a number of 'ifs' and 'buts' which make an unwelcome appearance, and after these are all taken into account the employment of airborne forces suddenly becomes a very restricted option. Among the drawbacks are firstly the vulnerability of the fly-in, even with air superiority; the vulnerability of the troops during the first few minutes of landing, before they have rallied and organized; the total reliance upon expert navigation by the air forces, something which is frequently absent; the light scale of weapons which must be carried by an airborne force in order to be airborne, which makes it vulnerable to heavier weapons in the hands of the enemy; and the difficulty of resupplying a force by air in combat conditions.

On the other hand, provided the time and place are chosen well, then an airborne attack can give an unsuspecting enemy a terrible shock, and if the airborne force can establish an initial superiority and claim the initiative against a weak enemy, then they have every chance of gaining whatever their objective may be — provided always that that objective is something well-defined and not too ambitious. Moreover any airborne operation must be based upon the assumption that ground forces will link up with the airborne troops within some specified time which is well within the self-supporting capability of the airborne force.

If, therefore, the pros are carefully organized and the cons are carefully assessed, then there is a fair chance of airborne success. But it is notable that few western nations place much reliance upon airborne forces today for anything other than raiding or rapid intervention forces. Except for Soviet Russia, who appear to be some thirty years behind the rest of the world in military thinking, the use of large airborne forces to intervene on the conventional battlefield is no longer thought to be worthwhile. The reason for this opinion is mainly the excessive vulnerability of a major air fleet in the face of modern missile systems. There are other objections, most of which can be traced back to lessons learned from wartime airborne operations. And the first of these was Operation Merkur, the German attack on the Mediterranean Island of Crete in 1941.

The terrain

The island of Crete is about 160 miles long and about 36 miles wide. At first sight it appears to be a single mountain spine, but this is in fact a combination of four mountain ranges which come together in the central mass of Mount Ida. The southwestern portion of the island is dominated by the Sphakia (or White) Mountains, which fall sheer to the sea in parts and make the whole area difficult of access. Rain from this range irrigates a northern coastal strip surrounding Suda Bay and supporting the town of Canea. There is then (moving eastward) a depression, after which the ground rises to the Mount Ida massif. After this there is another depression, and a northern strip which includes Heraklion, the principal town, after which the mountains rise again to the summit of Mount Dhikti.

The poor harbors (at least for small craft) and difficulty of access have made Crete a relatively isolated spot through most of its history, and in 1941 it was still well behind the rest of the Mediterranean in facilities. Communications were restricted to a few roads, only suitable for single-file traffic, with bridges unsafe for anything heavier than six or seven tons. There were three small narrow-gauge railways which ran in directions which made them of little military use, there was no major airport, and telephone and telegraph communications were minimal.

The background

Crete has always had strategic significance in the Mediterranean, which was greatly enhanced by the introduction of aircraft into war. An airfield on Crete could be used to raid deep into the Balkans and southern Europe and as a base for tactical air support of operations in Greece and the Balkans. In other hands it could similarly be used to raid into Egypt and Palestine and to support operations in North Africa. Moreover, in Suda Bay there was a harbor with great potential as a naval base. Obviously, whoever controlled Crete had considerable advantage.

Although the British were well aware of Crete's significance, they could not take advantage of it until Greece entered the war in October 1940 being invaded by Italy. Plans had been prepared by the Royal Navy for a Base Defence Organisation to move into Crete as soon as this became feasible, but when the time actually arrived there was such a shortage of troops and equipment due to other commitments in the Middle East that little more than a battalion of infantry, two batteries of anti-aircraft guns and some auxiliary forces could be spared to garrison the island. Their task was ill-defined, but principally they were there to forestall any Italian ideas of occupying the island.

The commander of this force set about doing the best he could to defend Suda Bay; at the same time a local force was raised and ten thousand rifles were sent to the island to arm them. Plans were made in Egypt to reinforce the island with an infantry division and extra heavy and light anti-aircraft guns, and a small number of guns were actually sent, bringing the total air defense strength up to 16 3.7in guns and 24 light 40mm guns, supported by one radar set and 24 searchlights. Work also began on laying out and grading five airstrips at various points on the island, but this work was held up by disagreement among the RAF as to the best locations and also because there was only one engineer on the island who had to allocate his time between airfields and other works.

This strength was somewhat improved when British troops were sent to Greece, when a Marine Naval Base Defence Organisation was sent to the island to organize the protection of a naval base which had been developing in Suda Bay. An anti-submarine boom had been constructed but no other facilities yet existed.

All this was suddenly upset by the failure of the campaign in Greece and the subsequent evacuation of Allied troops. The evacuation began on 25 April 1941 and lasted until the 29th; altogether about 25,000 men, mainly from the 6th Australian and 2nd New Zealand Divisions, disembarked at Suda Bay, most of them with nothing more than the clothes they stood up in and their personal weapons.

By now it seemed fairly certain that Crete would be invaded by air or sea; there appears to have been some debate over whether or not to defend the island, but the basic fact was that there were troops there, that there was little or no facility to evacuate them, and therefore they had little choice but to stay where they were and fight. General Wavell, commanding in the Middle East, flew to Crete on 30 April to review the situation there and placed General Freyberg, the New Zealand commander in charge of the defense.

Freyberg, a man of energy and ability, immediately set about extracting whatever he could from the Middle East Command in order to improve his defenses. By this time further evacuation had given him a total of some 30,000 Commonwealth troops, 11,000 Greek troops and 15,000 Italian prisoners-of-war. With a further 400,000 civilians on the island, Freyberg calculated that he required something in the order of 25,000 tons of supplies every month. This in the face of depleted shipping, poor port facilities and the threat of air raids.

A DFS-230 GLIDER NEAR MALEME AIRFIELD, WITH SOME OF ITS OCCUPANTS. THE DFS-230 CARRIED ONLY EIGHT AIRBORNE SOLDIERS AND THEIR EQUIPMENT, PLUS TWO PILOTS, AND COULD NOT CARRY VERY MUCH EXTRA EQUIPMENT SINCE ITS MAXIMUM PAYLOAD WAS ONLY 1000KG.

On the credit side, some of the evacuation troops had managed to bring heavy equipment; he now had a troop of light field artillery, plus about 100 other guns in various degrees of repair from which about 50 serviceable field pieces could be assembled. Sufficient machine guns and mortars arrived to equip all the troops, and an additional battalion of infantry was sent from Egypt. Remarkably, Wavell even managed to find some tanks; 16 light Vickers tanks and six Matilda infantry tanks were shipped to the island, though on arrival they were found to be battered relics of the Western Desert and barely able to move.

There was a handful of RAF fighters on the island; but Freyberg, a realist, saw that they were insufficient to have any useful effect and he ordered them flown off to Egypt on 19 May. He then requested permission to spoil the airfields so as to make them unfit for landings, but the RAF, convinced that they would eventually return in strength, were able to prevent this.

The plan

The planning, in this case, was largely on the German side, since the garrison on Crete, like any victims of air attack, could do little other than stay flexible and prepare to react to the situation. The German plan aimed at gaining command of all the island's strategic points within the first 24 hours, but it was risky insofar as there could be no guarantee that the forces dropped at individual points would, in fact, land together; they might well be scattered and defeated piecemeal.

The German forces preparing for the invasion consisted of Fliegerkorps VIII and XI, with 22,750 men, 500 transport aircraft, 75 gliders, 280 bombers, 180 fighters and 40 reconnaissance aircraft. The men were to be landed in various ways; 10,000 would parachute in, 750 would be in gliders bringing heavy equipment and supplies, 5000 mountain infantry would be flown into the Maleme airfield on transport aircraft and a further 7000 troops of the 5th Mountain Division would be shipped across to Heraklion by sea once the initial landings had been made. The air assault would be in two waves; at dawn Group West would attack Maleme and Group Centre would attack Canea. In the afternoon the second and smaller wave would attack Retimo and Heraklion. These various groups, landing from ten to eighty miles apart, were to link up as soon as possible. On the next day the mountain infantry would be air-lifted in to airstrips captured by the initial assault, while the remainder of the mountain division would be shipped across to Heraklion, Suda Bay and any other available landing place.

The battle begins

In the early hours of 20 May the Assault Regiment Meindl (named, like most German *ad hoc* groupings, after its commander) loaded into its aircraft at Tanagra Airfield in Greece. Three detachments, about 500 men, flew in gliders; one was to land south of the Tavronitis bridge and capture it. Another detachment was to land

ORDER OF BATTLE

ALLIED

It must be borne in mind that much of the Allied strength on Crete was made up of troops who had escaped from Greece, and therefore most of the formations were incomplete. It is for this reason that the word 'elements' is so frequently used. Many units nominally a battalion, were actually in much lesser strength. Many corps troops were actually fighting as infantry.

Elements 2nd NZ Div (Commander: Gen Freyberg VC)

4th NZ Bde Gp
    18th, 19th NZ Inf Bns

5th NZ Bde Gp
    21st, 22nd, 23rd, 28th NZ Inf Bns

10th NZ Bde Gp
    20th NZ Inf Bn

Elements NZ Divisional Cavalry (on foot)

5th NZ Fd Regt (9 × 75mm)

Elements 6th Australian Div

19th Aust Bde
    2nd/1st, 4th, 7th, 8th, 11th Inf Bns
    2nd/1st Machine Gun Company
    7th Medium Artillery Regt (as infantry)

14th Inf Bde

2nd Bn Leicester Regt
1st Bn Argyll & Sutherland Highlanders
2nd Black Watch
2nd York & Lancs

15th Coast Regiment RA

52nd Light AA Regt

2nd Heavy AA Regt Royal Marines

234th Med Regt RA (13 Italian field guns)

1st Bn Rangers (King's Royal Rifle Corps)

1st Bn Welsh Regt (Force Reserve)

Northumberland Hussars (as infantry)

C sqn 3rd Hussars (16 Lt tanks)

B sqn 7th RTR (8 Med tanks)

106th Battery Royal Horse Artillery (as infantry)

2/2nd Royal Australian Artillery (as infantry)

2/3rd Royal Australian Artillery (partly as infantry)

Mobile Naval Base Defence Organisation (Royal Marines)

Elements Greek Army (6000 all ranks)
    1st Inf Regt
    6th Inf Regt
    8th Inf Regt

ALLIED cas: 1742 KIA; 1737 WIA; 11,835 POW; 15,000 evacuated to Egypt

AXIS

XI Fliegerkorps (Commander: Gen Student)

Luftland Sturmregiment (Commander: Gen Major Meindl)
7 Flieger Division (Commander: Lt-Gen Sussmann)

5 Gebirgs Division (Commander: Maj-Gen Ringel)

141 Geb Jag regt of 6 Geb Div

Total 25,000 all ranks

2 Bn Pz Rgt 31 as heavy support after landing

VIII Fliegerkorps (Commander: Gen von Richthofen)

Stuk Geschw 2 (150 Ju87 Stuka)
Kampfgeschwader 2 (120 Do17)
11 Gp of K Geschw 26 (40 Helll)
Jagdgeschw 27 (90 Me109)
Zerstorergeschw 26 (45 Me110)
Zerstorergeschw 27 (45 Me110)
2 Staffel, Fernaufklarungsgruppe 11 (Ju88 Recon)

AXIS cas: 1990 KIA; 1955 MIA

At 7.15 am on 20 May, 1941 the first gliders landed south and west of the Maleme airfield, followed almost immediately by gliders landing on the dry river-bed and on Hill 107. The airfield landing went relatively smoothly, and the anti-aircraft position was quickly over-run, but the third company, aiming to take the Tavronitis Bridge, landed in the middle of an area occupied by New Zealand troops who reacted quickly and inflicted heavy casualties on the invaders. Nevertheless, by skilled piloting the gliders landed within yards of the bridge and in spite of the hot reception the assault troops were able to secure the bridge and hold it.

While this was in progress, the parachute landings began. The 3rd Battalion, intending to drop around Maleme airfield, was dispersed by a strong wind and while several men were blown out to sea and drowned, the remainder landed among the 5th New Zealand Brigade, and, again, were severely mauled. Within 45 minutes the battalion commander and 400 out of the 600 men who had landed were dead and the battalion was no longer an effective fighting force, most of the paratroops being killed as they searched for their weapons containers. At that time it was standard German practice for paratroops to jump armed only with a pistol and a few hand grenades, and they relied upon being able to get to their containers in order to secure rifles and machine guns. Even so, it has been argued that the remnants of 3rd Battalion won the battle for Crete, as will be seen.

The 4th Battalion of the parachute force dropped west of Tavronitis; one company dropped a distance away from the rest of the battalion and found itself fighting desperately against a group of armed civilians, but soon had the situation under control. The 2nd Battalion landed safely east of Spilia, except for one platoon which, dropped too far west, landed among Greek troops and armed civilian bands who rapidly

at the river mouth, destroy the air defense guns located there, and so ease the way for subsequent landings by transport aircraft. The third detachment was to land on the slopes of Hill 107, commanding the Maleme airfield, and capture the field. The remainder of the assault force, about 2000 men, were to parachute down well clear of the defenses, form up and then move rapidly in support of the glider-borne detachments.

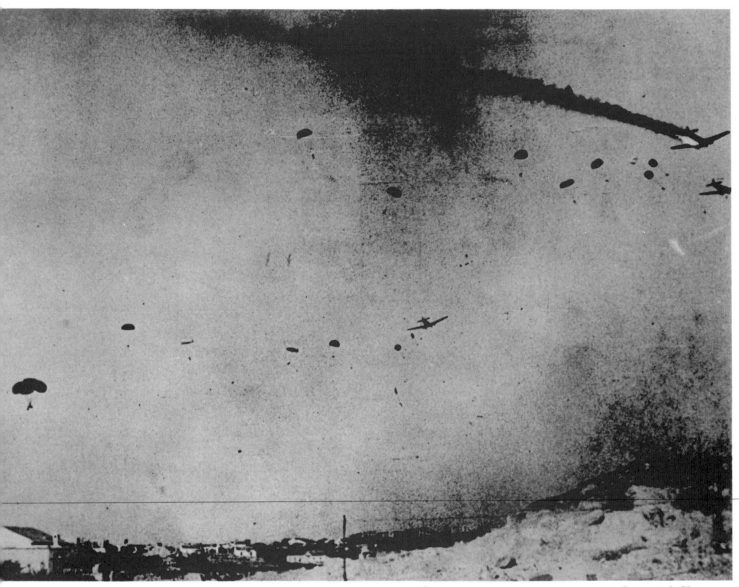

GERMAN PARATROOPERS DROPPING FROM JUNKERS JU52 TRANSPORTS. ONE JU52 HAS BEEN HIT BY ANTI-AIRCRAFT FIRE AND IS BURNING, ONE OF THE 170 LOST IN THE CRETE ACTION. THE JU52 COULD CARRY 13 PARACHUTE TROOPS WITH THEIR EQUIPMENT OR 5000KG OF CARGO, AND WERE ROBUST AND RELIABLE. THEY ALSO PERFORMED AS GLIDER TUGS, TOWING THE DFS-230 AT ABOUT 160KM/HR.

destroyed them; only 13 survivors were left, and they surrendered.

The attack on Canea was undertaken by Kampfgruppe Altmann, two companies of the 'Luftlande Sturmregiment' landing by glider, while Parachute Regiment 3 dropped southwest of the town. The 15 gliders of 2 company landed northwest of the town, on the Akotiri Peninsula, but they found that several of their objectives — anti-aircraft batteries — were dummies and the area was strongly held by the Northumberland Hussars. Of the 136 men who disembarked from the gliders, 108 became casualties within a very short time.

The 1st Company, in 9 gliders, landed southeast of Canea and captured their objectives — another anti-aircraft battery — but were then unable to link up with 2 Company due to the latter's destruction, and after spiking the captured guns the paratroops withdrew southwards in an attempt to link up with other parties which had dropped in that direction.

Parachute Regiment 3 had a bad drop, being widely dispersed, and they fell into an area held by 10 NZ Brigade reinforced by three Greek battalions, with the result that they met a very fierce reception. One company, carrying the heavy mortars, actually fell into a reservoir; several men were drowned and only a portion of their equipment could be salvaged from the water. Nevertheless, two battalions managed to capture the village of Agia and set up their regimental command post. The divisional staff had landed nearby in four gliders, but the divisional commander had been killed when his towrope had broken during the flight and the glider had crashed on the island of Aegina, not far from Athens. The staff linked up with the regimental headquarters, but beyond that they could achieve very little, being pinned to the village by the New Zealanders.

By midday things looked black for the Germans; none of their objectives, other than the Tavronitis Bridge, had been taken, casualties had been severe, many commanders were dead, and the various pockets of troops were pinned firmly in place with little prospect of breaking out. None of this, though, was known back at General Student's headquarters in Greece where the second wave was being readied for its flight. Due to the need to refuel all the aircraft by hand, their takeoff was delayed; this, in turn, led to dislocation between the planned air drops and their air support, with bombers and fighters making their preliminary attacks well before the second wave appeared. This alerted the Allied troops on the island to expect more paratroop attacks. Meanwhile the activity on the Greek airfields raised clouds of dust so that takeoffs had to be performed in small groups, which meant that the paratroops were going to be delivered to their objectives in small and scattered packets. In spite of the delays, though, the first of the second wave began taking off at about 1315hrs and by 1500hrs they were over their objectives in Crete.

Parachute Regiment 2, less its 2nd Battalion, dropped into an area held by the 19th Australian Brigade supported by four battalions of Greek Army, with the result that they were instantly pinned to their dropping zone with little chance to get at their weapons containers. Having landed close to a small hill to the east of the airfield, 1 Battalion managed to collect on the hill, dig in and hold on. The 3rd Battalion dropped east of Retimo and they too managed to collect themselves, secure a defensive position and dig in. Between them the regimental staff had dropped, with a company of infantry, and once again had managed to dig in; so that the attack on Retimo had now devolved into a matter of three independent small parties pinned down and waiting for either relief or obliteration.

Parachute Regiment 1, together with the 2nd Battalion of Parachute Regiment 2, dropped at Heraklion, intending to capture the town and airfield before nightfall. The various small parties forming the invasion force dropped in various localities around Heraklion, and found themselves immediately under fire from the 14th British Infantry Brigade which was defending the town, and at least one company was almost entirely killed.

By the evening of the first day, therefore, the situation was simply that the parachute troops were hanging on by the skin of their teeth, scattered all around their objectives, having suffered severe casualties — 1800 of the 3000 men dropped were dead — and they were in no shape to take very much offensive action towards their objectives. By this time General Student, at his HQ in Greece, was beginning to piece together various reports which were coming back by radio, and putting the tactical picture together. None of it was very encouraging, but it appeared that Maleme was the key point and, if this could be reinforced, it promised to allow some degree of exploitation. The 5th Mountain Division, which had originally been warned for action around Heraklion in support of Parachute Regiment 1, was now given fresh orders; it would land at Maleme, reinforce the paratroops there, and begin moving eastward with the object of eventually making contact with the force holding out around Heraklion.

The turning point

The night of 20/21 May was, in most respects, the time when Crete was lost, even though the battle went on for some days. Had Freyberg, who had an overwhelming superiority in men, artillery and armor, thrown in counter-attacks during the night against the exhausted paratroops, he could probably have wiped them all out or, at worst, so disrupted them that they would have been unable to act cohesively on the following day. Moreover, had he appreciated the significance of the German force around Maleme and reinforced the airfield, much of the subsequent course of the battle would have been impossible. Freyberg, however, seems to have taken a most pessimistic view of the situation; in a message to Wavell's HQ that night he reported that:

> "We have been hard pressed . . . fighting has been heavy and we have killed large numbers of Germans . . . the margin by which we hold them is a bare one. . . ."

A JUNKERS JU52 COMING IN TO LAND AT MALEME AIRFIELD AFTER ITS CAPTURE. ONE OF THE IMMORTAL DESIGNS, AND THE WORKHORSE OF THE LUFTWAFFE, THIS MACHINE WAS SEEN IN EVERY THEATER OF OPERATIONS AND WAS STILL IN USE FOR TRAINING PARACHUTE TROOPS IN THE SPANISH ARMY AS LATE AS THE 1960s.

GERMAN PARATROOPS IN CRETE

The German parachute force which landed in Crete surprised the world by the amount of specialized equipment which had been provided for its role. Everything had to be carried in the Junkers Ju52 three-motored transport, which could lift about 5.3 tonnes of payload, or in gliders. The recoilless guns were but one surprise; others included the SdKfz 2 Kleine Kettenrad — the half-tracked motor-cycle. This luxurious machine was based on the front half of a standard BMW motor-cycle, with a more powerful engine and shaft drive to the half-track suspension. Three or four men could be carried, and it could tow small trailers or, more particularly in Crete, the recoilless 75mm Light Gun, together with some ammunition and a couple of gunners.

German Paratroops differed from those of other countries in that they carried nothing more than a pistol or submachine gun when they jumped; all other armament either came by transport aircraft or was dropped in containers at the same time as the men. Hence, once on the ground the paratrooper's first task was to locate his weapon container and thus reach his rifle, machine gun, mortar or other equipment. If they were prevented from reaching all their containers, as often happened in Crete, they were fighting at a severe disadvantage, relying purely on their light weapons.

Other special equipment first seen with paratroops included shaped-charge demolition equipment (first used to silence the fortress of Eben Emael in Belgium in 1940) and a modification to the standard signal pistol to permit firing explosive grenades. With the cessation of the airborne role, however, all this equipment became standard for the German Army as a whole.

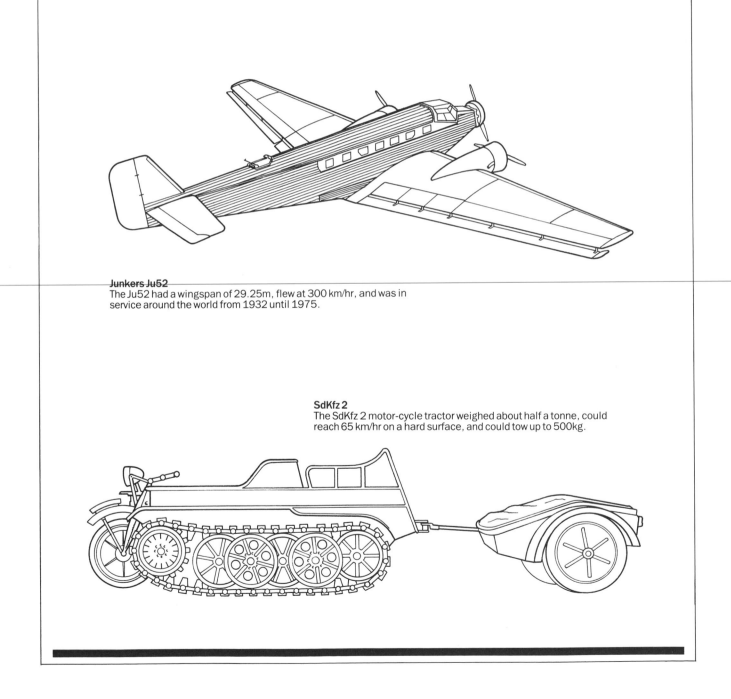

Junkers Ju52
The Ju52 had a wingspan of 29.25m, flew at 300 km/hr, and was in service around the world from 1932 until 1975.

SdKfz 2
The SdKfz 2 motor-cycle tractor weighed about half a tonne, could reach 65 km/hr on a hard surface, and could tow up to 500kg.

This lost opportunity was compounded early next morning when the commander of the 22nd NZ Battalion, mistakenly thinking his forward companies had been overrun by a determined German push against Hill 107, gave orders to pull back. In the confusion of an attempted disengagement and withdrawal, the New Zealanders were then genuinely overrun, and the hill was rapidly in German hands. This gave them command over the airfield, and with an additional 550 paratroops dropped shortly after this the Germans suddenly found themselves on a winning streak. Aided by the new arrivals the airfield was over-run and early in the afternoon a solitary Ju52 transport made a successful landing, even though much of the field was under machine gun fire from Allied troops. The pilot taxied to the far end of the field where he was screened from British fire, unloaded ammunition, took some wounded aboard, and then turned round and made a successful take-off. He immediately reported his success and the fact that the western end of the field lay in ground dead to defensive fire, and at about 1600 the first of a string of transports carrying the mountain troops made its landing.

The field was still under artillery fire, and it was only a small field; this meant that many of the transports soon became wrecks, either from shell fire or by simple collisions, but most of the troops got out safely, the wrecks were manhandled clear of the runway and the reinforcements kept on coming in. Within two hours the best part of 1000 troops were on the ground and dispersing ready for action. Their greatest fear was a concerted counterattack, but this failed to materialize; the New Zealanders intended to make one, but found only two companies available and by the time it began, four hours late, the Germans were in too great a strength to be pushed out. Maleme was now securely in German hands and they were not going to be dislodged.

The troops surrounding Heraklion were still in a difficult position, and in spite of attempting a number of attacks during the course of the day they made relatively small progress until a stroke of luck fell their way. Regiment 1 had consolidated their position overnight and during the morning managed to fight slowly into the outskirts of Heraklion. There they soon became bogged down in house-to-house fighting and their ammunition was running short. Then the Greek commander of the town suddenly appeared and offered to surrender the town. The German commander rapidly dictated terms, to which the Greek equally rapidly agreed, and the surrender was officially confirmed. Unfortunately, the British commander knew nothing of this, counterattacked fiercely then called upon the German to surrender, to which the reply was that "The German Army has been ordered to take the island. It will carry out this order."

While the airborne element had been making their bid, the seaborne reinforcements had begun their journey. Sixty-three fishing vessels had been requisitioned, and a first group of 25 were to lift some 2250 troops of the 5th Mountain Division to Maleme, to arrive on the evening of 21 May. These would be followed by a second group of 38 vessels carrying a further 4000 men to Heraklion.

The first group left the harbor of Piraeus on 19 May, as planned, and by the evening of 20 May had reached the island of Milos and anchored for the night. It set sail again the next morning, and at the same time the second group left Piraeus, now with its orders changed and heading for Maleme. At about 2300, as it rounded Cape Spatha and came in sight of Maleme, the first flotilla was surprised by a British naval force of three cruisers and four destroyers. In spite of valiant efforts by an Italian torpedo-boat which was escorting the German flotilla, the powerful British force hunted down and sank almost every one of the fishing vessels. The 3rd Battalion of the 100th Mountain Regiment was destroyed as a fighting force, over 500 officers and men being drowned, plus a large number of parachute troops who were travelling in the flotilla. About 250 survivors were picked from the sea by German and Italian aircraft and launches, while a handful of mountain troops managed to reach the shore, still carrying their weapons. (This episode still rankles with the German mountain troops; an officer who was on Crete and watched the destruction from a hilltop told the author in 1985 "This employment was irresponsible and will never be forgotten; a mountain infantry battalion was destroyed. . . .")

The second group left Milos on 22 May but soon came within range of another Royal Navy force, four cruisers and three destroyers. Before they could engage, however, German fighters and bombers swarmed over, and the British withdrew under the increasing weight of the German air attacks. But, mindful of the fate of the first group, the second was recalled to Piraeus rather than risk them at sea, and reinforcement by sea was forthwith abandoned until the outcome of the battle was more certain. Meanwhile a major air assault by the Luftwaffe was mounted against any Royal Navy ships which could be found, and very quickly the cruisers

THE JUNKERS JU87 'STUKA' DIVE-BOMBER; IT NORMALLY CARRIED A 500KG BOMB BETWEEN THE WHEELS, ON A RETRACTING LAUNCH FRAME, AND FOUR 50KG BOMBS ON WING RACKS. A TERRIFYING MACHINE TO GROUND TROOPS, IT WAS HIGHLY VULNERABLE TO AIR ATTACK BY FIGHTERS.

Gloucester and *Fiji* and the destroyers *Juno* and *Greyhound* had been sunk, and the cruisers *Naiad* and *Carlisle* and the battleships *Warspite* and *Valiant* severely damaged. It became obvious that the naval forces could no longer operate within flying range of the German airbases during daylight.

During the night of 21/22 May the New Zealanders decided on a counterattack to take Maleme airfield. Unless it was taken the landing of airborne reinforcements would quickly turn the balance in the German favor. The attack was to go in from the east, astride the coast road, but before this force got within striking distance of the airfield it found itself crossing rough ground which was infested with the remnants of the 3rd Parachute Battalion. These, it will be recalled, had landed on the morning of the 20th and had been severely dealt with. But the survivors had hidden in the rough ground and were obedient to the Eighth Imperative of the German Parachutist Code: "You must grasp the full intention of every operation, so that if your leader is killed you can fulfil it yourself." In this case they had simply held their ground, and now that the New Zealanders attempted to advance through this ground they began exacting a price for that passage. There was nothing for it except that the New Zealanders had to slow down and search out every one of these tiresome defenders. By the time dawn came, the New Zealanders were still far from their objective, and with the dawn came the Stukas and the fighter-bombers to drive the New Zealanders back into their original positions. The counter-attack against Maleme had failed, due entirely to the tenacity of the survivors of 3rd Parachute Battalion, and because of that the loss of Crete was now inevitable.

On 22 May the air transport of mountain troops to reinforce the island continued, even though Maleme airfield was still under artillery fire. The Mountain Division commander, Major General Ringer, also arrived and immediately assumed command of all the German troops in the Maleme area, dividing them into three 'Kampfgruppe'. KG Schaete was to defend the Maleme area from attacks while also expanding westward to capture Kastelli; KG Ramcke was to move north to the sea and then begin extending eastwards along the coast; and KG Utz was to move eastward across the mountains in the hope of outflanking the Allied positions.

These moves began at dawn on 23 May and were generally successful. KG Utz moved into the mountains and by afternoon had reached the village of Modi, where they were stopped by a position held by New Zealanders. KG Ramcke, in its advance towards Kastelli, came up against fierce, but uncoordinated, opposition from armed civilians, including women and children. By this time it was apparent to the Germans that whilst fighting Allied regular troops was hard, fighting the Cretans was considerably worse, since they had no qualms about mutilating any German dead or wounded who fell into their hands. Eyes were gouged

THREE PHOTOGRAPHS SHOWING STAGES IN THE SINKING OF THE CRUISER HMS *GLOUCESTER* ON 22 MAY. ATTACKED BY SUCCESSIVE FLIGHTS OF STUKA DIVE BOMBERS AND HIT THREE TIMES, *GLOUCESTER* WAS FIRST SET ON FIRE, HER GUNS PUT OUT OF ACTION, REDUCED TO 12 KNOTS AND FINALLY SENT TO THE BOTTOM WITH ALMOST ALL HER CREW.

out, sexual organs cut off, and other forms of torture were generously applied. Eventually the Germans announced that for every tortured German found, ten Cretans would be executed, but this appears to have had little effect.

After fierce fighting had swayed back and forth over the Modi position, the New Zealanders were forced to pull back as elements of the mountain division outflanked them and reached a position threatening Platanias. This necessitated the withdrawal of the covering artillery to a more secure position during the night, which meant that Maleme airfield was now no longer within range and the Germans could now fly troops in without fear of interruption.

The German edge

By the 24th the German forces had been reinforced and resupplied to the point where they could now begin to think of orthodox tactical moves, advances in strength supported by tactical air attacks from Stuka dive-bombers and with the aid of their own artillery. For, to the intense surprise of the Allies, the air landings had brought artillery in to the island. This was previously unheard of in 1941; artillery was cumbersome and was not considered a suitable armament for air-landed forces, but artillery the Germans now had. The answer to this puzzle was that the German forces were deploying the first recoilless guns which had been seen in the west.

The recoilless gun had first been developed during the First World War by an American naval officer, Commander Davis. His design was extremely basic; he reasoned that if two guns were placed back to back and fired simultaneously, then the recoil of one would cancel that of the other and the combination would remain still. He applied this reasoning in practice by making a gun with a single central chamber and two barrels facing in opposite directions. One barrel carried an explosive projectile, the other an equivalent weight of grease and lead shot. When the central cartridge was exploded the two projectiles were sent down their respective barrels at identical speeds, making the entire structure free from recoil. The explosive shell went to its target, while the wad of grease and shot simply disintegrated in the air once it had left its barrel. The Davis gun was purchased by the British and experiments were made in fitting it to aircraft as an anti-submarine weapon, but the war ended before the trials were completed, and in post-war years the idea was abandoned and forgotten.

The German Rheinmetall company continued to experiment with the Davis idea and eventually reduced it to a far simpler form. Their reasoning was that if two opposite and equal weights produced a recoilless effect, then if the 'countershot' was half the weight and ejected at twice the velocity, the result would still be no recoil. Carrying this to its utmost, they arrived at a design in which the shell was counterbalanced by a stream of gas moving at extremely high velocity through a nozzle in the gun breech. A similar device was developed by the

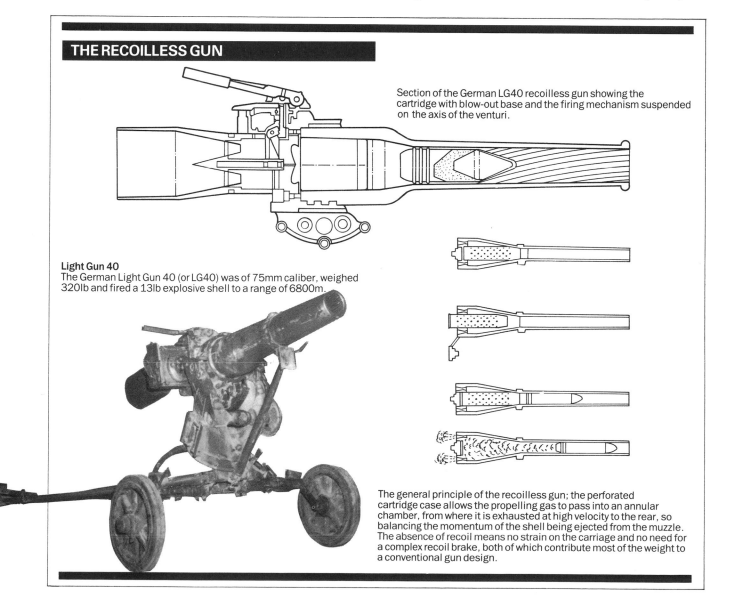

THE RECOILLESS GUN

Section of the German LG40 recoilless gun showing the cartridge with blow-out base and the firing mechanism suspended on the axis of the venturi.

Light Gun 40
The German Light Gun 40 (or LG40) was of 75mm caliber, weighed 320lb and fired a 13lb explosive shell to a range of 6800m.

The general principle of the recoilless gun; the perforated cartridge case allows the propelling gas to pass into an annular chamber, from where it is exhausted at high velocity to the rear, so balancing the momentum of the shell being ejected from the muzzle. The absence of recoil means no strain on the carriage and no need for a complex recoil brake, both of which contribute most of the weight to a conventional gun design.

Russians, probably from Rheinmetall's work, and used by them in Finland in 1939—40, but none of this was known outside Russia at that time, and as a result the German deployment of these remarkable recoilless guns on Crete came as a severe shock.

The 'Light Gun 40' (to use the official German terminology) was of 75mm caliber, weighed 320lbs, and fired a 13lb high explosive shell to a range of 6800m. The conventional 75mm gun of the German Army weighed 2470lbs and fired the same shell to a range of 9425m. There, in a nutshell, was the advantage of the recoilless gun; it allowed firepower almost the same as a conventional gun at one-eighth the weight. The only drawback was the loss of about 3km of range, but for the close-quarter action expected of airborne troops this was no great loss. Accompanied by a tracked motor-cycle which towed the gun and carried a few rounds of ammunition, and with the paratroop gun crew hanging on to the gun and tractor wherever they could, the airborne troops had a highly mobile and powerful artillery support which astonished the Allies when it went into action.

Throughout 24 May heavy air attacks were put in against Galatas and Canea, while a fresh battle group was formed and ordered to march 50 miles across the mountains in a flanking move which would cut the Canea-Retimo road east of Suda. Late in the day elements of the 100 Mountain Regiment made contact with Heidrich's paratroops who had been surrounded in their drop zone southeast of Canea since their arrival on the 20th.

The decisive battle for Crete

At noon on 25 May, the decisive battle for Crete began. This was a concerted German attack against the blocking position at Galatas. After bitter hand-to-hand fighting the New Zealanders were eventually ousted from the village and the Germans moved in, only to be thrown out by a determined New Zealand counter-attack led by two 3rd Hussars tanks. But the New Zealanders knew that they could not hold the village, since their numbers were now far too depleted, and during the night they withdrew, so that at dawn the German mountain troops were able to move back in, secure the village, and thus open the road for their advance on Canea.

On the evening of the 26th Freyberg signalled again to Wavell:

> ". . . in my opinion the limits of endurance have been reached by the troops under my command . . . from a military point of view our position here is hopeless. A small, ill-equipped and immobile force such as ours cannot stand up against the concentrated bombing that we have been faced with during the last seven days . . . from an administrative point of view the difficulties of extricating this force in full are insuperable. Provided a decision is reached at once, a certain proportion of the force might be embarked.''

That was the end for the Allied forces in Crete. On 27 May the decision to evacuate the island was taken,

and the defenders began to make preparations and to withdraw southward. The Germans, for their part, failed to realize what was happening and continued their attacks against Canea, throwing in two fresh mountain regiments which had arrived by air. To the southwest of Suda violent counterattacks by Australian and New Zealand troops occupied all the Germans' attention, and they failed to see this sudden activity for what it really was — a rearguard action intended to cover the withdrawal of the remainder of the Allied forces.

The Kampfgruppe Krakau, which had been making the forced march across the mountains in order to cut the Canea-Retimo road, approached the village of Stilos early in the morning of 28 May and came under sudden heavy fire from a blocking position occupied by the 23rd New Zealand battalion supported by artillery and tanks. While this battle raged, a small task force of German mountain troops outflanked the fight and captured intact the bridge on the main coast road south of Kalami. Having captured the bridge they rapidly removed the demolition charges and dug in, since the possession of this bridge was vital for the success of the Germans' eastward movement. Meanwhile recoilless guns and mortars had been brought forward to Stilos, and with the aid of their shaped-charge shells the tanks were rapidly put out of action, after which the German artillery turned on the Allied artillery and began a duel which ended with the German victorious. Once the support was silenced, the infantry had little choice of action, and, leaving rearguards to screen the movement, the Australians and New Zealanders disengaged and began retreating southwards.

Late on the 27th, Maj Gen Ringel had formed another Kampfgruppe, KG Wittmann, and sent it along the coast road with the object of relieving the hard-pressed paratroopers who had, all this time, been holding out in their scattered positions around Heraklion and Retimo. Once there, they would combine with the paratroops to capture Heraklion airfield, since German intelligence assumed that British aircraft were still using this field. The positions at Heraklion had been reinforced by small numbers of paratroops dropped on the 23rd and 24th, and several of these scattered units had managed to combine to set up defensive areas in which they sat tight and waited for relief.

KG Wittmann moved off early on 28 May, but were stopped some three miles beyond Suda by a party from 'Layforce', a force of British Commandos which had been landed at Suda during the nights of the 24th—26th. Together with two battalions of New Zealanders, Layforce held up the advance for several hours, but eventually they were beaten back, and KG Wittmann was able to make contact with KG Krakau, who were then fighting around Stilos. As the New Zealand and Australian troops withdrew, so the two Kampfgruppen were able to restart their eastward march. But within a few miles they were again embroiled in a bitter fight when they ran into the main body of Layforce

ADVERSARIES ON CRETE

General Sir Bernard Freyberg, VC (1889–1963)

Freyberg was born in England but raised in New Zealand, and as a young man had fought with Pancho Villa in the Mexican Civil War. He then joined the British Army and fought at Gallipoli and on the Western front, where he won the Victoria Cross and three DSOs and was wounded nine times. He was a Major General in 1939 and commanded the 2nd NZ Division. He took his troops to the Mediterranean theater, where they rapidly acquired a reputation as tough and skilful soldiers.

His force was sent to Greece, and then fell back to Crete where they were able to inflict severe casualties on the German parachute troops, to the extent that they were never used in the airborne role again. Returning to Libya, the division took part in almost all the operations in the Western Desert up to the capitulation in Tunisia. Though wounded in July 1942, Freyberg was back in action in time to lead 2 NZ Div at the Battle of El Alamein. They then went to Italy as part of the 8th Army, but were later detached and placed under command of the US 5th Army. Their principal action in Italy was the Battle of Cassino, at which Freyberg was the Corps Commander. In 1945 he occupied Trieste and took the surrender of the German garrison.

As might be gathered from the above record, Freyberg was a fighting soldier — Churchill compared him with a salamander since he 'thrived in the fire' — and although something of a martinet he was well-liked by his men since he was frequently to be seen in the front line and was always careful of their welfare.

General Kurt Student (1890–1978)

Student began his career as a soldier but during the First World War became a pilot, and when the Luftwaffe was formed was one of its first staff officers. He was selected by Goering to form and train the first experimental parachute infantry force and also supervised the development of specialized gliders and transport aircraft. Under his command the parachute arm performed well in the invasion of the Low Countries in 1940.

The success of the Crete operation was marred by the heavy casualties, and as a result although Student continued to command the parachutists, they were rarely used in airborne roles thereafter. However, since they were an elite force with high morale and a very high standard of training, they continued to expand during the war in their infantry role, eventually reaching a strength of 10 divisions.

Student was in the vicinity of Arnhem at the time of the Allied landings there and his expertise in airborne tactics and their limitations undoubtedly helped the German Army to defeat the Allied assault. Appointed commander of Army Group G in Holland, he retained this post until the end of the war.

GENERAL FREYBERG AND AN AIDE.

accompanied by a company of Australian infantry. KG Wittmann was stopped by sharp counter-attacks and hand-to-hand fighting, but eventually KG Krakau, using its mountain skills, was able to outflank the fighting area and turn the Allied position. During the night Layforce withdrew once more, and in the morning the eastward advance was resumed. Delayed by road-blocks, demolitions and mines, the Kampfgruppen finally reached Retimo at about 1300 on 29 May, to make contact with the first group of paratroopers. But the town, even though in German hands, was an unhealthy place, since Australian troops, well-provided with heavy machine guns, were in positions in the hills around, and it was decided that no further advance could be made until heavy artillery and armored cars, delivered by sea, could be brought up. The remainder of the day was spent in securing Retimo and shipping prisoners back to Maleme.

Orders for evacuation had been issued by Freyberg on the 27th, and the garrison at Heraklion embarked during the night of the 28/29th aboard two Royal Navy cruisers and six destroyers. After leaving Heraklion one destroyer had to be abandoned due to a failure in her steering gear, and another was sunk by air attack. Other ships were damaged by air attacks and many of the evacuated soldiers became casualties. Meanwhile the German troops moved on Heraklion on the 29th and, finding no resistance, took the town.

At Retimo the heavy artillery had arrived and shortly after dawn on 30 May began a bombardment of the heights around the town. Orders for evacuation had never reached these troops, and they could see no way out of their predicament other than surrender. Within a short time some 700 British and Australian troops had surrendered, and with them came a number of German paratroops who had, until then, been their prisoners. After splitting off a detachment to guard the prisoners and another to move into the mountains to round up any further Allied troops who might be there, KG Wittmann moved off eastwards once more, and by 0900hrs had made contact with the next parachute outpost, a party from 2nd Parachute Regiment. Moving on once more, by midday contact was made with a patrol from 1st Parachute Regiment which had been holding out close to Heraklion, and shortly after that the vanguard of the advance reached Heraklion airfield. The advance continued, joined by a small Italian force which had landed at Sitia on the previous day, and at 2200hrs the village of Ierapetra on the south coast was reached.

The Germans had made a simple error which, in the event, proved to be salvation for many Allied soldiers. They assumed that the Allies were retreating eastwards when, in fact, the main retreat had been southwards to Sphakia, from which port the Royal Navy were evacuating troops as fast as they could. But once KG Wittmann had reached Ierapetra, and once they had made contact with the Italians who had come westward from Sitia, it was obvious that the British forces could not possibly be in the eastern part of the island. Therefore it became necessary to move south in order to bring the battle to a conclusion.

On 29 May the German advance to the south began, two battalions of the Mountain Division leading. They were stopped at Kares by a determined rearguard and spent the night there, resuming the advance next morning as the rearguard disengaged and fell back. The next check was at the Imbros pass, but this was soon secured, and by the evening of 30 May the leading elements were within three miles of Sphakia. By that time the whole of the island except for a small perimeter around Sphakia was in German hands.

By now close to 12,000 Allied troops had been removed by the Royal Navy from Sphakia, and this evacuation now continued, in the face of severe air attacks by Stuka dive-bombers. Two anti-aircraft cruisers were sent from Alexandria to give protection, but one of these, HMS *Calcutta*, was sunk by Ju 88 members. General Freyberg was extracted by flying boat on the evening of 30 May, leaving General Weston in charge. Weston was then ordered out, handing over to Lt Col Colvin commander of Layforce with orders that the remaining Allied troops should surrender at 0900hrs on 1 June. In accordance with these orders, British troops began to surrender, and by 1600hrs the German forces were in complete control and the battle for Crete was over.

The lessons

Crete was a German victory but a costly one. Some 6000 German troops had been killed of the 22,000 which had arrived on the island, while the Allied troops lost 1742 killed, 1737 wounded and 11,835 made prisoner. 7000 British, 3000 Australian and 4500 New Zealand troops were successfully evacuated to Egypt. How many Greek soldiers and Cretan civilians died in the fighting has never been determined. The Royal Navy suffered one aircraft carrier, three battleships, six cruisers and nine destroyers severely damaged, three cruisers and six destroyers sunk, with the loss of over 2000 sailors.

But the most significant feature was the conclusions drawn by Hitler. He had been a fervent admirer of airborne forces since their formation, and he had been impressed by their performance in Belgium in 1940. Now the fearful casualty list appalled him, and two months later he ruled that:

> "The day of the parachutist is over. The parachute arm is a surprise weapon, and without the element of surprise there can be no future for airborne forces."

The German parachute troops were henceforth to be employed as light infantry, and apart from one or two minor raids were never again used in the airborne role.

When this became known to the Allies, it was considered to be a typical Hitler mistake. But in view of the casualties incurred by British and American airborne troops in Normandy, and the fiasco which was Arnhem, perhaps he was not so far wrong after all. It is noticeable that massive airborne forces are no longer a commonplace in Western armies, and those which do exist are largely seen as rapid intervention forces to secure political objectives rather than combat forces to turn the tide of battle.

Most of all, Crete was lost by indecision. The Allied troops originally outnumbered the Germans by a considerable margin, and rapid and ruthless decisions, followed by rapid and ruthless action could have eliminated the German threat within the first 24 hours. But, not for the first time nor for the last, Allied commanders paused to consider their options, waited for better intelligence, made plans and discussed plans, then finally issued orders. And when the orders were issued the battle was not forced to the utmost; the handful of German parachutists who held up the entire New Zealand counter-attack for those crucial few hours on the night of 21/22 May were the pivot around which the entire battle revolved. Had the counter-attackers had the same dedication and resolve as the defending paratroopers, the whole subsequent sequence of events could well never have taken place. But in 1941 the iron had not yet entered into the souls of the British and Dominion troops.

There was also too much dependence upon orders from Egypt, which was a long way away and had little knowledge of or sympathy with events in Crete. Freyberg, having got rid of his RAF aircraft on 19 May wanted to spoil the airfields to prevent them being used as landing grounds, but pressure from the RAF command in Egypt led to his being ordered to preserve the airfields for future use by the RAF. In the event they were of no further use to the RAF but were the principal means of delivering the German troops. Had Freyberg simply gone ahead with the courage of his convictions and blasted the airfields without further reference to Egypt, he would probably have given his troops sufficient advantage to have saved Crete.

CHAPTER TWO

OPERATION CRUSADER WESTERN DESERT

ARMORED WARFARE
NOVEMBER – DECEMBER 1941

Overleaf

The guns of 4th Regiment, Royal Horse Artillery, beating off a
Panzer attack at Sidi Rezegh. (*Battle of Sidi Rezegh, 1941* by T Cuneo, OBE)

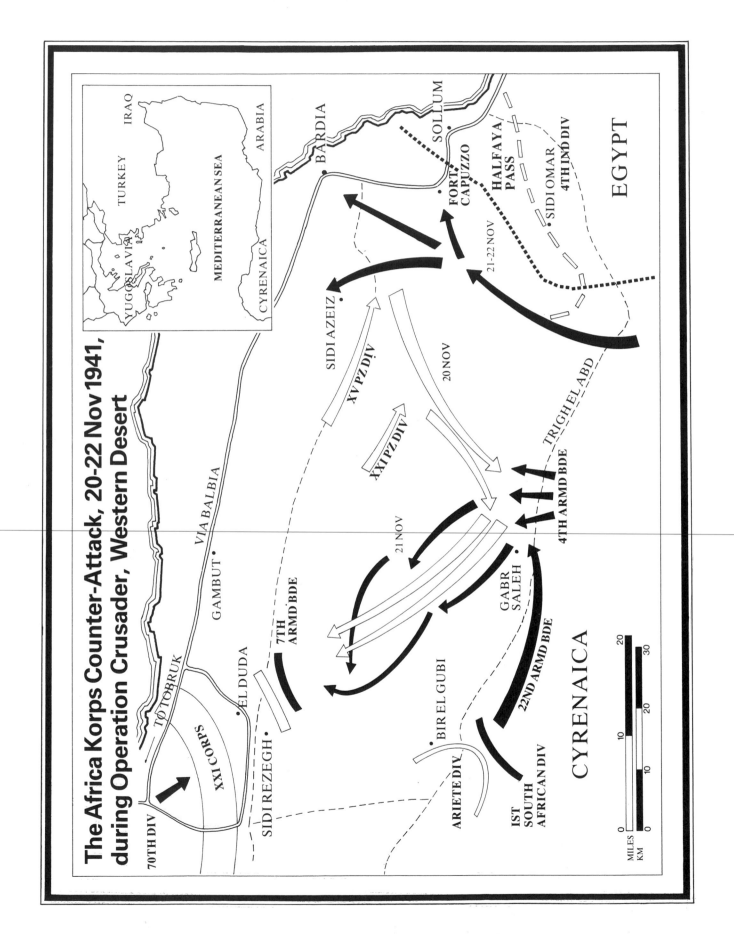

The Africa Korps Counter-Attack, 20-22 Nov 1941, during Operation Crusader, Western Desert

Legend has it that it was Rommel's supply officer who said that the desert was a tactician's paradise and a quartermaster's hell, and a short examination of the theater of war soon shows why he said that. The North African desert was a perfect place to fight a war; vast open spaces, little or no urban areas, a thinly dispersed civilian population, all of which permitted the opposing armies to maneuver and fight with little regard for anything but each other. On the other hand these same features, together with the immense distances, the general isolation of the theater from each combatant's production facilities and the paucity of supply ports, meant that keeping these moving armies fed, watered and supplied was a gigantic task.

On the face of it war in the desert was the ideal opportunity to permit armored formations to operate in the manner that the theorists of the 1930s had enthused about; fleets of tanks moving about the desert just like fleets of ships operating on an ocean, able to move in any direction they chose, adopt fighting formations which might spread for miles, swooping on their enemy, fighting, withdrawing, flanking . . . the opportunities were endless. Unfortunately it didn't work out that way.

The background

That the British (and Commonwealth) armies fought in the Cyrenaican Desert at all was due to Italy's late entrance into the war in 1940. Prior to that, Egypt was a convenient place to keep troops to guard the Suez Canal and to train in a warm climate, but once Italy declared war their African colonies immediately became potential objectives for British military action. In fact it was the Italians who moved first, in an indecisive manner; Marshal Graziani, with 200,000 troops, garrisoned Libya, and in September 1940, with a large proportion of these troops he advanced some sixty miles into Egypt and encamped to await further orders. Before these came, in December 1940, General Richard O'Connor, with the Western Desert Force attacked him with 36,000 highly-trained men and 57 tanks. A night attack, coupled with an encircling movement, soon routed the Italians, and they were then pursued along the Mediterranean coast until they were finally trapped and destroyed at Beda Fomm. The Italian garrison was no more and Libya was open to British occupation.

Unfortunately, the Italians were also occupying Eritrea and Abyssinia with another 200,000 troops, and General Wavell, Commander-in-Chief of the Middle East forces, now moved the major part of his victorious Libyan force to expel the Italians from their East African colonies. By May 1941 this had been achieved and the Italian Empire in Africa was no more. But this now meant that the British forces had to be stretched thinly in all directions in order to retain a grasp of what had been won, and the further they got from Cairo, the thinner they became. As a result, the front line (such as it was) in Libya was little further than where the Italians had been beaten at Beda Fomm, and the complete occupation of Libya was ignored.

This phase of the war was followed by the Italian expedition into Albania, which in turn led to the Greek campaign and its consequent disasters which are dealt with in more detail elsewhere. But in the attempt to stiffen Mussolini's backbone, and also secure his right flank preparatory to his forthcoming invasion of Russia, Hitler sent German troops to salvage what might be possible of Italy's lost empire. And since there was a large area of Libya unoccupied by any troops at all, the way was open for them to land in North Africa. On 12 February, 1941 two German Panzer divisions led by Lieut-General Erwin Rommel landed in Tripoli. Meanwhile the experienced British troops who had ejected the Italians had largely been shifted to Greece, where they were expected to do the same again, and their places on the Libyan boundary had been taken by new troops fresh from Britain.

Rommel's arrival had not gone unnoticed by the British, but measuring others by their own standards, they confidently assumed that Rommel would spend two or three months acclimatising his troops, finding his way around, liaising with the Italians, making plans, having discussions and generally 'playing himself in'. This, though, was not Rommel's way; within a week he had sent his formations forward to test the British defenses. Finding them wanting, he continued his advance and by April had chased the British back to the Egyptian frontier at Mersa Matruh. Only a mixed garrison at Tobruk held out, a standing threat to Rommel's flank which, try as he might, he was unable to capture. Apart from that, the triumph of 'Wavell's Thirty Thousand' had been expunged in just over a month by the new German commander.

THE CRUSADER TANK, OR CRUISER MARK 6, WAS THE LAST OF A LONG LINE OF PRE-WAR DESIGNS TO SEE SERVICE, AND THE 'FAMILY LIKENESS' LAY IN THE PECULIAR LOZENGE-SHAPED TURRET, DESIGNED TO DEFLECT SHOT. WIDELY USED IN THE DESERT, IT SUFFERED FROM UNRELIABILITY.

A GERMAN 88MM FLAK 18 ANTI-AIRCRAFT GUN DUG INTO AN AMBUSH POSITION IN THE HALFAYA PASS AREA. FIRING A 9.5KG PIERCING SHELL AT 850M-SEC, IT COULD DEFEAT ANY BRITISH ARMOR AT RANGES UP TO ONE KILOMETER, AND WITH A HIGH EXPLOSIVE SHELL COULD ACT AS A DIRECT SUPPORT GUN AGAINST INFANTRY AND TRUCKS.

In an endeavor to push Rommel back, 'Operation Brevity' was hurriedly planned and launched, but this lived up to its name and was rapidly spurned by Rommel, who was sitting in good defensive positions. A worried Churchill then despatched a special convoy, codenamed 'Tiger' to deliver 238 new tanks to Egypt in order to stiffen the armored force; these were the 'Crusader' model, a fast and highly maneuverable vehicle but one which had been insufficiently developed and tested, due to the pressure of events, a vehicle which was completely strange to the troops who were to use it, and which demanded a good deal of preparation and modification — notably to such things as engine air filters — before it could be used in the desert.

The next attempt to repel Rommel was 'Operation Battleaxe', which was 'Brevity' all over again but with rather more muscle thanks to the 'Tiger' convoy's tanks. This came to grief when Rommel seeded the Halfaya Pass area with concealed anti-tank guns, including a number of 88mm air defense weapons. He then caused his armor to maneuver in front of this ambush and then retire, causing the British armored units to race after him and thus into the jaws of the trap. Those which escaped slaughter by the guns largely fell victim to their own mechanical unreliability, and once this had happened Rommel's Panzers came roaring back to deal with whatever was left. Within 48 hours of its start 'Battleaxe' was over and the survivors were back at their start line leaving two-thirds of their armor wrecked on the battlefield.

It is axiomatic in Britain that when the team loses, the manager is changed; Churchill had been contemplating a change in desert command for some time, and Wavell was now removed and replaced by General Auchinleck. 'The Auk', as the rest of the army came to know him, was an ex-Indian Army officer and little-known among the officers in the desert forces; moreover he brought in a fresh set of commanders, picked from officers he scarcely knew and not, therefore, necessarily the best choices available. General Cunningham, selected to lead the newly-formed Eighth Army, had conducted a sparkling campaign in East Africa against the Italians but had no experience of handling armor, while General Ritchie, who later replaced him, had not commanded in battle since 1918.

Auchinleck's strong suit was his refusal to be prodded into premature action by Churchill, who was over-fond of firing off peremptory telegrams of detailed instruction to commanders in the field. After consideration of what he found, he decided that there could be no offensive action by the desert army until its strength had been built up and some vital training carried out, which meant early November before battle could be resumed. During this period Rommel, too, was consolidating, training and building up his strength, and generally getting ready to drive into Egypt. But Tobruk was a thorn in his side since it was a constant potential source of a cutting-off flank attack, and moreover it was an attractive goal because it would give Rommel a supply harbor much closer to his front than Tripoli and thus reduce the distance his fuel, ammunition and supplies had to be hauled. Rommel therefore decided that he would launch an attack on Tobruk some time in November.

Auchinleck's instruction to Cunningham was simple: go out and capture Cyrenaica. And from this came 'Operation Crusader'.

The plan

In fact Cunningham arrived on post to find two sets of plans in existence; all he apparently had to do was choose between them. The first plan suggested a drive deep into the desert, along the northern side of the Great Sand Sea, from Jarabub to Jalo Oasis, and then a swing back north to end up in El Agheila and so cut off the whole of the Cyrenaica bulge in one swoop. With the wide open spaces of the desert to play with this was the sort of plan which looked very good when described with suitable sweeping gestures over a map, but one which, on closer examination, promised some fearful logistic problems. Moreover while this grand maneuver was in progress Rommel might well take it into his head to ignore it and drive through what little was left of the British forces to his east and occupy Cairo.

The alternative plan may have been less adventuresome but it was more practical, and after some minor adjustments Cunningham put it forward to Auchinleck and had it approved as 'Crusader'. The ultimate aim was to bring Rommel's armor to battle and destroy it,

ORDER OF BATTLE

BRITISH & COMMONWEALTH

8th Army (Commanders: Gens Cunningham/Ritchie)

13 Corps (Commander: Gen Godwin-Austen)

NZ Div (Commander: Gen Freyberg)
4th, 5th, 6th NZ Bdes

4th Indian Div (Commander: Messervy)
5th, 7th, 11th Indian Inf Bdes

1st Army Tank Bde (130 tk)

30 Corps (Commander: Norrie)

7th Armd Div (500 tk) (Commander: Gen Gott)
4th Armd Bde Group, 7th, 22nd Armd Bdes

1st SA Div
1st, 5th SA Bdes

22nd Guards Bde

29th Indian Indep Bde Gp

Reserve: 2nd SA Div
4th, 6th SA Inf Bdes

Oasis Force (Commander: Reid)

29th Indian Inf Bde Gp
6th SA Armd C Regt

Tobruk Garrison (Commander: Scobie)

70th Inf Div
14th, 16th, 23rd Inf Bdes

Polish Carpathian Inf Bde Gp

32nd Army Tk Bde (130 tk)

British cas: 18,000 K/M/W, 278 tks

AXIS

GERMAN

Deutsche Afrika Korps (Commander: Gen Cruewell)

15 Pz Div

21 Pz Div (Commanders: Stephan/von Ravenstein)
5 Pz Rgt

ITALIAN

20th Corps

Ariete Div (Armored)

Trieste Div (Motorized)

21st Corps

Bologna, Brescia, Pavia, Trento Inf Divs

Axis cas: 38,000 K/W/POW, 300 tks

---

since once the Panzers were out of the way the task of rolling up the infantry component of the Axis forces would be relatively simple.

The force available for Crusader was two Corps, XIII and XXX. XIII Corps under Lt Gen Godwen-Austin consisted of the 4th Indian and New Zealand infantry divisions and the 1st Army Tank Brigade with 135 tanks. XXX Corps under Lt Gen Norrie consisted of 7th Armoured Division (the original 'Desert Rats'),

1st South African Division, the 22nd Guards Brigade, and the 4th Armoured Brigade Group. In addition to these major units there were the troops of Tobruk and Matruh 'fortresses' and a detached force known as the 'Oasis Group'.

The basic plan now put forward was for the infantry of XIII Corps to capture the Axis positions along the coast between Sollum and Sidi Omar; for the armor of XXX Corps to cross the frontier south of Sidi Omar and head for Tobruk; and for the Oasis Force to stage a diversion in the Jarabub area so as to draw attention away from the north. If all this went well, the armored sweep would draw and destroy the Panzers, everybody would meet at Tobruk and relieve the garrison there, and the whole force would then sweep to the west, overcome the Axis defenses in the Gazala area and drive the remnants of the German and Italian forces out of Cyrenaica once again.

According to the best intelligence estimates British armor outnumbered Axis armor by a significant degree; the British now had 736 tanks in first-line condition, while the Germans had 240 assorted Panzers, the Italians 150 medium and 160 light tanks, a grand total of 550 vehicles. Unfortunately the British armor was not to be employed as a mass, but was split up across the arena, largely due to the demand for armored support from the various infantry formations. The 4th Armoured Brigade Group was part of XXX Corps and was to locate itself close to the New Zealand Division; but the 7th Armoured Brigade, accompanied by the 22nd Armoured Brigade (which had just arrived in the theater and had no experience of warfare) was to drive out into the desert and, instead of going hell-for-leather for Tobruk, was to come to a stately halt after the first day's cruising and take up defensive positions around Gabr Saleh, an entirely un-noteworthy piece of desert about one third of the distance between the frontier and Tobruk. Here, it was confidently predicted, would be the bait which would draw Rommel's armor to battle, though why Rommel should respond to this particular gambit was never satisfactorily explained. There was no tactical or strategic feature about Gabr Saleh which would encourage anyone to commit a corporal's guard to capturing it, let alone loose the entire Afrika Korps into battle, nor was it even a piece of ground well-adapted to defense. It was simply a piece of desert, no different to the desert which stretched for miles in all directions around it.

The battle begins

If the plan for Operation Crusader was simple enough — some might say too simple — the execution was something else. One commentator later said that the whole affair 'resembled an American Sandwich' with layers of opposing troops fighting in different directions, formations moving every which way, some making contact, some missing contact, and the general air of a disturbed anthill. It is, without doubt, one of the most difficult battles of the Second World War to fol-

ITALIAN GUNNERS OF THE ARIETE DIVISION LOADING A 152MM GUN. INTRODUCED JUST BEFORE THE WAR THIS FIRED A 45KG SHELL TO A RANGE OF 20 KM AND WAS AMONG THE BEST MEDIUM ARTILLERY WEAPONS AVAILABLE TO EITHER SIDE IN THE DESERT. FORTUNATELY FOR THE BRITISH THERE WERE NOT MANY OF THEM.

low, since so many things were happening in different places at the same time.

Rommel had decided to move against Tobruk at the end of November, and so on 14 November he flew to Rome to attend a conference, and then flew on to Greece. On the 18th, while he was in Athens, the British attack began, the tanks of 7th Armoured Division rolling steadily forward from the frontier all day with no opposition or anything more than the occasional enemy armored car which appeared in the distance and immediately withdrew. Moreover, a furious thunderstorm accompanied by highly unseasonable rain during the previous night had temporarily grounded the air forces of both sides so that there was no interference from the Luftwaffe. By 1730hrs that day the armored formations had reached their appointed places around Gabr Saleh. The New Zealand infantry had crossed the frontier and swung around to take the static defenses in the rear, and the 4th Indian Division was in position to attack the Axis troops at Sidi Omar and Sollum. All was going well. But during the day Rommel had flown from Athens and taken up his post in his advanced HQ at Gambut.

Among the various German reconnaissance units which had been rebuffed by the mass of armor during the drive to Gabr Saleh, one had been so upset as to radio back that he was being attacked by 200 heavy tanks. Rommel dismissed this out of hand; this, together with the maneuvring of the 4th Indian Division before the Sidi Omar positions, was obviously some sort of diversionary gambit intended to panic the Italians and cause them to demand succour from the Afrika Korps, so disrupting Rommel's planned move

on Tobruk, due to begin in two days time.

Consequently, the laagered armor spent a quiet night, and, since the expected concentration of Rommel's armor had not taken place, and since idle troops tend to lose their momentum, General Gott, commanding 7th Armoured Division, decided not to wait upon events any longer but push forward. The 22nd Armoured Brigade would move to investigate Bir el Gubi, which the Italian Ariete division were believed to be occupying; 7th Armoured Brigade would push forward in the direction of Sidi Rezegh; and 4th Armoured Brigade would also advance, guarding the right flank and also looking out for the left flank of XIII Corps when it arrived.

22nd Armoured Brigade duly motored across the desert towards Bir el Gubi, their leading tanks easily driving back the Italian outposts. There was a halt while more tanks arrived, after which an attack was launched on what was thought to be a minor defensive position. In fact, and to everyone's surprise, this turned out to be the major Italian defensive line, backed by the entire strength of the Ariete Armoured Division, firmly supported by artillery. The initial advance, described by one onlooker as the nearest thing to a cavalry charge ever seen during the war, appeared to be highly successful, but the decision to attack with nothing but armor meant that there was no infantry to consolidate the gains, and artillery and minefields began to take their toll of the 22nd Brigade tanks. A counter-attack by the Italian 132nd Tank Regiment proved decisive, and by evening the 22nd Brigade were retiring, sadder and wiser and with 40 of its 136 tanks burning in the desert and several more broken down and abandoned.

7th Armoured Brigade, on the other hand, had an eminently successful day. Having driven northward, preceded by their outlying screen of South African armored cars, late in the afternoon they crested a ridge to see before them the Italian airfield at Sidi Rezegh, with several aircraft dispersed around it and everyday maintenance activities in progress by the unsuspecting aviators. A swooping rush by 6th Royal Tank Regiment and the South Africans soon wrecked every aircraft by either gunfire or collision. Having secured the airfield and captured 80 or so prisoners, a squadron was then told off to make a further advance to secure the higher ground of the Escarpment beyond the airfield. There they fell in with two battalions of Afrika Regiment 361, well dug in and prepared to argue over possession. And since, again, no British infantry had accompanied the tanks, the squadron retired back to the airfield to spend the night with the rest of 7th Armoured Brigade.

4th Armoured Brigade left behind at Gabr Saleh, had an unfortunate day. General von Ravenstein of 21 Panzer Division was apprehensive of what might be happening to his south, after reports from some of his armored cars, and he requested permission to send a force down to have a look. By this time Rommel was beginning to suspect that there might be more to the British move than a simple spoiling maneuver, and at 1145 von Ravenstein was given orders to send a reinforced Panzer regiment south. 'Kampfgruppe Stefan',

composed of 85 medium tanks, 35 light tanks, a battery of field howitzers and four 88mm guns, moved off shortly after noon and by 1430 arrived at Gabr Saleh to be greeted by some 50 or so M3 Stuart tanks of the 8th Hussars coming to meet them.

Tank versus tank

This was to be the first purely tank versus tank encounter in the desert — probably the first anywhere in which the opposing forces were in some strength. Here, at last, was the situation which the theorists and pre-war tank enthusiasts had contemplated as the future method of waging war, with no infantry to slow down the lightning maneuver, no artillery to complicate the issue, but two fleets of tanks with all the space in the world in which to disport themselves. Now they could take up battle formations, skirmish, deploy, advance, retreat, encircle and generally live up to the promise which had been held out so long.

But it didn't happen. The glorious theories expounded by Liddell Hart, Swinton, Fuller and their disciples were blown to shreds within the first five minutes. Whatever the opposing commanders may have intended, the dust and smoke, a veritable 'fog of war' soon put an end to advanced tactical ideas. Instead of coordinated operations in which this troop covered that, this squadron encircled while that squadron engaged with gunfire, the whole affair rapidly turned into a mad melee in which tanks pounded around in a blinding, choking cloud of dust and smoke, shooting whenever they got a glimpse of anything they could identify as enemy.

The momentum of the British charge carried the Stuart tanks clean through the panzer formation, whereupon they about-turned and charged back once more. By that time the dust was up and thereafter any

THE AMERICAN M3 LIGHT TANK

THIS TANK WAS CALLED THE 'STUART' OR THE 'HONEY' BY BRITISH TROOPS AND IT GRADUALLY REPLACED THE UNRELIABLE CRUISERS. FIRST USED AT SIDI REZEGH, WHEN THEY EQUIPPED THE 4TH ARMOURED BRIGADE, THEY WERE POPULAR BECAUSE OF THEIR RELIABILITY AND COMFORT, BUT THEIR HIGH SILHOUETTE, THIN ARMOR AND 37MM GUN MEANT THAT THEY RELIED ON SPEED FOR SAFETY.

ARMOR AND ANTI-ARMOR IN THE DESERT

The PAK 38 5cm Gun was the mainstay of German anti-tank operations in the desert. Later replaced by 75mm and 88mm guns, at this time it was the master of most British armor since it could outrange the British 40mm gun used on tanks and could stand off and shell British 40mm anti-tank guns into silence. In addition to being towed, a modified version was later fitted to the Panzer III tank.

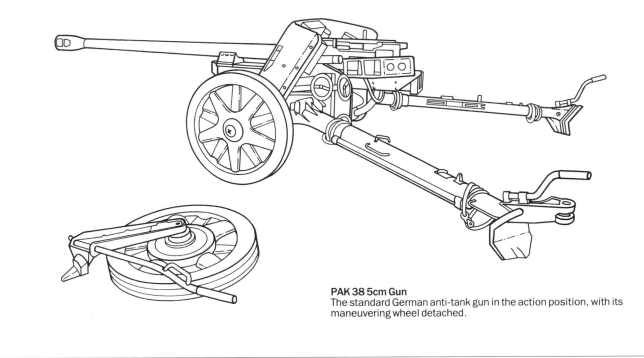

PAK 38 5cm Gun
The standard German anti-tank gun in the action position, with its maneuvering wheel detached.

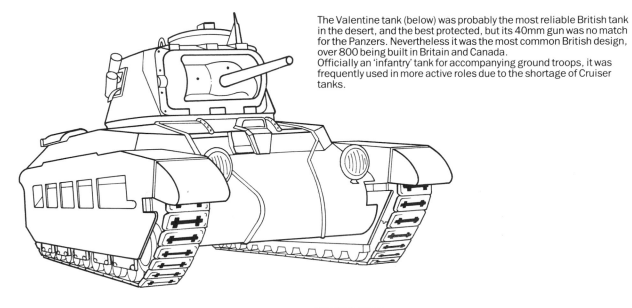

The Valentine tank (below) was probably the most reliable British tank in the desert, and the best protected, but its 40mm gun was no match for the Panzers. Nevertheless it was the most common British design, over 800 being built in Britain and Canada.
Officially an 'infantry' tank for accompanying ground troops, it was frequently used in more active roles due to the shortage of Cruiser tanks.

Valentine tank
The Valentine weighed 16.26 tonnes, had a speed of 25 km/h and range of 145 km, with a crew of 3 or 4.

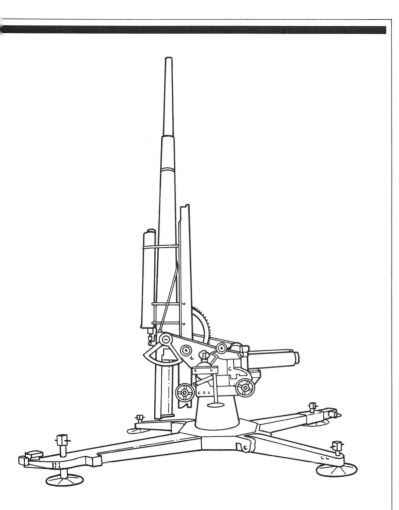

8.8cm Flak 18 Gun
The standard German anti-aircraft gun, seen here fully elevated in its air defense role.

The 8.8mm gun was one of the first weapons to appear when Germany began re-arming. Designed in the late 1920s, it was an excellent weapon and was gradually improved during the war years. As an air defense gun it fired a 9.4kg shell to a maximum ceiling of 9900m; in the ground support role it could fire the same shell to 14,800m. Its potential as an anti-tank gun had been seen during the Spanish Civil War and special armor-piercing ammunition was provided before 1939. The standard armor-piercing shot weighed 9.5kg and could go through 105mm of armor at 1000m range when striking at 30° from the vertical. It was later given a tungsten-cored shot which enabled it to achieve greater penetration at short ranges, though at 1000m the performance remained the same. Its success in this role led to a special 8.8mm anti-tank gun being developed by Krupp which, with improved ammunition, could penetrate 175mm of armor at 1000m range. This gun was then adapted to a number of tank and tank destroyers, including the celebrated Tiger tank. In the air defense role the gun was steadily improved, and the final model, the 8.8cm Flak 41, could send the same 9.4kg shell to a maximum height of 10,675m and a maximum ground range of 19,735m.

semblance of order vanished. Even the German anti-tank guns, which, in their standard drill had emplaced themselves to a flank in order to pick off the British tanks, found they could not distinguish targets, and they, in their turn, were to suffer from chance encounters as Hussar tanks roared out from the dust cloud, saw an anti-tank gun, sprayed it with machine gun fire or a quick round of high explosive, and then vanished back into the murk.

As the day drew to a close the two sides disengaged, each thinking they had defeated the other. In fact the result was in the nature of a draw, though the Hussars had suffered more tank casualties, losing about 20 tanks to the German loss of only three. More German tanks had been put out of action in the course of the battle, but their highly efficient recovery troops had been able to remove these for repair. In hindsight, it is apparent that the Germans were the victors insofar as material loss went, but at that time there was no certain idea of what the scale of loss had been, and the British troops were quite convinced that they had given the Panzers a beating.

Altogether the day showed a profit to the British side, and the commander of 4th Armoured Brigade, confident that tomorrow would bring an opportunity to deal decisively with Kampfgruppe Stefan, ordered 3 and 5 Royal Tank Regiments, which had been sent north towards Sidi Azeiz and Bardia, to return to Gabr Saleh in order to ensure success. The Support Group, a mixed assembly of artillery and infantry, was ordered north to join 7th Armoured Brigade at Sidi Rezegh, and the South African Division was sent to Bir el Gubi to take over the attack on the Ariete Division, while 22nd Armoured Brigade was to disengage and reconnoiter northwards towards Tobruk. In a signal sent to Churchill that night, Auchinleck was in no doubt that things were going well:

> "It seems that the enemy was surprised and unaware of the imminence and weight of our blow. Indications, though they have to be confirmed, are that he is now trying to withdraw from the area Bardia/Sollum. Until we know the area reached by our armored troops today it is not possible to read the battle further at the moment. I myself am happy about the situation. . ."

Rommel was determined that all this activity was not going to prevent his forthcoming attack on Tobruk, and in order that he might devote all his energies to that operation, he gave General Cruewell, commander of the Deutsches Afrika Korps, a free hand to disperse these gadflys which had crossed the frontier. Cruewell had an incomplete picture; he appears not to have been aware of the presence of 7th Armoured Division at Bir el Gubi and Gabr Saleh, but his reconnaissance armored cars had reported British tanks around Sidi Azeiz and Bardia. In fact this was 3rd RTR, who were now on their way back to Gabr Saleh. Cruewell therefore sent 15 Panzer Regiment east towards Sidi Azeiz, and 21 Panzer Division southeast to take up a position near Sidi Omar so as to cut off any formation retreating

THE DESERT COMMANDERS

General Sir Alan Cunningham (1887–)

The younger brother of Admiral Cunningham, General Cunningham led the forces which evicted the Italians from Ethiopia in 1940–41. In August 1941 he assumed command of the 8th Army in North Africa and one of his first tasks was to conduct Operation Crusader. Here he failed to exhibit his customary dash and, in the words of one critic, 'lost the battle in his mind'. Failing to press home his attack, he was relieved by Auchinleck and for the rest of the war was employed in administrative roles. At the close of the war he became the last High Commissioner in Palestine.

Brigadier 'Jock' Campbell, VC (1894–1942)

Campbell was an officer in the Royal Horse Artillery who devised and commanded 'Jock Columns', mobile columns of infantry and artillery, in the Western Desert 1941–42. He was awarded the Victoria Cross for his handling of the Support Group of 7th Armoured Division in the Battle of Sidi Rezegh, during which he was wounded. He had just been appointed Commander 7th Armoured Division when he was killed in a road accident on 26 February 1942.

General William Henry Ewart Gott (1897–1942)

General Gott was a relatively unknown British officer who came to prominence as a corps commander in the Desert campaign in 1941. He was nicknamed 'Strafer', not from any personality trait, since he was a mild-mannered man, but simply from the First World War German phrase 'Gott Strafe England'. In 1942 he was appointed to succeed Ritchie and command the Eighth Army, but flying forward to his new headquarters,

BRIGADIER JOCK CAMPBELL (LEFT) WITH MAJOR GENERAL W H E GOTT.

he was killed when the aircraft crashed.

Field Marshal Erwin Rommel (1891–1944)

Erwin Rommel was commissioned into the infantry during the First World War and rapidly made his name as a fearless and skilled leader of men. A company commander at the Battle of Caporetto he was awarded the Pour le Merite, the highest German decoration for bravery. He remained in the shrunken postwar army and became a valued instructor, writing 'The Infantry Attacks', one of the most useful books ever written on small-unit tactics. He was an early supporter of Hitler and the Nazi party, and was commander of Hitler's personal guard battalion in Austria, Czechoslovakia and Poland.

In 1940 he was given command of 7 Panzer Division, which he led in the subsequent invasion of France. His operations in France were conducted with flair, as a result of which he was selected to command the newly-formed Afrika Korps in February 1941. His handling of this force, and his brilliant conduct of the war in North Africa came within a very short distance of defeating the British, who probably respected and revered him more than did his own

before 15 Panzer's attack. 21 Panzer was also to rendezvous with Kampfgruppe Stefan and add them to their force.

Cruewell was not alone in misreading the available information. General Cunningham, whilst daunted by the reports that 22nd Armoured Brigade had suffered a heavy loss of tanks, felt that this was counter-balanced by reports from 4th Armoured Brigade that they had soundly defeated a heavy force of Panzers, and as a bonus the 7th Armoured were firmly in possession of Sidi Rezegh, well forward. Following the rule of exploiting success, it seemed the next move was to beef up the presence at Sidi Rezegh by moving 22nd Armoured there, leaving Bir el Gubi to be taken by the South Africans. The South Africans were less than enthusiastic about this idea, their General Peinaar pointing out that an armored formation had been repulsed, which didn't argue that an infantry forma-

tion would necessarily succeed. His point being taken, the orders were amended to a holding role, to keep the Ariete Division pinned down and thus out of the remainder of the activity.

Out of all these plans, those of the Germans came into effect first. At first light on 20 November, Cruewell's panzers moved off and by 0830 were well ahead on their allotted routes, with the infantry of 21st Panzer already calling for assistance from armor since he could see enemy tanks in front. This, though, turned out to be nothing but a reconnaissance force of armored cars and the German advance continued on schedule.

Kampfgruppe Stefan had received orders to move up and connect with 21 Panzer; but due to the late arrival of its fuel and supply column the move-off was delayed. Fortunately so was the counter-move of 8th Hussars and 5 RTR, since the return of 3 and 5 RTR from their forward locations near Sidi Azeiz had been done slowly troops. He was rapidly christened 'The Desert Fox' by his enemies, but he gained their respect for his absolutely correct treatment of prisoners and his undoubted skill in handling his forces.

Although eventually beaten by Montgomery, he extracted a high price for the victory and he rarely allowed Montgomery to dictate his subsequent moves as he retreated towards Tunisia.

By the time of the Normandy invasion Erwin Rommel had achieved a considerable degree of fame for his activities in North Africa, though in point of fact his name was probably better known in the British Army than in the German.

He had been given sick leave from Tunisia, since his health had been affected by the campaigns, and thus was not present for the surrender there. Upon returning to duty he was given command of a reserve army in Northern Italy for some months and was then appointed to the post of Inspector of Coast Defenses, France. In this his brief ran well beyond pure coast defense to encompass the entire

defense against invasion, and his initial tour of inspection revealed many deficiencies. He set to work to construct a full system of defenses based on the premise that any invasion had to be defeated on the beaches before the Allies could gain a toe-hold. He visited every sector and imbued the defending troops with some of his own spirit, building up morale as he built up the defensive works.

In the summer of 1944 he was given command of Army Group 'B' in northern France, but disagreed fundamentally with Rundstedt over the employment of the armored reserve. On 17 and his henchmen should

be removed from power — though he did not advocate assassination. Unknown to him, the Plotters had decided to name him as head of state after their coup, in the hope that, being known to the Allies, he would be able to negotiate reasonable surrender terms. When the Bomb Plot failed and Rommel's name appeared Hitler, wishing to avoid scandal with such a well-July his staff car was attacked by a British fighter-bomber and Rommel was severely wounded in the head.

He had been approached, some time previously, by the Bomb Plotters, and he appears to have agreed with them in

principle — that Hitler respected name, gave him the choice of a 'People's Court' and execution, or suicide and a hero's funeral. He chose the latter course, the public being informed that he had died of complications from his wound.

General Ludwig Cruewell (1892–1958)

Cruewell was commissioned into a dragoon regiment in 1912, served through the First World War and was a member of the postwar army. In 1938 he was given command of 6 Panzer Regiment and in December 1939 was promoted Major General. In 1940 he received command of 11 Panzer Division and in 1941 was appointed commander of the German Afrika Korps. He served well under General Rommel and during Rommel's absence in 1942 commanded Panzer Armee Afrika. Captured on 29 May, 1942 whilst commanding on the Italian front, he spent the remainder of the war as a prisoner.

FIELD MARSHAL ROMMEL POINTS OUT SOMETHING OF INTEREST.

and they were therefore late in reaching Gabr Saleh and later still in being ready to move against Stefan. Thus, by the time 5 RTR and 8th Hussars had advanced to do battle, Stefan had already moved off to make his rendezvous, and the two forces met and had a running battle as Stefan crossed the front of the British force. In the midst of this Stefan received orders from von Ravenstein to hurry up and make his appointed meeting with 21 Panzer, so the German force disengaged and made off, a move which the British, understandably, interpreted as a retreat. They gave chase for about six miles but then decided to stop and allow the rest of 4th Armoured to catch up.

By this time 15 Panzer had reached Sidi Azeiz to find nobody there, and reported this to Cruewell. He soon realized his error, and concluded that, after all, the reports of a British force at Sidi Rezegh which he had assumed to be a mere reconnaissance party, must be the

main thrust of a British attack. Therefore, it followed that the force at Gabr Saleh, which Kampfgruppe Stefan had mauled the previous day and brushed with this morning, could be no more than a flank guard intent on keeping the Germans from discovering the main body. Now all was clear. Now was the time to launch 21 Panzer, which had now assimilated Kampfgruppe Stefan at their appointed rendezvous at Gabr Lachem, against this troublesome flank guard and despatch it, thus leaving the way clear to deal with the main British force.

Except that he now received a brief message from 21 Panzer to the effect that they were almost out of fuel and ammunition, and without an immediate supply by air they would be in no condition to go into battle.

The British Army's radio intercept service was working moderately well at this time, and they had managed to pick up and decipher an exchange of signals between

Cruewell and Rommel which laid bare Cruewell's plans, though the vital message from 21 Panzer had not been intercepted. As a result Cunningham was aware that on the morrow he would probably be hit by a mass of panzers; here at last was the Afrika Korps coming out to battle, but unfortunately Cunningham's forces were now dispersed all over the desert and not in the right place to perform their declared aim of destroying the German armor when it arrived. 22nd Armoured was therefore ordered to get across to Gabr Saleh as fast as possible so as to reinforce 4th Armoured in time to meet the onslaught. But 22nd were in much the same state as 21 Panzer, and until they were fuelled and supplied, they were unable to do very much.

It was at this stage of the battle that XIII Corps suggested that since they had the New Zealand Division but ten miles away from Gabr Saleh, it might be a good idea if this force was added to the defense. Brigadier Gatehouse, commanding 4th Armoured Brigade, turned the offer down. This was going to be a tank battle, fought by tanks, and no assistance from foot troops was required thank you. The fact that the New Zealanders had, in addition to their three infantry brigades, a full divisional artillery and a battalion of Valentine tanks from the 1st Army Tank Brigade cut no ice whatever. It is said that later, General Freyberg, the commander of the New Zealand Division, sent a signal to Gatehouse asking if he was fighting a private war or could anyone else join in?

Cruewell was not prepared to wait for 21 Panzer; he ordered 15 Panzer to move against Gabr Saleh forthwith, with 21 Panzer to catch up on the following day. And at about 1630 the 8th Panzer Regiment, accompanied by two infantry regiments and an artillery regiment, came up against 4th Armoured, well positioned on a slight rise, with the sun behind them.

For about half an hour the battle raged as the Panzers attempted to overcome the British armor which was in well-sited and dug-in positions. Honors were about even, the German superiority in numbers being matched by the British superiority in position, but then the German artillery arrived and began to add its weight to the battle. Soon the British were being forced back, leaving 26 tanks wrecked. At this moment 22nd Armoured Brigade, having finally disentangled themselves from Bir el Gubi and refuelled, arrived on the scene, and this sudden reinforcement was enough to make the Germans pull back under cover of strong artillery fire. Darkness fell and the two forces separated and settled down for the night.

Battle lines are drawn at Sidi Rezegh

At Sidi Rezegh things had begun to hum. The Afrika Regiment which had repelled the exploratory attack on the previous day had called for reinforcements and artillery and infantry had been sent to strengthen their position. At dawn on 20 November this force felt sufficiently confident to mount a sharp attack on the airfield positions of 7th Armoured Brigade, though this

was beaten off. Then another and heavier attack was launched by the Germans, this time aided by heavy artillery fire, and it became obvious that 7th Armoured, on their open airfield, were a sitting target. The second attack was also beaten off, but for the rest of the day there was sporadic shelling of anything which looked remotely military around the airfield. Cunningham had ordered an attack on the German position, but it was now apparent that because of their increased strength they were unlikely to be upset by anything 7th Armoured could muster, and that an attack would have to wait for the arrival of the Support Group and for 5th South African Brigade, neither of whom would be ready for any attack until the following morning.

Late in the day, shortly after a German Stuka raid had added to 7th Armoured's troubles, General Gott (commanding 7th Armoured Division) arrived with the information that orders had been sent to the Tobruk Garrison to make their break-out on the following day. Therefore the infantry now concentrating at Sidi Rezegh were to advance and clear the Germans from the ridge to the north, opening the way for the armor to drive ahead to El Duda where they were to meet the tanks of 32nd Army Tank Brigade which would be spearheading the breakout from Tobruk. 5th South African Brigade would then come up and join them, and this combined force would then move west to secure the area between El Duda and the Tobruk-El Adem highway.

Even allowing for the recent accretion of strength in the German infantry positions on the ridge, there is good reason to think that this maneuver might have worked exactly as planned. But that evening the cat came out of the bag with a flourish: the BBC Overseas Broadcasting Service announced to the world that the Eighth Army had invaded Libya and was about to destroy the Afrika Korps. This, of course, was picked up by the Germans and immediately passed to General Rommel, upon whom it acted like an electric shock. All now became clear, and he immediately dropped all plans for an attack on Tobruk and urged Cruewell to move as fast as possible against Sidi Rezegh. By 0300 on 21 November the Panzers were on the move.

As dawn came up, it found the Tobruk Garrison commencing their breakout. Plans had been laid to deal with various of the beseiging strongpoints by a combined tank and infantry sortie, and this progressed well. During the night engineers had crept forward to lift mines and cut wire, so that as first light came the routes were prepared. The first objectives fell relatively easily, but after that things got progressively more difficult, until at 1430, the appointed time of rendezvous at El Duda the sortie was fighting bitterly to keep what it had gained and prevent being driven back into Tobruk.

Dawn at Sidi Rezegh had seen the Support Group moving out to attack the German infantry positions on the ridge. Following a very short bombardment by artillery, a smokescreen concealed the British movements until the leading infantry, the Rifle Brigade in

Bren gun carriers, debouched from the smoke on to the crest of the ridge. One platoon was immediately shot to pieces by anti-tank guns, but the remainder de-bussed their infantry into a ditch from which they were able to enfilade much of the German defended area. More infantry now moved up on foot, through the smoke-screen, and the battle became a close-quarter affair of bayonet and grenade. Here Rifleman Beeley, sole survivor of his section, took a Bren light machine gun and, firing it from the hip, charged a German post containing an anti-tank gun and two machine guns. He killed seven of the occupants, thus opening the way for another section to complete the destruction, but was himself killed by a grenade as he closed with the post. He was subsequently awarded a posthumous Victoria Cross.

By noon the Rifle Brigade had taken the ridge, at the cost of 84 dead, and the armor was free to move on. Crusader tanks of 6th Royal Tank Regiment swept over the ridge, heading for El Duda. Minutes later they were brought to an abrupt halt by a concentration of 50mm and 88mm anti-tank guns. The leading tanks were instantly destroyed, and the remainder rapidly made their way back over the ridge to the slope behind; but before they could decide what to do next, they were recalled to the airfield, where more trouble was brewing.

At Gabr Saleh the night had passed quietly and the 4th and 22nd Armoured Brigades were ready for the forthcoming battle. They were quite sure they would deal with the Afrika Korps, required no further assistance from any quarter, and the only outstanding question appeared to be in what direction the Germans would retire. In fact when day came all they saw of the

BRITISH INFANTRY IN BREN GUN CARRIERS ON THE COAST ROAD. THE CARRIER HAD BEEN ORIGINALLY INTENDED AS A METHOD OF MOVING THE SQUAD MACHINE GUN OVER BULLET-SWEPT GROUND, BUT IN THE IMMENSE SPACES OF THE DESERT IT BECAME THE PRIMARY METHOD OF MOVEMENT FOR MOST INFANTRY BECAUSE OF ITS CROSS-COUNTRY ABILITY.

Afrika Korps was the tail-end of 15 Panzer Division vanishing over the horizon in the far distance as it hurried off to Sidi Rezegh. 22nd Armoured set off in pursuit, followed shortly afterwards by 4th Armoured, but their intended flank attack was delivered too late and they merely brushed with the rearguard. After regrouping 22nd Armoured made another dash forward, intending another try at a flank attack, but this time they ran on to the usual anti-tank screen of 88mm guns and lost seven tanks before breaking off the action. After following 15 Panzer on its flank for about an hour 22nd Armoured then decided to stop and refuel. 4th Armoured did likewise, and they watched the rearguard of 15 Panzer vanish into the haze, convinced that the defeated Germans were retiring as hard as they could go; after all, they were moving in the right direction for a retreat.

By that time Sidi Rezegh was under attack. Brigadier Davy, commanding at Sidi Rezegh, was warned of the approach of German armored forces just as the Support Group began its attack. He knew that the break-out from Tobruk had begun and that everything hinged on the meeting at El Duda, so nothing could be allowed to interfere with the northward thrust. All he could do was muster what remained of his force and prepare to stave off the Panzers until the link-up at El Duda was made. A battery of Royal Horse Artillery 25-pr guns was deployed as a screen, backed by his reserve of 2nd Royal Tank Regiment, while the tanks of the 7th Hussars went forward to locate and delay the advance of the German force. According to the best information Davy had, he was faced with a single panzer division which, in all probability, would have 4th Armoured Brigade harrying its progress, and in any case he was expecting 22nd Armoured to appear at any moment; nobody had told him of the change in plan which had sent 22nd Armoured to Gabr Saleh the previous night.

To Davy's horror, he was confronted now by an entire German Panzer Corps which proceeded to destroy his armor systematically. Deploying a screen of anti-tank guns to keep 2 RTR at arms length, the two Panzer Divisions hunted down and destroyed every tank of 7th Hussars; the regiment was smashed beyond recovery and was never to be reformed in the Western Desert campaign. Having completed this bloody morning's work, the Panzers refuelled, and prepared to sweep the length of the valley and clear the remaining British troops from the airfield and its environs.

The first German tanks moved forward to reconnoiter an area occupied by 2 Rifle Brigade which was strengthened by two 2-pounder anti-tank guns and six 25-pr guns of 60th Regiment RA. The 2-pr anti-tank gun was, by that time, outclassed by the German armor; to succeed it had to be close, but the guns mounted on the German tanks could out-range it, and thus they generally managed to discover the 2-pr and shoot it up before they got into danger. But here the 2-prs managed to get a few shots in before they were put out of action.

The 25-pr field artillery gun was, as events were to

A COLUMN OF GERMAN ARMY PANZER II TANKS MOVING ACROSS THE DESERT. THE PANZER II WAS INTENDED AS A TRAINING TANK, BUT USE IN SPAIN SHOWED THAT IT WAS A GOOD BATTLE TANK EVEN THOUGH ONLY ARMED WITH A 20MM GUN. AGAINST THE BRITISH CRUISERS IN THE DESERT IT SERVED WELL, BUT THE RUSSIAN CAMPAIGN ENDED ITS USEFUL LIFE.

prove during this battle, the salvation of the Eighth Army. Not simply for its usual role as supporting weapon but for its formidable anti-tank performance. It was equipped with a 20lb solid steel armor-piercing shot which was fired at 1700 feet per second, and this was, at that time and against the tanks of the day, a lethal projectile; there was not a tank in existence which could survive against a 25-pr gun at 800 yards range. Four German tanks were now wrecked by the guns of 60th Regiment and the remainder moved hurriedly back out of danger.

It is worth pausing for a moment here to visualize the situation, one which is totally unique in the Second World War. Taking a slice of North Africa we have, running from north to south, firstly the British and Polish troops breaking out of Tobruk. Beneath them we have a layer of Germans and Italians who are fighting northwards against the Tobruk sortie and southwards against the attempted break through by the Support Group. Below them is the Support Group fighting north and 7th Armoured Brigade fighting southwards against the Panzer Corps, and at the same time the Panzer Corps are warding off attack from the 4th and 22nd Armoured Brigades. And as time went on the edges between these layers became more and more ragged and the various contestants became more and more inextricably mixed.

The Rifle Brigade signalled the imminence of an armored attack back to 7th Armoured Brigade HQ but were disbelieved; they were roundly abused, indeed, for mistakenly firing on the tanks of 7th Hussars, for the HQ were as yet unaware of the complete destruction of that regiment. But before they could do anything about correcting the misapprehension, the forward position was attacked by a squadron of Stukas, followed by a heavy artillery bombardment. In the middle of this they managed to get another message back to HQ which left HQ in no doubt as to the accuracy of the riflemen's tank recognition, as a result of which five Crusader tanks drove forward to the battalion area. They were forthwith destroyed by long-range anti-tank guns. The German panzers came on again, the 60th Field Regiment engaged them, and the battle resolved into a straight duel between tanks and guns. Inevitably the six guns were overwhelmed by the far greater number of tanks, and every gun was eventually destroyed or the gunners killed.

Gradually the Panzers moved down the valley, resisted by more of the 60th Field Regiment's guns, and gradually these guns were silenced. All that now remained of the British force was the Brigade HQ, a handful of guns, a few infantrymen, and the remnants of the 6 RTR tanks which had been repulsed by the anti-tank guns in their attempt to break through to El Duda. At this moment 21 Panzer found itself short of ammunition, and 15 Panzer found itself under pressure from the tanks of 2 RTR; these, it will be recalled, had been held off during the morning battle while 7th Hussars were wiped out and they had moved out of range, circled, and were about to make an attack on 15 Panzer's flank. And then, at the eleventh hour, 22nd Armoured Brigade appeared, followed by 4th Armoured. They were still some distance away from Sidi Rezegh, having no cause to hurry — had they not seen the Afrika Corps in retreat? — but outlying reconnaissance units of the Panzer Corps reported their approach, and this was sufficient to make the Panzers pause and reduce the force of their attack, making preliminary moves to counter this new threat. Somehow the British managed to survive until nightfall when, under cover of darkness, they were able to disengage.

Taking stock

Altogether, the Afrika Korps had had a good day; they had stalled the attempted breakout from Tobruk, destroyed an entire British cavalry regiment, severely damaged two other armored regiments and inflicted heavy casualties on the Rifle Brigade. Nevertheless, both Rommel and Cruewell were far from happy, since they both were sure that the forces arrayed against them were far more powerful than they were in reality. Cruewell therefore pulled 15 Panzer back from Sidi Rezegh and ordered them to take up a position to the south where they could block 22nd Armoured's advance, and ordered 21 Panzer to move around the airfield ridge and concentrate at Belhammed, from where he was to clear the ridge on the following day. As a result the remaining British were once again astonished to see the German threat melt away before their eyes.

Moreover when the results of the day were added up at XXX Corps HQ, the balance appeared to be in favor of the British. This was due firstly to exaggerated claims for the number of German tanks knocked out, and secondly to an optimistic type of arithmetic which said

'If we have lost x tanks, then surely the Germans must have lost at least x and possibly x + y tanks, therefore we must be winning.' The official estimate, indeed, was that German losses were as three to one against British losses, a fine piece of optimism. The only people who appear not to have been happy were the unfortunates inside Tobruk; at 1600hrs their commander had given up hope of the promised link-up and had thereafter confined his endeavors to holding on to what had been gained.

On the British side, though, one notable thing had happened during that day; on the orders of General Cunningham the New Zealanders had at last been given leave to join the war, and by late afternoon they had reached Sidi Azeiz and were pushing ahead towards Bardia and Fort Capuzzo. The 7th Indian Brigade, of 4th Indian Division, had also moved up, had swung behind the Italian positions at Sidi Omar, and were preparing to assault them next day.

On the morning of the 22nd the infantry, accompanied by armor, attacked the German-Italian positions at Libyan Omar and Sidi Omar and, though losing their lead tanks to a combination of mines and 88mm guns, took their objectives by early afternoon. 5th New Zealand Brigade took Fort Capuzzo at about the same time, while 4th New Zealand Brigade reached the outskirts of Bardia. 6th NZ Brigade had reached the

A STUART TANK PASSES A WRECKED PANZER III IN THE DESERT. THE PANZER III WAS THE MOST FORMIDABLE GERMAN TANK OF ITS DAY, ARMED WITH A POWERFUL 50MM GUN AND CAPABLE OF OUT-RANGING ANY ALLIED TANK OR ANTI-TANK GUN IN 1941. THOSE USED IN AFRICA WERE SPECIALLY MODIFIED FOR 'TROPICAL' CONDITIONS.

heights of the Trigh Capuzzo ridge and were moving along it westwards by noon, headed towards an area into which Cruewell had directed 15 Panzer. Rommel descended on 21 Panzer and directed them to assault the ridge which the Rifle Brigade had won on the previous day, while 5 Panzer Regiment were to head towards El Duda and then come back into the Sidi Rezegh valley from the other end and sweep through it to remove whatever might be left of the British.

There was, by this time, a considerable increase in British strength around the airfield. 22nd and 4th Armoured Brigades had finally arrived and taken up positions during the night, though in the morning they had both moved out into the desert in order to try and locate reported German armor, without success. General Cunningham decided to thicken his move towards Tobruk with more infantry and ordered 1st and 5th South African Brigades to move to the Sidi Rezegh area, their task of masking the Ariete Division being taken over by 22nd Guards Brigade who, until then, had had to be content with guarding field maintenance areas and supply dumps which were rapidly coming into existence behind the battle area. 1st SA Brigade would take time to arrive, since they would need to hand over to 22nd Guards, but 5th SA Brigade were to move as quickly as possible so that they could thicken up the Rifle Brigade position on the ridge; there were indications that German forces were building up and might be preparing to attack.

The battle for Sidi Rezegh
Before the South Africans could even begin to move, however, the First Battle of Sidi Rezegh began. At 1415 fifty panzers were seen to be advancing from the west,

with more tanks crowding along behind them and their usual accompanying anti-tank guns rolling along on their flanks. The first line of British defense was the guns of 4th Regiment RHA, and these were soon in action at point-blank range. Though they fired valiantly and took a toll of the advancing armor, the relentless pressure was bound to overcome them shortly unless relief arrived. And, surprisingly, relief did arrive, just in time. 22nd Armoured Brigade came roaring in from their desert tour, across the airfield, between the guns, and began to engage the panzers.

It was a short-lived relief; 22nd Armoured were rapidly shattered by the mass of German tanks, but it was sufficient of a respite to permit the gunners to bring up more ammunition, clear away the empty cartridge cases, attend to their wounded, and then plunge back into the battle as the last of 22nd Armoured went down fighting or limped back from the battle. The pressure was on once more, and one by one the guns fell silent.

On the ridge, too, disaster struck. Attacked from the rear and without any anti-tank defense remaining to them, the Rifle Brigade were flushed from their positions, killed or captured, and by nightfall the ridge was in German hands.

On the airfield more relief appeared. At 1530 4th Armoured Brigade drove in from its abortive desert trip with 108 Stuart tanks. At first they found it difficult to grasp what was going on in the confused melee around the airfield. They were soon taken in hand by Brigadier Jock Campbell, commander of the Support Group who had, for most of the day, been directing the defense of the airfield, and the 108 Stuart tanks vanished into an enormous cloud of dust and sand to do battle with whatever they could find.

By this time the Panzers were running dangerously short of ammunition, and it was necessary for them to disengage from this riotous assembly and replenish their tanks. And so, to the surprise of the battered British forces on the airfield, the dust cloud gradually cleared and revealed the panzers withdrawing towards the ridge. The tanks of 4th Armoured stopped on the edge of the airfield, and there set up a defensive line, which was soon stiffened by the few remaining guns and infantrymen. And as the day drew to a close, General Gott came up to assess the position. Since 7th Armoured and 22nd Armoured could muster less than 50 tanks between them, and since 4th Armoured had 100 tanks left but these were only light tanks and no match for Panzers in a straight fight, it seemed that the wisest course was to withdraw from this exposed and totally undefensible position. By moving south they could gain the comforting presence of the South African Division and then re-form to continue the battle.

The 5th South African Brigade had been given the task of clearing the ridge to the South of Sidi Rezegh, but had run into trouble. The German opposition had been far more severe than they had bargained for, plus a Stuka attack had caused severe casualties before they

had even begun their attack. As a result instead of clearing the ridge they were pinned down and in no position to do much to assist the British troops who now began falling back towards them from Sidi Rezegh. To add to the day's toll of disaster, 8 Panzer regiment of 15 Pz Division blundered into the HQ of 4th Armoured Brigade, sitting out in the desert awaiting the return of their squadrons. The Germans were quicker off the mark than the British, jumped from their tanks with submachine guns and within minutes the Brigade Second-in-Command and his staff, 35 tanks, artillery and vehicles were all taken by the Germans.

By a strange coincidence, though, this loss was equalized on the following day. The New Zealanders had been delayed by minefields in their move westwards during the afternoon, had stopped to refuel and eat after nightfall, and at 0300 had moved on again. Close to dawn the column halted to allow reconnaissance parties to move out and establish their position. As dawn broke it revealed firstly that they were not where they thought they were, and secondly that they had managed to form a laager completely surrounding General Cruewell's Afrika Korps headquarters. This time the New Zealanders were quicker to the draw than the Germans, and Cruewell's HQ was rapidly rounded up and sent back to the prisoner-of-war cages. The only flaw was that Cruewell, together with his Chief of Staff Bayerlein, had left the HQ about thirty minutes before the New Zealanders arrived.

Rommel, on the morning of 23 November, was at last sure that he knew what was going on and that he held the initiative. His troops held Sidi Rezegh airfield and the southern ridge, and south of them was what remained of the British and South African force. He

SOUTH AFRICAN INFANTRY ADVANCING THROUGH A SMOKESCREEN DURING THEIR ATTEMPT TO TAKE THE SOUTHERN END OF THE SIDI REZEGH ESCARPMENT ON 22 NOVEMBER, 1941. THE ATTACK FAILED, CASUALTIES WERE HEAVY, AND THE BRIGADE WAS WITHDRAWN.

therefore ordered 15 Panzer to move south, towards Bir el Gubi, and the Ariete Division to move north from El Gubi, the two to meet somewhere south of the British position and then, concentrated, to sweep back northwards, encircle the British, trap them against the German troops holding the ridge, and destroy them.

15 Panzer duly set off at dawn, followed by 21 Panzer who were slower in moving away, and in their course across the desert blundered into the British 'B Echelon' — the collection of trucks and soft vehicles which contained the supply group and such things as gun tractors and maintenance vehicles not required in the front line. The sudden intrusion of a Panzer division into this cosy domestic encampment scattered them to the four winds, while the few tanks and guns which were attached for protection purposes did their best to stem the flow, though to little avail. Guns and tanks raced to the scene from the concentration area to the north, attempting to take the Panzers in flank, and while there was little sense of organized opposition, certainly these miscellaneous attacks here and there caused the Panzers some problems. Nevertheless, they had thoroughly scattered the 'B Echelon' and taken vast quantities of prisoners, though because of the drag these parties would have been on the German advance, many were later simply released and allowed to wander back to their own lines at their own convenience. At last, after an hour or so of this melee, the Panzers pulled clear and continued on their ordained route to Bir el Gubi.

It was obvious to the British and South Africans that the Panzers were going to vanish into the desert, regroup, refuel, stock up with ammunition, and then come back to repeat the performance, and therefore the entire force set about organizing defenses against the coming storm. 25pr, 2pr and even a couple of ancient 18pr field guns were accumulated from all parts of the concentration area and moved to form a barrier in the south, and the whole area below the ridge was put into a state of defense. All the time German artillery in the Belhammed area was pounding the British and South African positions with random gunfire.

Shortly after noon the Germans and Italians made contact and after some debate (since, strictly speaking, the Italian Ariete Division was not under Rommel's command) some two-thirds of the Italian armor was combined with the Panzer corps and the accumulated troops were being positioned ready for their attack. In defiance of normal tactics, Cruewell decided that strange situations warrant strange dispositions; he simply formed all his armor into a long line of some 260 tanks and followed this with two regiments of lorried infantry. At 1500 Cruewell signalled the advance, and these two long lines swept forward across the desert towards 5th South African Brigade.

All this preparation had, uniquely, been carried out in full sight of some of the defenders, who had used artillery in an endeavor to break it up, though without much success. But as soon as the advance began, it was rapidly within range of the artillery in the defensive line, and a storm of fire broke against the moving tanks. The Italians, on the left flank, were badly mauled and fell back, so exposing the flanks of 5 Panzer Regiment, while the lorried infantry suffered enormously from gunfire, both directed at them and haphazard shots intended for the tanks in front of them.

The tanks broke through the gun line and wheeled round to assist their infantry, and numerous isolated small fights began as sections of German infantry attempted to prevent guns being withdrawn to new positions and sections of South African infantry tried to stop them. Soon almost all the guns were silent, and the panzers were able to work their way systematically through the South African position, destroying as they went. Crusader tanks of 22nd Armoured came up and attempted a flank attack, but this was repelled, and at one stage of this small battle both sides were fighting and maneuvering around and through the South African field hospital. To the astonishment of the medical staff, the tanks of both sides were particularly careful not to damage any of the hospital facilities, were careful not to run over men lying on the ground, and generally went out of their way to avoid any damage to the non-combatants. But no sooner had the tank battle moved away than German infantry followed up and the entire hospital was made prisoner. Brigade Headquarters, some distance behind the Field Hospital, was made prisoner shortly afterwards.

Eventually the Germans secured the entire area and the Panzers pushed through to make contact with the German infantry holding the northern edge of the arena. 5th South African Brigade lay shattered, but the cost to the Germans had been terribly high, some 60 or 70 tanks and a high proportion of their battle-seasoned officers and senior NCOs. What was left of the mixed British and South African force withdrew southwards; 7th Armoured Division now had about 70 tanks in running order. General Cunningham now realized that he no longer had the overwhelming superiority in armor with which he had begun the battle, and if Rommel maneuvered so as to get between the British and the Egyptian frontier there would be nothing to stop him driving straight to Cairo. The decision had to be taken; either continue the battle in the hope of recouping something, or disengage entirely and withdraw back to Egypt. Disinclined to take such a responsibility, Cunningham asked Auchinleck to come forward, see the situation at first hand, and take the necessary decision.

Auchinleck was in no doubt once he had heard all the reports; the battle would continue. XXX Corps would reorganize and refit, but continue to protect the New Zealanders from armored attack; XIII Corps, which had been hardly affected by the events of the past two days, was to assume responsibility for relieving Tobruk, capturing the Sidi Rezegh El Duda ridge in the process. The Oasis Force (still maneuvering away in the south) was to turn and make for the coast road to form a road-block against any Axis retreat.

But all this was to be thwarted by Rommel. After a meeting with Cruewell on the morning of the 24th, Rommel came to the conclusion that the British had shot their bolt; XXX Corps had been destroyed and the whole of 8th Army must, by this time, be in a state of chaos. He was therefore intent upon driving eastwards to deal with the New Zealand and Indian divisions before they were ready to assault Tobruk, capture Habbata and Maddalena and thus acquire the 8th Army's supplies, and finally retake Sidi Omar and generally relieve his hard-pressed frontier troops.

The dash to the wire

Thus began what the British were later to call 'The Dash to the Wire', 'the Wire' being the Cyrenaica-Egypt frontier line. Leaving a small force to block the New Zealanders' advance, Rommel led 21 Panzer eastward along the Trigh el Abd track headed for Bir Sheferzen on the frontier. Behind came 15 Panzer, and accompanying them were elements of the Ariete Division (now formally transferred to Rommel's command by Mussolini) and two German infantry regiments who were hoping, as they went along, to accumulate sufficient abandoned British transport to replace their own losses. The route took them from a point south of Sidi Rezegh in a south-easterly arc, and this, inadvertently, swept them past a number of B Echelon encampments.

Rommel now had the same view which 5 Panzer had had the previous day, of British and South African supply trains suddenly galvanized into activity by the appearance of Panzers and furiously dashing off in all directions in order to get out of the way. In this way they scattered elements within the 1st SA Brigade area, XXX Corps HQ units, 7th Armoured Division, 1st SA Division, 7 Support Group and the remains of 7th Armoured Brigade. Had Rommel not been insisting on speed to the frontier, the Afrika Korps could have made a fine haul during the course of their cruise across the desert. As it was, almost all the startled formations managed to get clear and live for another day.

By 1600 Rommel had arrived at the frontier at Gasr el Abid and ordered von Ravenstein with the forward elements of 21 Panzer Division to carry on to Halfaya. The following day they were to turn towards Sollum and then attack westwards while 15 Panzer, straddling the frontier, would drive North to complete an encirclement. The Italian Ariete and Trieste divisions were to attack Fort Capuzzo. But due to the Ariete Division being slow to arrive, the orders had to be changed almost as soon as they had been given. Now 15 Panzer would attack between Sidi Omar and Sidi Azeiz.

About one hour later Cruewell arrived, less confident than Rommel; from his position with the rear of the German column, Cruewell had been able to see that the British formations, after their initial scattering, were coming together very quickly and were able to do some damage to the rear end of the column. And if the British had been disorganized, so now was the Afrika Korps, spread across miles of desert, with vehicles breaking down or running out of fuel, formations leapfrogging each other instead of staying in their allotted places, others falling out to refuel or eat from time to time and then attempting to catch up.

Moreover, when Rommel and Cruewell sat down to digest the accumulated status reports from their various formations which were now beginning to come in, a pretty dismal picture began to emerge. 21 Panzer now had only 20 tanks left in battleworthy condition; the 21st Panzer's Divisional Reconnaissance Regiment now had no armored cars left; over 70 tanks had been lost in the previous day's battles, and instead of the efficient Afrika Korps recovery service collecting these from the battlefield for repair, they were actually part of the 'Dash to the Wire' and were fully occupied trying to deal with the day's breakdowns.

The morning of the 25th found Rommel's men on the frontier moving off in their assigned directions. It also found the British and Commonwealth troops realizing that with Rommel away, there was a chance that the relief of Tobruk might actually become a reality. Two brigades of New Zealanders were moving towards Tobruk, intending to take the principal high features in the area — Zaafran, El Duda, Belhammed and the Sidi Rezegh ridge. Since there was little armor left to accompany the infantry, General Freyberg decided on a night attack, with his remaining tanks following the infantry to assist in consolidation. The attack began at 2100 and, in that broken and unmapped

ITALIAN GUNNERS FIRING A 75MM ANSALDO MODEL 37 FIELD GUN. THIS FIRED A 6.4KG SHELL TO 12,580M RANGE, BUT ONLY A SMALL NUMBER WERE BUILT AND IT WAS ONLY USED BY THE 'FAST DIVISION' IN AFRICA, BEING ONE OF THE FEW ITALIAN GUNS DESIGNED FOR MOTOR TRACTION.

country, soon took on a confused appearance. In spite of bitter fighting the New Zealanders had not taken their objectives by dawn.

But at the same time the Tobruk Garrison had decided that it was time to break out and by dawn they had cut through an Italian division, beat off a counter-attack during the morning, and by early afternoon had arrived at El Duda. This spurred on the New Zealanders, who could watch the Tobruk force taking El Duda, and as soon as darkness fell another spirited attack was put in. By the morning of the 27th the entire Sidi Rezegh area was firmly in New Zealand hands. Another battalion of the New Zealanders had bypassed the battle and linked up with the Tobruk force at El Duda, and the relief had been finally completed.

The Germans, during the day, had seen their plans go somewhat awry. 21 Panzer had attempted to recapture Sidi Omar, but had run up against dogged resistance from the Indian Brigade who were happily located behind the excellent wire and minefields originally built by the Germans themselves. 5 Panzer Regiment were badly mauled when they ran up against 1st Field Regiment RA and 4/11 Sikh Regiment in an outpost in the desert south of Sidi Omar, losing 18 tanks to the guns while the infantry, with no part to play in the engagement sat in their slit trenches and threw their steel helmets in the air with cheers every time a German tank caught fire. The Royal Air Force, which throughout Crusader had been assiduous in providing support by ground attack and bombers, caught a column attempting to attack the British railhead and dump at Mis Heifa and destroyed it. 15 Panzer were stalled in their attempt to reach Sidi Azeiz due to supply problems, and the Ariete Division was delayed by a brush with 1st South African Brigade.

General Auchinleck, reviewing the situation, considered that whilst there was yet the possibility of success if the momentum of attack was kept up, there seemed to be something lacking in the command and direction by General Cunningham. Put at its simplest, Cunningham was looking over his shoulder too much, contemplating methods of defense when he ought to be thinking more of attack. A replacement was needed, and after reviewing the possibilities, Auchinleck appointed Major-General Ritchie, his Deputy Chief of Staff in place of Cunningham, who flew back to Cairo and was admitted to hospital suffering from acute exhaustion. Ritchie took command of the 8th Army on 26 November.

By now Rommel had reached the conclusion that his 'Dash to the Wire' had been a fruitless exercise, particularly in view of the reports he was receiving about activity around Tobruk and Sidi Rezegh. He therefore decided to wind up the various activities on the frontier, turn his Panzers westwards once more, and return for another battle around Sidi Rezegh. Early on 27 November the move west began; after initial problems when various regiments became entangled, this was sorted out and then 15 Panzer unexpectedly ran head on

SOUTH AFRICAN TROOPS ATTACKING A STRONGPOINT NEAR SOLLUM. ONE MAN IS ABOUT TO THROW A GRENADE WHILE HIS COMPANIONS WAIT TO FOLLOW UP THE EXPLOSION. WHILE THE SOUTH AFRICAN COMMANDERS TENDED TO BE SLOW OFF THE MARK, THERE WAS NOTHING TO FAULT IN THE SKILL AND BRAVERY OF THE TROOPS THEMSELVES.

into a New Zealand B Echelon which, among other things, contained the HQ of 5 NZ Brigade. The entire contents of this area were captured, including the New Zealand commander, Brigadier Hargest.

The battle is rejoined

News of the German advance went before them and the British forces around Sidi Rezegh made their preparations. By now the supply and repair services had been able to put some strength back into the badly battered armored units. 4th Armoured Brigade now had 77 M3 Stuart tanks, 22nd Armoured had 42 assorted Cruiser tanks, though 7th Armoured Brigade had been so badly mauled that they had been withdrawn. XXX Corps were in good shape, and from all this it was decided that an ambush could be laid. 22nd Armoured would move down into the German's path, while 4th Armoured would lurk several miles south in the desert so as to be able to move in at speed and take the rear of the column when it had been stopped by 22nd. To screen all this from surprise by any other German units moving around in the area, the Support Group split up into separate small columns and fanned out to the eastward.

22nd Armoured took up hull-down positions, their vulnerable vehicles screened by earthworks and only their light 2pr guns showing; they were backed by two batteries of 25pr field guns to act as long-range anti-tank weapons and thus keep the Panzers as far from the ambushing tanks as possible. No sooner was the position occupied than the head of the German column appeared and the ambush was sprung. The tanks played havoc with the advance guard armored cars while the field guns stood off the heavier tanks. As might be expected the German force reacted violently and began deploying for the inevitable counter-attack, but before this could be started 4th Armoured raced over the horizon and fell on the rear of the stalled column. Finally squadrons of Desert Air Force fighters and bombers appeared overhead to add to the confusion.

Had the day lasted longer, 15 Panzer would undoubtedly have been destroyed. But night fell at about 1715 and, as was the tribal custom, the British armor broke off the action and retired some five miles into the desert, there to form their laager and settle down for the night. Much relieved by this kindness, 15 Panzer collected their remaining men and vehicles and drove off on their original course; after about seven miles they, too, decided to bed down for the night.

On the following day 15 Panzer crossed the ridge and swept down the Sidi Rezegh valley, bypassing the various British and New Zealand units there, turned north at the end and attacked El Duda in an attempt to close the 'Tobruk Corridor'. The position was held by three battalions of infantry and 26 tanks of 4th RTR. Inside three hours the Panzer attack rolled over the infantry, destroyed all the anti-tank guns and 15 tanks, but was then brought up short by running into the concentrated fire of a battery of RHA 25pr guns. This firmly pinned the tanks down as night fell and prevented further advance. After pausing for a while, shortly before midnight the artillery loosed a fierce bombardment, and under cover of this the 11 remaining 4 RTR tanks, shoulder to shoulder, and accompanied by two Australian infantry companies, charged the astonished Panzers. Two hours later the position was in the hands of its former owners and the Germans were either prisoners or dead.

The next day started badly for the Germans when von Ravenstein accidentally drove into a New Zealand position and was taken prisoner, together with various documents revealing German and Italian locations and the daily cipher changes for the week. Things improved later in the day when a powerful attack on the Sidi Rezegh ridge finally drove the New Zealanders from their position. The remnants of 22nd Armoured Brigade were handed over to 4th Brigade and 22nd HQ retired back to Egypt, and the new composite force attempted to repel the German advance. By this time, however, both men and machines were feeling the strain, and the verve and dash with which attacks had been put in during the first days of Crusader was no longer in evidence. The appearance of a force of Italian light tanks in the distance was enough to halt the advance, an artillery duel began, and when night fell the armor, as usual, fell back to a night laager.

The first day of December saw a violent attack by 15 Panzer on the New Zealanders holding Belhammed. Mist and smoke confused the battlefield, the artillery could see nothing, even the tanks found themselves blinded, and the affair resolved itself into an infantry battle which ended in the complete vanquishing of the New Zealanders and the cutting of the 'Tobruk Corridor'. What particularly irked the New Zealanders was the fact that during their tenacious grasp of the corridor, 4/22nd Armoured and 1st South African Brigade had maneuvered pointlessly around the desert to the south instead of coming up and reinforcing them.

In spite of this setback, Ritchie was determined to keep up the pressure on the German forces, and planned to attack El Adem, an important communications center for the Afrika Korps some 15 miles west of El Duda and a short distance from the Tobruk perimeter. XXX Corps was given this task and was to be made up from 7th Armoured Division, 1st South African Brigade, 22nd Guards Brigade and 4th Indian Division who were to be relieved on the frontier by 2nd South African Division. But before this advance could take place it would be necessary to eliminate a strong German position some six miles north of Bir el Gubi. 11th Indian Brigade, supported by armor was sent to do this, but the attack failed and the Indians suffered heavy casualties.

Rommel's weaknesses

Rommel, for his part, was acutely aware of his forces still left on the frontier, and so leaving a strong force to watch the British around Sidi Rezegh, he sent out two columns eastwards to clear the lines of communication to his frontier positions. Both these were spotted from the air; the northern column was ambushed and destroyed by 5th New Zealand Division, while the southern was similarly caught and destroyed by 4th Indian Division.

Having seen the failure of this move, Rommel now decided on an all-out attack against the British force near Bir el Gubi. Stripping the masking troops from the eastern Tobruk perimeter, and ordering 15 and 21 Panzer plus the Ariete and Trieste Italian divisions to assemble north of Bir El Gubi, the attack was scheduled

A SOUTH AFRICAN MARMON-HERRINGTON ARMORED CAR DUG INTO THE DESERT IN A RECONNAISSANCE POSITION. THE MARMON-HERRINGTON WAS AN AMERICAN DESIGN BUILT BY THE FORD MOTOR COMPANY IN SOUTH AFRICA AND WAS ARMED WITH THE .55IN ANTI-TANK RIFLE, THOUGH MANY WERE SOON UP-GUNNED WITH CAPTURED ITALIAN AND GERMAN WEAPONS.

A VICKERS LIGHT TANK CONTEMPLATES A DUST STORM. THE VICKERS DESIGN WAS THE LAST OF A SERIES WHICH BEGAN IN THE LATE 1920S AND THE DESERT WAS THEIR LAST BATTLE. WITH NO MORE THAN 15MM OF ARMOR AND ARMED WITH A .50IN MACHINE GUN THEY WERE NO MATCH FOR THE GERMAN ARMOR, BUT WITH LITTLE ELSE AVAILABLE AT THE OUTBREAK OF WAR THEY HAD TO BE USED. EXPERIENCE IN FRANCE SHOWED THEM TO BE RELATIVELY USELESS EXCEPT AS RECONNAISSANCE MACHINES AND THE DESERT REINFORCED THIS VIEW; THEY WERE RAPIDLY REPLACED BY STUARTS.

to take place on 6 December, but not for the first time, the Italians found an excuse not to appear and Rommel was forced to cancel the whole thing.

Rommel was now beginning to receive disturbing reports of serious deficiencies in his strength. Sixteen commanding officers had been killed or seriously wounded, there had been heavy losses in regimental officers, 3800 soldiers were lost, 142 tanks, 25 armored cars and 390 trucks had been destroyed, 42 anti-tank guns, 41 artillery guns and 60 mortars had gone, and the Korp's stock of fuel was rapidly shrinking. Moreover the Italian supply directorate reported that Allied attacks on shipping had now reached such a pitch that over fifty percent of ships carrying supplies from Italy to North Africa were being sunk en route. Not until the end of December, when German Luftwaffe squadrons would have been brought down and based so as to give protection to convoys, would the situation show any sign of improvement. Until that time Rommel would receive the bare minimum of supplies to keep him moving but he could expect no reinforcements, no new tanks, little ammunition. Faced with this shattering information Rommel, with 40 tanks under his command and dwindling stocks of fuel and ammunition realized that the only course left to him was to withdraw.

A fall-back position existed at Gazala, and it was into this which Rommel now withdrew his forces. He was pursued by XXX Corps but they were repulsed fairly easily. Tobruk, though, was again opened up and fully relieved — a success which escaped the headlines it might have made had it not occurred on 7 December, just as the Japanese were making their attack on Pearl Harbor.

On 9 December, Ritchie decided to pull XXX Corps back and put them to mopping-up operations among the scattered German and Italian outposts on the Egyptian frontier. He passed the responsibility for Rommel across to General Godwen-Austen and XIII Corps. Godwen-Austen felt that the Gazala position would fall to a solid attack and put Rommel out of the war once and for all, and he planned a concerted attack using the Polish Carpathian Division, fresh from their long stay in Tobruk, the 4th Indian Division, and 4th Armoured Brigade with about 90 tanks, who would make a wide sweep around Rommel's position and attack from the rear.

The attack opened on 15 December, and some progress was made at first. Then 4th Indian Division were stopped by fierce armored counter-attacks. 4th Armoured Brigade had to make a 70-mile trip across rough country and by the time they approached their planned position were dangerously low on fuel. They waited until the following day, by which time fuel had reached them, and then moved slowly against the rear of Rommel's defenses. They achieved very little and the attack was called off. Now plans were laid for an advance by 4th Armoured Brigade towards Mechile and by 4th Indian Division to a point west of Derna, the objective being to set everything up for a lunge against Benghazi. This move was to commence on 19 December. But it never took place, for during the night of 16/17 December Rommel, using all his customary skills, disengaged, slipped from his position at Gazala, and vanished into the desert.

Caught by surprise, XIII Corps set out in pursuit, but hampered by a shortage of fuel and by rough country on their chosen route, they were almost a week before they caught up with Rommel near Antelat. Here they ran up against another strong position and also discovered that Rommel had managed, in spite of the Supply Department's gloomy forecast, to strengthen his Panzers with 22 new tanks. 3rd RTR, the vanguard of the British force, were stopped and thrown back; 22nd Armoured Brigade were ordered forward but ran out of fuel en route and sat for a day awaiting supplies before they could respond to the call. From then on Operation Crusader simply ran itself down as Rommel, taking his time and picking his stopping places, cautiously retired, fending off every attempt by the British to bring matters to a conclusion. Eventually, by the end of December, the Afrika Korps was back in El Agheila, from whence they had begun their adventures in February.

The lessons

There were a number of lessons to be learned from Operation Crusader, principally by the British. The first was simply that the pre-war notions of unrestricted tank warfare were pipe dreams; tanks operating in a vacuum could not survive against an enemy who operated them as part of a balanced all-arms force. The ideas of using tanks as an independent force were finally exploded, although it was to take some time for the lesson to sink in.

An extension of this lesson was the example given by the Germans of using anti-tank guns in ambush to destroy armor instead of attempting to destroy it with more armor. Unfortunately the belief that the natural enemy of a tank is another tank is one which still obtains in many quarters, forty-odd years after Crusader and in spite of innumerable examples to the contrary. Which is why the tanks of the 1980s are highly specialized weapons for destroying other tanks but precious little use for their original purpose of accompanying and supporting infantry. It is likely that the future will show that the true tactical descendant of the original tank is actually today's 'infantry fighting vehicle', but this is, as yet, a matter of speculation.

The next important lesson to be extracted from Crusader is that of organization. For reasons which are involved and would demand very long and detailed explanation, the British forces in the desert became convinced that the division — that building brick of armies — was an unwieldy formation, and the fashion for 'Brigade Groups', 'Battle Groups', 'Columns', and other fragmented formations took over. As a result, British formations tended to be fed into battle piecemeal, battalions and brigades at a time, chewed up, and replaced by more of the same. On the other side the Germans kept their divisions together as much as possible, rarely broke them down into smaller formations and then only for special purposes, and thus managed to produce more power at the point of decision. As a side-issue from this fragmentation of formations, the British also demolished their artillery organization; instead of a divisional artillery which could be switched around from target to target with massive effect, regiments and batteries were detached and sent hither and thither about the desert in formations too small to have really decisive effect. It has to be admitted that much of this was due to the shortcomings of the 2-pounder anti-tank gun, which meant that infantry always insisted on having their attached artillery in positions where it could form their anti-tank defense. Once in these positions, they were rarely properly sited for indirect fire and concerted action.

The lesson of tank armament had also been learned in an expensive manner. British tanks were armed with the 2-pounder gun, the same gun that was being used as the anti-tank gun. This stemmed from pre-war reasoning which argued that since both the tank gun and the anti-tank gun had the same target, both should be the same. It overlooked the need for a gun capable of supporting infantry as well as shooting tanks, though lip-service was paid to this proposition by equipping a few tanks with 15-pounder shell-firing howitzers. Moreover, although a good high explosive shell existed for the 2-pounder, it seems that none ever managed to reach the troops in Egypt. On the other side the German tanks were equipped with a good 50mm gun capable of firing either solid shot or high explosive shell and with a far better range and penetrative performance than had the 2-pounder. Unfortunately, although this defect was realized by the British, the dimensions of the existing tanks precluded the fitting of any larger weapons into their turrets.

In one area, though, the British got it right; the support given to the ground troops by the Royal Air Force was far better than anything which had hitherto been experienced. Fighters patrolled the desert daily, fought the Luftwaffe and kept them off the backs of the soldiers whenever they could, while bombers and ground attack fighters made significant inroads into German columns and formations on the ground. It was this experience of what air power could do to assist the ground forces when properly directed which laid the foundation for the outstanding performance of the Tactical Air Force in Normandy three years later.

Crusader was a great step forward for the British, insofar as they relieved Tobruk and chased the Afrika Korps out of Cyrenaica. But it was an inconclusive victory; there was no smashing defeat for Rommel, no decisive encounter from which the British emerged as obvious winners and the Germans as obvious losers.

CHAPTER THREE

STORMING CORREGIDOR

SIEGE WARFARE
DECEMBER 1941 – MAY 1942

Overleaf

The last days of Corregidor when, virtually safe from retaliation, the
Japanese brought up heavy artillery close to the Marivelles shore and bombarded the island fortress round
the clock. (*Japanese Guns Pound Corregidor* by T Hadler)

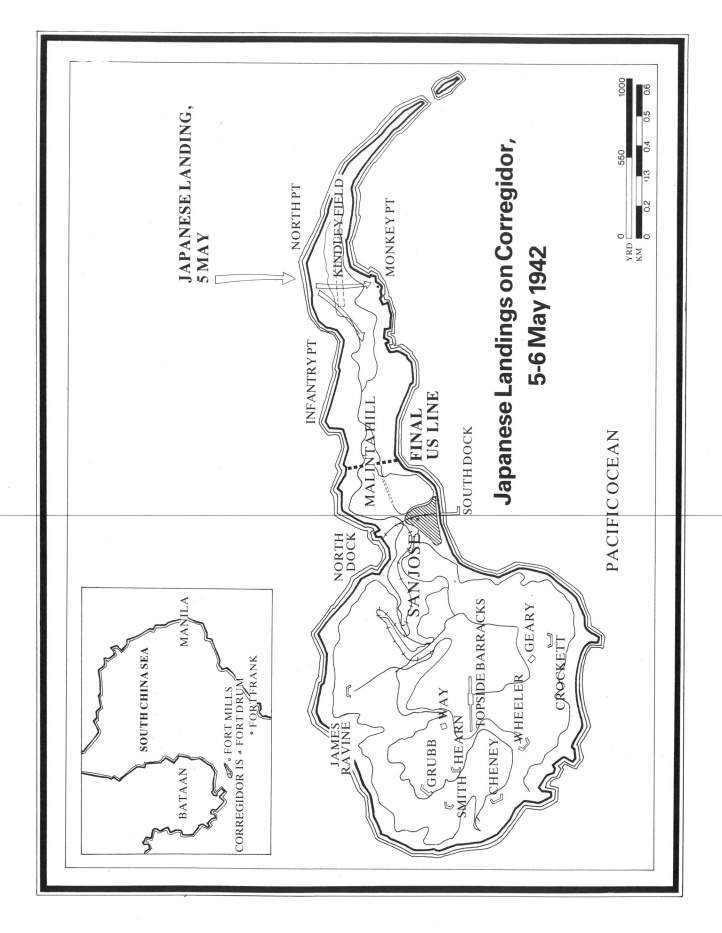

Japanese Landings on Corregidor, 5-6 May 1942

JAPANESE LANDING, 5 MAY

NORTH PT

KINDLEY FIELD

MONKEY PT

INFANTRY PT

MALINTA HILL

FINAL US LINE

SOUTH DOCK

NORTH DOCK

SAN JOSE

PACIFIC OCEAN

JAMES RAVINE

GRUBB

SMITH

HEARN

WAY

TOPSIDE BARRACKS

CHENEY

WHEELER

GEARY

CROCKETT

SOUTH CHINA SEA

MANILA

BATAAN

FORT MILLS

CORREGIDOR IS

FORT DRUM

FORT FRANK

KM 0   0.2   0.3   0.4   0.5   0.6
YRD 0   550   1000

At the end of the Spanish-American War in 1898 the United States found itself with a number of dependencies on its hands, and in the fashion of the day these had to be protected against seaborne attack by coast artillery batteries. In conformity with tactical teaching, coast batteries were not simply spread across the coastline — such a policy would rapidly bankrupt any power — but concentrated so as to protect attractive targets. And in the Philippine Islands the only attractive targets were Manila and the US Naval installations which were brought into being at Cavite on Manila Bay and in Subic Bay. As a result, the mouth of Manila Bay was turned into one of the strongest fortresses in the world by the building of four forts which between them mustered 70 pieces of artillery ranging from 3in anti-torpedo-boat guns to massive 14in rifles firing shells weighing half a ton.

The guns

The prime site was the island of Corregidor, which was transformed into Fort Mills. Corregidor was on the western side of the bay, close to the peninsula of Bataan and it was formidably armed with fourteen batteries of guns and mortars. Batteries Cushing, Hanna, James and Maxwell Keys each had two 3in rapid-fire guns to protect against close-in attack from high-speed small craft. Batteries Crockett, Cheney and Wheeler each had two 12in guns mounted on disappearing carriages; these were enormous structures which carried the gun barrel on top of pivoted arms, the lower end of the arm carrying an enormous counterweight. As the gun fired, so the force of the recoil caused the barrel to move back and turn the pivoted arm, lifting the counterweight. The barrel continued its movement and gradually dropped down behind a protective parapet, coming to rest close to the floor of its emplacement where it could be reloaded under cover. A raised sighting platform allowed the gunlayer to continue tracking the target while loading was in progress, and as soon as the gun was ready, a catch was released, the counterweight pulled on the end of the pivoted arm, and the gun barrel soared through the air to come to rest with the muzzle just above the protecting parapet, ready to fire.

Battery Grubb had two 10in guns on disappearing carriages, while Batteries Morrison and Ramsay had respectively two and three 6in guns on the same type of carriage. Battery Hearn and Battery Smith each had a single 12in gun on a barbette carriage, more modern than the disappearing type and one which held the gun in a cradle, allowing it to recoil but without any concealing movement. Finally came Batteries Geary and Way, with respectively eight and four 12in mortars, stubby breech-loading guns which fired at high elevation so as to drop their piercing shells down on to the lightly-armored decks of any warship within range. These mortars were in groups of four, each group in a steep-sided concrete pit about twenty feet deep, impossible to detect from the sea (as were the disappearing guns) and

capable of firing in any direction.

Powerful as these weapons were, they could not entirely seal off the entrance to the Bay, and on the eastern side two more small islands were converted into works of defense. Carabao Island became Fort Frank, and Caballo Island became Fort Hughes.

The design of Fort Mills had begun in about 1902, and its armament was a result of this early planing. In 1905 the 'Taft Board' on fortification met to discuss the defenses of the new possessions, and one of the recommendations of this board was that the 12in gun should be superseded by a new and more powerful weapon, a 14in gun. Stemming from this, Forts Frank and Hughes were designed in accordance with the Taft Board's ideas, and both used these new weapons. Fort Frank contained Batteries Crofton and Greer, each with a single 14in gun, plus Battery Koehler of eight 12in mortars and Battery Hoyle with two 3in rapid fire guns. Fort Hughes had Batteries Gillespie and Woodruff, each with one 14in gun, Battery Craighill with eight 12in mortars, Battery Leach with two 6in guns on disappearing carriages, and Battery Fuger with two 3in rapid fire guns.

TOP: A 12IN DISAPPEARING GUN OF BATTERY CROCKETT AS FOUND BY THE US FORCES WHO RE-TOOK THE ISLAND IN 1945. DURING THE WAR THE JAPANESE DID NOTHING TO FORT MILLS AND THUS THE 1945 PICTURES ARE VIRTUALLY THE ONLY RECORD OF WHAT THE FORT LOOKED LIKE AFTER THE SURRENDER. ABOVE: PHILIPPINE SCOUTS LOADING A 12IN DISAPPEARING GUN IN FORT MILLS IN 1940. NOTE HOW THE CREW WERE PROTECTED BY THE WALL FROM FIRE FROM THE SEA DURING LOADING BUT NOT FROM AERIAL ATTACK.

Outside Manila Bay — 'around the corner' as it were — lay Subic Bay, in which the US Navy were building a major repair facility. Protection for this was assured by turning Grande Island into Fort Wint, providing it with Battery Warwick of two 10in guns, Batteries Hall and Woodruff each with two 6in guns on disappearing carriages, and Batteries Jewell (two 3in) and Flake (four 3in) of rapid fire guns.

All this gave the US Engineer Corps something to occupy themselves with for several years, but the planners were not entirely satisfied. Although the guns could cover every inch of the width of Manila Bay, it was possible to sail a ship up the middle of the channel at night without it being seen by the forts. Although the guns could reach such a target, it was impossible to detect it because the searchlights on the forts could not project their light for the necessary distance. And so in order to close the gap, placing guns and lights closer to the center of the bay's entrance, it became necessary to plan for an artificial island.

Artificial islands for forts was not a new idea; Britain had built several in the 1870s — at Plymouth and Portsmouth in England, and also at Bermuda — and the Russians had also built them at Kronstadt, guarding the entrance to St Petersburg. But these had been in waters which, compared to Manila Bay, were sheltered, smooth and shallow, and which were also relatively close to the manufacturing facilities. The prospect of trying to build a similar iron-armored island in Manila Bay was mechanically daunting; and, moreover, nobody was very sure of just what sort of a hell-hole an iron fort might be in that climate.

But as luck would have it, in almost the ideal spot was a tiny stump of rock called El Fraile Island. The Spanish had placed a battery of three 12cm guns there during the Spanish-American War, and it was generally agreed that this gun strength was not arrived at by any tactical formula; it was simply the maximum number of guns which could fit on to the small flat area of the island. It was obviously impossible to mount heavy artillery on it.

In 1908 a Lieutenant Kingman of the Corps of Engineers suggested encasing the island in concrete and putting two armored cupolas on top. The idea was examined, then modified; the top of the island would be blown off with explosives, then the remains would be encased in a block of concrete, on which two gun turrets each carrying two 14in guns would be installed. Work began on this plan in 1909, and the result was Fort Drum, more familiarly known to the US Army as 'The Concrete Battleship', since its shape was based on that of a ship. The concrete was shaped into a long prow facing out of the bay, with a blunt stern; the two turrets sat on the 'foredeck' with a naval-type lattice mast behind them carrying searchlights and rangefinding equipment. Inside the concrete block were living quarters, fire control rooms and magazines, and at each side of the 'hull' were two 6in guns in armored sponsons. The forward turret became Battery Marshall, the rear

Battery Wilson, and the two sponson batteries were named MacRea and Roberts. Fort Drum was handed over to the Coast Artillery Corps late in 1918, and with that the Harbor Defenses of Manila and Subic Bays were completed.

There was, however, one unfortunate feature about these defenses, a feature in common with coast defenses of that era all round the world. They were built with a seaborne or land-bound enemy in mind; they were built before the age of the aeroplane, and thus the gun emplacements were enormous open concrete pits with the guns sitting in the middle, open to the sky. What did the sky matter to the fortress engineer of the 1900s? His concern was to conceal the guns from observation by an enemy fleet, a fleet armed with flat-trajectory artillery which would never be able to drop shells vertically into the emplacements. Except for Fort Drum, every gun in the fortress was open to attack from the air, and the general opinion of aircraft even in the post-war years was not so high that anybody gave very much thought to the problem of protecting the guns. Which was, perhaps, just as well, since it would have been a formidable engineering problem and one which would probably only have produced a solution which would, by 1940, have been overmatched by the armor-piercing bomb.

After World War One, the Washington Naval Conference was held to settle various disputes about relative naval strengths, and one of its clauses restricted fortification in the Pacific Ocean area. This effectively prevented the US Army from moving in any heavier guns (a 16in had by that time been decided on as standard for future installations), so that the defenses of Manila were to remain at the same strength as they had been built. The only possible improvement was to bring the

A BATTERY OF 12IN MORTARS FIRING; THE CAMERA HAS CAUGHT A SHELL IN MID AIR. MORTARS WERE FIRED IN FOURS SO THAT THE FALL OF SHOT WOULD STRADDLE THE TARGET, DROPPING STEEPLY SO TO PENETRATE THE THIN DECK ARMOR OF WARSHIPS WITH THICK SIDE ARMOR.

rangefinding and fire control systems up to date. In passing, it should be said that the same restrictions prevented the British from improving the defenses of Hong Kong, but since Singapore was outside the restricted area the new naval base there was able to be fortified with the very latest equipment. Similarly, the restrictions should have applied to the Japanese, but they, secure in their ability to conceal whatever they were doing from prying eyes, were able to install powerful 16in and 12in turrets covering the area between Japan and Korea and also fortify several other Pacific island areas.

The plans

On 7 December 1941, as is well known, the Japanese aircraft carrier fleet made their surprise attack on the US Naval facility at Pearl Harbor in Hawaii. This attack, in many respects, was to seal the fate of the Philippine garrison, since it immediately destroyed one of the fundamental factors upon which the defense of the Philippines had been based, the availability of the US Navy. Pre-war planning for the defense of the islands had originally been devised by the US War Department as 'Plan Orange', and this envisaged defending Manila and its Bay and Subic Bay and the naval base there, staving off Japanese attacks until relieved by reinforcements brought by the US Navy. MacArthur, who assumed command in the Philippines on 26 July 1941, was able to have this plan amended to 'Plan Rainbow' which called for vigorous defense throughout the islands, but which still relied upon navy aid coming before the defenses ran out of reserves. With the destruction of the US Navy at Pearl Harbor it became obvious that any invasion of the Philippines by the Japanese could only have one end, since there was no way in which relief could be provided.

The Japanese, for their part, detailed off their Southern Army, under General Terauchi, to 'Seize American, British and Dutch possessions in the southern area' as soon as war was declared, and in September 1941 Terauchi began making plans for taking the Philippines, assigning the task to the 14th Army under General Homma. 14th Army consisted of 16th and 48th Divisions and 65th Brigade, totalling some 50,000 troops, and it was to be assisted by the 5th Air Group (Army), the 3rd Fleet and the 11th Air Fleet (Navy).

The general plan called for simultaneous air attacks on the first day of war against all known American installations. While these were in progress, Army and Marine units would land on Bataan Island, north of Luzon; at three locations on Luzon Island; and at Davao on Mindanao Island, and would seize airfields close to these landing points. These fields would then be occupied by Japanese air forces, from which they would be able to concentrate their attacks, particularly against airfields and US Army Force installations. Once US air strength was crippled, the main force of the 14th Army would land along Lingayen Gulf, north of

A 14IN DISAPPEARING GUN DURING ITS ACCEPTANCE AND PROOF TRIALS AND BEFORE INSTALLATION INTO ITS EMPLACEMENT, ALLOWING THE CONSTRUCTION AND METHOD OF OPERATION TO BE SEEN MORE CLEARLY. THE GUN LAYER REMAINED ON HIS PLATFORM, TRACKING THE TARGET, DURING THE GUN'S DISAPPEARANCE, LOADING AND RE-APPEARANCE.

Manila, while another force would land at Lamon Bay, southeast of Manila. These two forces would advance on Manila from two directions, and it was anticipated that they would then trap the major US Army strength and defeat it close to Manila. Once this had been done, the islands defending Manila Bay were to be captured, after which the remainder of the Philippines would be occupied. The entire programme was expected to last no more than fifty days — General Homma considered he could do it in 45 — after which about half of 14th Army and most of the air units would be withdrawn for operations in Thailand leading to the attack on British troops in Burma.

The attack

The events which led up to the incarceration of the garrison of Corregidor can be briefly recited. The Japanese attack proceeded entirely in accordance with Homma's plans; first the aerial bombardment, which quickly destroyed most of the US air strength and wrecked most of the airfields, as well as disposing of most of the light naval craft which were all that the Philippine Navy owned. Destruction of the US Naval base at Cavite by bombers led the US Navy commander, Admiral Hart, to evacuate his remaining naval vessels.

While these attacks were under way, the first landings were made by ground troops in the north and south of Luzon, as well as on Mindanao, their aim being to secure advanced bases from which close support aircraft could operate in connection with the forthcoming major landings. In this they were fully successful, being undisturbed by the defending force. On 22 December the main attack began with 45,000 troops being landed in Lingayen Gulf, to the northwest of

COAST DEFENSES OF CORREGIDOR

Fort Mills, built between 1905 and 1912, was representative of the most up-to-date thinking on coastal fortification, and its defenses revolved around three types of installation — the anti-torpedo-boat light gun, the long-range bombardment gun and the high-angle mortar. The drawing (below) shows a typical emplacement for four 12in mortars. The mortars are on turntables in the pit, which is about 8-10m deep and walled with reinforced concrete. On each flank of the pit are earth 'traverses' which separate adjacent pits and prevent enfilading fire dropping into the pit. Beneath the traverses are the magazines, with separate rooms for shells and for powder, from where the ammunition was trolleyed to the individual mortars. The magazines were of heavy reinforced concrete surmounted by earth and designed to prevent the heaviest naval shells from penetrating. Also beneath the traverse was the fire direction center, and on top of one traverse was an observation cell from which it was possible to see the field of fire and from where the battery commander controlled his mortars. Orders from the observation post would be sent to the fire direction center where they were converted into range and direction data for the mortars, and, after firing, the fall of shot would be spotted and corrected. A battery usually consisted of eight mortars, and four would be fired, followed by the other four on corrected data, so as to drench the target area with shot.

TYPICAL EMPLACEMENT FOR 12IN MORTARS

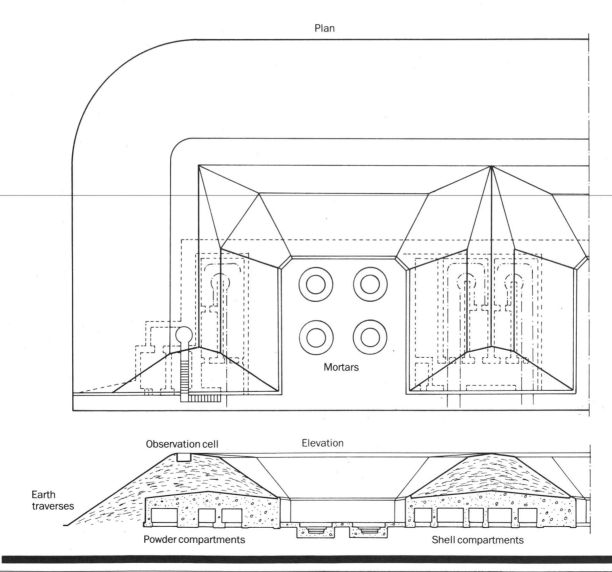

Plan

Mortars

Observation cell

Elevation

Earth traverses

Powder compartments

Shell compartments

Typical of the emplacements for disappearing guns is this plan of Battery Gillespie, Fort Hughes. The battery itself can be seen in the picture (left), perched high on the spine of the island; a similar battery was built at the other end of the rock. The drawing (below) shows the plan and elevation; the circular gunpit has a well beneath it to take the 100-ton counterweight of the disappearing mounting. To the left are the magazines, separate compartments for powder and shell which were carefully ventilated to keep the ammunition at a constant temperature, the plotting room and crew accommodation and the power supplies for the gun. All these ancillaries were protected by thick concrete and a layer of earth, and an exceptionally thick concrete parapet ran around the sea side of the emplacement, designed to be thick enough to keep out naval gunfire.

BATTERY GILLESPIE, FORT HUGHES

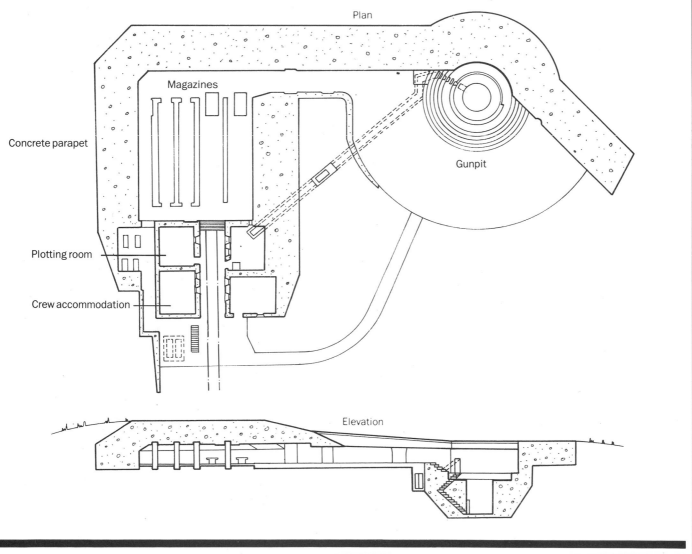

Manila, and, on the following day, a further 7000 at Lamon Bay, to the southeast.

MacArthur had some 10,000 US troops, 12,000 regularly-enlisted Philippine troops, and a further 100,000 or so newly-enlisted Philippine troops with little or no experience or training. He had high hopes of the Filipinos in action, but these were soon dashed as units broke and ran before the sustained Japanese attack, leaving gaps in the line by which US troops were rapidly outflanked. Within 24 hours MacArthur abandoned any idea of fighting a pitched battle in Luzon, arranged for a withdrawal to the Bataan Peninsula, and declared Manila an open city. On 24/5 December he moved his headquarters on to Corregidor, and by 7 January the whole of his Luzon army was backed up into the Bataan position. Elements remained on the other islands and they were left virtually to their own salvation.

In spite of the fact that a retreat into Bataan had been a feature of operational plans for several years, the preparations were curiously inept. Some 30,000 tons of ammunition, plus gasoline and other stores were stockpiled or collected, but the situation with regard to food was much different. Due to civil regulations which for-

FORT DRUM BEFORE (TOP) AND AFTER (ABOVE). THE UPPER PICTURE WAS TAKEN WELL BEFORE THE WAR AND SHOWS WHY IT WAS NICKNAMED THE 'CONCRETE BATTLESHIP'. THE CAGE MAST AND BARRACK WERE JETTISONED AS SOON AS COMBAT BEGAN. THE LOWER PICTURE, TAKEN IN 1945, SHOWS THE ENORMOUS DAMAGE DONE TO THE OUTER CONCRETE SHELL THOUGH WITHOUT AFFECTING THE OPERATION OF THE TWO TWIN-14IN GUN TURRETS OR THE INTERIOR OF THE FORT.

bade the movement of rice or sugar between provinces in the islands, insufficient of these items had been placed in storage in Bataan. Moreover, the proposal, by one officer, to commandeer 2000 cases of tinned food from Japanese-owned warehouses was abruptly refused by MacArthur's headquarters with the threat of court-martial if the officer failed to obey. As a result, Bataan had food stocks sufficient to issue a reduced field ration to 100,000 men for 30 days, and from the start the 80,000 troops and 26,000 civilians were on half rations — 2000 calories a day.

The Japanese threw in heavy attacks and soon maneuvered the defenders out of their first lines and back to the 'rear battle line' by 22 January, 1942. Homma then tried to outflank this line by a series of amphibious landings on the west coast of Bataan but these were repulsed by the US and Philippine troops, and not one Japanese escaped alive. By this time Homma's 45th day had come and gone, and Imperial HQ was breathing down his neck, demanding the return of some of his forces for the forthcoming attack on Burma. Homma withdrew to a secure line and reorganized, then sat down to wait until fresh troops could be sent to replace those removed. During this time the defenders began to feel the pinch of short rations, coupled to poor supply organization, disease, and lack of clothing and equipment.

On 12 March, on orders from President Roosevelt, MacArthur was evacuated from Corregidor by motor-torpedo-boat to an airfield on Mindanao, from where he was flown to Australia. With a fine sense of priorities he took with him his wife and child, the child's nurse, and 17 of his staff, including his public relations officer. He left the command of the resistance in the Philippines in something of a chaotic mess, since he intended to direct operations from Australia and thus deputed his Chief of Staff as overall commander, with General Wainwright commanding the forces on Bataan. Unfortunately he failed to make this clear, and when Wainwright began receiving messages from President Roosevelt which appeared to confirm him as overall commander, and when he was promoted Lieut-General, MacArthur took umbrage. General Marshall, Chief of Staff in Washington, was quick to point out that MacArthur could scarcely command tactically from such a distance, and Wainwright was confirmed as the de facto commander in the Philippines.

On 3 April, Good Friday, General Homma began his final attack. Weakened by disease and hunger, the defense crumbled rapidly, and on 9 April General King, commanding the troops on Bataan, surrendered his force to the Japanese. 78,000 troops went into captivity, only about 2000 managing to escape across the water to Corregidor, there to join the garrison. Then began the infamous 'Death March' of the captives, northward out of the Bataan and into prison camps, during which march a high proportion died of ill-treatment; for this, among other things, Homma was to be executed after the war.

What Are You Fighting For?

A JAPANESE PROPAGANDA LEAFLET, ONE OF MANY DROPPED
FROM THE AIR ON TO THE BESIEGED ISLAND. IT DEPICTS THE
STARVING GARRISON, TRAPPED INSIDE THEIR OWN DEFENSES AND
SURROUNDED BY AMPLE FOOD AND DRINK, SUPPOSEDLY THEIRS
IF THEY SURRENDERED. AS WITH MOST PROPAGANDA ATTACKS,
IT FAILED IN ITS OBJECT, AMUSING THE TROOPS RATHER THAN
TERRIFYING THEM.

The siege opens

Corregidor Island is invariably described as being
shaped like a tadpole; the 'head' was high, with steep
cliffs, and on top was a plateau which contained the
barracks, parade ground, golf course and most of the
heavy gun batteries. Below this, towards the body, was
'Middleside', another plateau with hospital, officers
and NCOs quarters and other facilities. Then came
'Bottomside', almost at sea level, with the 'barrio'
(village) of San Jose, docks, power station, cold-
storage plant, and stores. And finally came the 'tail',
with another rise of ground to a plateau on which was
Kindley Field, a small airstrip. Beneath Malinta Hill,
which began the 'tail', was a series of tunnels, branch-
ing from a 1400ft long central tunnel wide enough to
have two railway lines running down its center. Twenty-
five lateral tunnels opened off this, and to the north of
the complex was an underground hospital with a
separate tunnel system of its own and a separate
entrance. On the other side of the central complex was
the Navy tunnel system, connected to the main system
by a partially-completed passage. The railway was an
electric system which ran all the way up to Topside and
had branch lines to every gun battery for the supply of
ammunition and also linked various other facilities.
There were about 65 miles of roads.

The pre-war gun batteries had, by this time, been
somewhat augmented by mobile artillery. Nineteen
155mm guns had been emplaced on 'Panama Mounts',
concrete emplacements which allowed them to be
swung from target to target over a wide arc, 28 3in anti-
aircraft guns had been emplaced in prepared pits, and
a number of 75mm field guns, ex-World War One

wooden-wheeled pieces, were dotted around the island
as beach defenses. (It might be noted that the US
Official History is in error in crediting the defenses with
two 8in guns; these were railway guns, and one had been
shipped to Corregidor, removed from its railway truck
and anchored into a concrete emplacement. But somebody forgot the fire control equipment, and it never
fired a shot. The second gun never arrived.)

The prewar garrison of Fort Mills was principally
artillery, both the gun batteries and the harbor defense
command, plus a small number of service troops —
cooks, bakers, signallers, mechanics. The four forts in
the mouth of the Bay mustered about 6000 men between
them, and in peacetime the greater part of this number
would be on Corregidor, leaving merely maintenance
parties in the other three forts. Fort Wint, being some
distance away, was rather more independent and also
served as the gunnery school.

After the declaration of war the personnel on
Corregidor increased dramatically. First came survivors from the bombed-out and closed-down naval base
at Cavite, then, with MacArthur's headquarters came
military police, ordnance and engineers, and a host of
service and headquarter troops from Manila. The 4th
Marines arrived to swell the crowd, and eventually
came the 2000 escapees from Bataan.

The forts went to their action stations several days
before Pearl Harbor, but in spite of sundry air-raid
warnings they were undisturbed for the first three weeks
of the war. The first attack on Corregidor came shortly
after the fall of Manila and the arrival of MacArthur
and his entourage on the island. It is probable that after
the rapid fall of Manila Homma felt that he would be
moving against the island quite soon, and he therefore
set about 'softening it up', ordering a massive air raid to
commence at noon on 29 December, first by Army aircraft and then, an hour later, by Navy bombers.

Some six minutes early, 18 bombers appeared over
Corregidor, covered by 19 fighters, broke into smaller
formations, and passed back and forth over the island
dropping about fifty 100kg and 250kg bombs on barracks and store buildings. As they flew off, they were
replaced by a further 22 heavy bombers accompanied
by 18 dive bombers. The heavies scattered 100kg bombs
on prominent buildings on Topside and Bottomside,
while the dive-bombers aimed their 20kg bombs at gun
emplacements as well as buildings. As the dive-bombers
left at 1300hrs, so the Navy bombers came in their
wake, 60 strong, scattering 100kg and 250kg bombs
from one end of the island to the other.

The Japanese did not have everything their own way;
the anti-aircraft defenses of Forts Mills and Hughes
opened fire and claimed 13 bombers shot down for the
expenditure of 1200 rounds of ammunition, which is a
remarkably good ratio, whilst heavy machine guns
managed to bring down four dive bombers.

When the raids ended, it was found that half the barrack and headquarters buildings were demolished, the
empty hospital, the service club and the officers' club

COMMANDERS ON CORREGIDOR

General Douglas MacArthur (1880–1964)

MacArthur was the son of a Civil War hero who later became military governor of the Philippines, a factor which undoubtedly influenced the son in later life. Douglas MacArthur's first military service was as a survey officer in the Philippines in 1903, and he travelled extensively in China, Japan and Korea prior to the First World War. During the war he was chief of staff of the Rainbow Division, then commanded the 84th Infantry Brigade and was twice wounded. He then commanded the US Occupation Force in Germany until 1919, returning to the USA to become Superintendent of West Point. In 1922–25,

as a Brigadier-General, he again served in the Philippines, and again in 1928–30. Promoted General in 1930 he served as Chief of Staff of the US Army to 1935, after which he went back to the Philippines as Field-Marshal of the Army. Retiring from US service in 1937 he continued with his duties in Manila, but was recalled to the US Army in July 1941 as commander of Far East forces.

After leaving Corregidor he became Supreme Commander South-West Pacific. In this role he developed the 'island-hopping' tactic of advance against Japan, which he persisted in seeing as the principal enemy, being strongly opposed to Roosevelt's decision that Germany

GENERAL MACARTHUR AT HIS DESK IN HIS MALINTA TUNNEL HEADQUARTERS.

must be defeated first and Japan later. He took his ejection from the Philippines as a personal insult and was determined to recapture the islands, which he eventually did in January 1945. After the war he became Supreme Commander of the

occupation forces in Japan and ruled the country as virtual dictator for five years. Given command of the UN forces in the Korean War he flouted the orders of his Commander-in-Chief and was relieved of duty.

MacArthur was a supreme egoist and self-publicist who managed to convince large sections of the populace that he was

---

were all wrecked beyond repair, and Bottomside was a shambles of corrugated iron from the many structures which had been shattered. Fires broke out in so many areas that observers on Bataan said that the entire island was enveloped in a cloud of dust and smoke. Two gun batteries were slightly damaged, but were back in action within 24 hours, but some sixty percent of all the wooden buildings on the island were destroyed in this first raid, and MacArthur's HQ moved into the Malinta tunnel next morning.

The bombing continued, intermittently, for a further six days, and by the end of it there was very little of any consequence left standing. The garrison water tanks, the wharves, shops and stores in Bottomside, the diesel oil dump — almost every building on the island was demolished, and bomb craters were so thick that one report said that it was impossible to walk more than twenty-five yards in any direction without encountering one. What the blast of the bombs failed to destroy, fire consumed; the electric railway was so often damaged that eventually it was abandoned; every telephone cable was broken, repaired and broken again, since all the communications were strung on poles and there was never time or labor to spare to set about burying them. Fortunately the gun installations went relatively unscathed, since their magazines and crew shelters were

all designed to be proof against naval shells and shrugged off bombing.

The cessation of the bombing attacks on 6 January was due to withdrawal of the Japanese 5th Air Group for the forthcoming attack on Burma, and the aircraft remaining to General Homma were now required for support of the army in its attacks on Bataan. But in order to keep up the pressure, Homma now ordered artillery to be emplaced so as to bring the forts under attack. Towards the end of January reports began to reach Corregidor of Japanese activity on the southern shore of Manila Bay, around Ternate, the closest point to Corregidor. Four 105mm guns and two 15cm howitzers were being emplaced there and in spite of counter-battery fire from Fort Frank, aimed at likely sites, these six guns were ready by the beginning of February. At 0800hrs, 5 February, the artillery bombardment began.

The principal target on the first day was Fort Drum — the 'Concrete Battleship' — and over 100 shells landed on its surface. This did very little damage to the basic structure — it was a 30ft thickness of concrete — and since the Japanese guns were to the east of Fort Drum the early-morning sun shone into the eyes of the Americans and made it impossible for them to spot the location of the Japanese guns. Nevertheless the 14in turret guns fired in the general direction, and they were the finest commander of the Second World War. His record, on close examination, does not substantiate such claims.

General Jonathan Wainwright (1883–1953)

Wainwright entered the US Army as a cavalry officer and served in the Philippines in 1909–10. During World War One he was on the staff of an infantry division in France, and he held various command and staff posts in the inter-war years. He was sent to the Philippines in September 1940 and was given command of the Northern Luzon sector. Outmaneuvered by the Japanese selection of landing places, Wainwright and his men were forced to retire into the Bataan peninsula in order to avoid being completely isolated from the rest of the defenders. When MacArthur was ordered to leave, Wainwright was promoted Lieut-General and given command in the Philippines by direct order of President Roosevelt.

He held out on Bataan far longer than anyone expected, and was ordered to move to Corregidor on 8 April. Eventually forced to surrender on 6 May, he accompanied his men on the infamous Death March, and survived to be held as a prisoner in a Manchurian camp until released in 1945. Still a sick man from his imprisonment, he nevertheless stood alongside MacArthur on board the USS *Missouri* in Tokyo Bay to watch the Japanese surrender on 2 September, 1945. He returned to the USA to receive the Congressional Medal of Honor.

'Skinny' Wainwright, as his men called him, conducted an epic defense; it is to America's honor that he was never denigrated after the war as were so many generals who had the misfortune to fail against a far stronger enemy.

General Masaharu Homma (1888–1946)

Homma spent most of his military career in intelligence, but in spite of his lack of combat experience he was selected to command the attack on the Philippines. His seasoned troops were able to defeat the Filipino and American forces confronting them, and Homma found himself faced with the choice of either securing Manila which he knew to be undefended or cutting off the retreat to Bataan; he elected to head for Manila, wasting time and allowing a large number of US troops to escape into the peninsula.

He then made a gross under-estimate of the American strength in Bataan and allowed many of his forces to be withdrawn for operations elsewhere, retaining only nine battalions for the Bataan campaign. After a month of severe fighting he had made little headway and was relieved of command for incompetence, subsequent operations being controlled by General Yamashita, though Homma remained in place as a figure-head. After the surrender of the Bataan force, the survivors were force-marched 65 miles through the jungle to a prison camp, an ordeal in which some 16 000 US and Filipino troops died. After taking Corregidor, Homma was then retired to Japan where he spent the rest of the war in administrative posts. He surrendered to US forces in Tokyo in September 1945, was taken to Manila, tried, and executed for his part in ordering the Bataan Death March.

A SOMEWHAT INDISTINCT JAPANESE PHOTOGRAPH SHOWING A FLIGHT OF MITSUBISHI G4M 'BETTY' BOMBERS APPROACHING CORREGIDOR FROM THE DIRECTION OF BATAAN. THE DISTINCTIVE TAIL OF THE ISLAND, WHICH CONTAINED THE AIRFIELD AND MUCH OF THE AIR DEFENSE ARTILLERY, CAN BE SEEN TO THE LEFT, 'TOPSIDE' TO THE RIGHT.

aided by the 12in mortars on Fort Frank, but they appeared to have no effect.

This shelling continued daily until the middle of the month. Its only effect was to make the men on the island forts more wary in their daily routine, and on Fort Drum the wooden barrack built on the deck in peacetime was rapidly demolished and pushed over the side into the sea, soon followed by the lattice mast. In mid-February two additional 15cm howitzers joined the Japanese gun line, and Homma gave orders that the 'enemy must be demoralized', so the rate of fire was increased. The shelling reached its climax on 20 February, when the Japanese guns fired at one minute intervals from 0930 until late in the afternoon, though doing very little serious damage to the forts. After that the intensity died down, and in subsequent days a few rounds might be fired at odd times during the day, simply, apparently, for nuisance value.

Japanese forces regroup

This slackening, though, was merely a pause to allow the Japanese to strengthen their forces. Roads and tracks in the Ternate area were improved and new tracks driven through the jungle to make new gun positions in the Pico de Loro hills, southwest of Ternate. The Americans got wind of this and began firing at roads and bridges in the area but they did little damage and by 15 March the Japanese had installed two batteries of 24cm howitzers. At 0730 that morning they opened fire on all four island forts and continued hammering two of them throughout the day. Fort Frank took some 500 shells, destroying one battery of 155mm guns of Panama Mounts and a battery of 3in anti-aircraft guns and putting two other batteries out of commission for the rest of the day. Fort Drum received another 100 shells, though the only damage was from one shell which penetrated one of the side casemates protecting a 6in gun.

The attack continued on the following day and, with rather less intensity for another five days. At the end of this time Fort Drum was battered but undamaged, apart from having anything from 8-15ft of its concrete surface 'planed away', but Fort Frank had two serious incidents. In the first, a 240mm shell penetrated the concrete protection of a 12in mortar battery, delved underneath one of the powder magazines and exploded. The floor of the magazine was shattered and the powder canisters inside thrown around, but by a miracle there was no explosion or fire. On the second occasion a shell penetrated the 18in concrete roof of a tunnel inside which a queue of men were waiting for their routine yellow fever inoculations; 28 men were killed and 46 wounded.

The American guns attempted to reply to the Japanese but the latter had chosen their gun positions with care; their howitzers were behind the Pico de Loro hills, firing with a high trajectory. The American guns, designed purely for attacking ships, had a maximum elevation of 15° and could not attain a high enough trajectory to reach over the hills. The only weapons capable of matching the Japanese howitzers were the 12in mortars, and these were fired at every opportunity.

A 12IN MODEL 1890 MORTAR OF BATTERY WAY BEING MAINTAINED IN PRE-WAR PEACE. THE MORTAR IS MOUNTED ON SPRING ARMS WHICH ABSORB THE RECOIL, AND SET ON A TURNTABLE ALLOWING IT TO FIRE IN ANY DIRECTION. THE MORTAR FIRED A 493KG DECK-PIERCING SHELL TO A RANGE OF 10,900M WHEN ELEVATED TO 65°.

However, they lacked observation facilities near the target, so were firing blind, and moreover their projectiles were designed to pierce armor and burst inside a ship. When striking something as soft as soil, they simply went down in the ground before detonating, so making a small crater and doing very little damage. Attempts were made to modify the delay fuzes to burst on impact, but since this type of shell had a very small bursting charge even impact bursts had relatively small effect. A small number of high explosive shells with nose impact fuzes were on hand, but these, it was decided, might have their most important role if and when the Japanese appeared on the Bataan peninsula, and therefore their use was restricted.

The artillery duel came to an end on 22 March; the guns were needed for more important duties in preparing for the final Japanese attack against the American positions on Bataan. The 24cm and 15cm howitzers were removed, with only the four 105mm guns remaining, and their intermittent fire was no more than a minor irritant after the pounding of the heavies.

If nothing else, the artillery bombardment had given the defenders on the various forts a focus in life; they rapidly began taking an interest in protecting themselves. More tunnels were excavated on Corregidor, sandbag protection was used liberally around gun positions, command posts and communications centers, concrete bomb-proof cover was laid over fuel stores and overhead protection was built for the many 75mm guns positioned for beach defense in order to give them some protection against dive bombing. Slit trenches, shelters and tunnels were dug in the various gun batteries and trenches and dug-outs were excavated for the beach defenses.

The garrison of Corregidor were, apart from their digging activities, virtually unemployed. They had nothing at which to shoot, and once their defenses were organized they had little to do but sit around and grumble about the food. They had some grounds for complaint, insofar as the ration was halved from their peace-time standard, but in comparison with the troops on Bataan, those on Corregidor were well off. The men on the gun batteries and beach defenses at least had some purpose in life, but for the remainder, mostly cooped up in Malinta Tunnel, they had very little to do. The tunnel was the focal point of Corregidor's life; it contained what remained of the Philippine Government, the remains of MacArthur's headquarters, a 1000-bed hospital, and several thousand otherwise homeless troops and civilians who had little more than a suitcase or kitbag and a wooden bunk to call their own.

When the Japanese prepared their final attack on Bataan, they were alive to the possibility of the evacuation of troops to Corregidor, and in order to try and reduce this, an air attack on Corregidor was again ordered. Homma had received reinforcements to replace the 5th Air Group, and at 0925 on 24 March the first attack by Army bombers came in, releasing a shower of 250kg and 500kg bombs. Five more Army

ORDER OF BATTLE

US

HQ USAFFE (Commanders: Generals MacArthur/Wainwright)

Service troops
4th Marine Regt
Philippine Division
26th Cavalry Regt
43rd Infantry Regt
86th Field Artillery Regt
88th Field Artillery Regt
192nd Tank Bn
194th Tank Bn
200th CA (AA)

Harbor Defenses of Manila & Subic Bays (Commander: Maj-Gen GF Moore)

59th CA
60th CA (AA)
91st CA
92nd CA
200th CA

Total US strength 30 Nov 1941: 31,095, incl 11,957 Philippine Scouts

Total defensive strength 15 Apr 42: 14,728

JAPANESE

14th Army (Commander: Gen Homma)

4th Division
16th Div
48th Div

1st Heavy Artillery Regt

V Air Group Army (Commander: Lt-Gen Obata)

XI Air Fleet

squadrons followed, and then came two Navy squadrons, and a total of 71 tons of bombs landed on the island during the course of the day. The same sequence was followed on the next day, and after that Army and Navy squadrons appeared in turn, with smaller formations making nuisance raids between the bigger attacks, for the next week.

The casualties produced by the bombing were few, since the period of pause which allowed the garrison to complete their protection work had paid off. Nevertheless, considerable damage was done to whatever had not been demolished in the earlier raids; the men's theater, the Post Exchange, the bakery were totally wrecked and the Naval radio station severely damaged. Several ammunition dumps were blown up, and most of the roads cratered, though these were soon repaired. Those lucky few who had accommodation on the surface saw it smashed, and were driven to take their beds and go into Malinta Tunnel to join the displaced who were already in residence there.

On 9 April, as we have seen, the US troops on Bataan surrendered, and General Homma then began planning his final move, the elimination of Corregidor and the island forts. Planning took time; it was necessary to assemble landing craft and train the assault parties, and the Japanese plans were upset when a large proportion of the men of the 4th Division, earmarked for the attack, were hospitalized with an epidemic of malaria. Homma had originally boasted that he would take Corregidor within a week of the collapse on Bataan; he later revised that and planned to attack on 27 April, but in the event he was unable to make any move until early in May.

A concerted Japanese attack

The plan as finally evolved called for a combined air and artillery bombardment to soften up the target area, then two separate infantry assaults by sea to be made on successive nights at opposite ends of the island. The two forces would then turn inwards and sweep into the island to meet in the area of Bottomside, so that Corregidor would be in Japanese hands within two days of landing. The force would then turn its attention to Fort Hughes, after which Forts Drum and Frank would be taken. The Japanese hand was strengthened by a very precise knowledge of the gun defenses of all the islands; air photographs, intelligence and interrogation of prisoners had given them the most complete information on all but two of the major coast batteries, most of the smaller gun positions, the water supply, communications system, power installations and storage dumps. They knew about Malinta Tunnel, though they were unaware of its size or importance, and they were in the dark over much of the infantry and beach defenses, since these had been developed since the start of hostilities and thus little information had leaked off the island about them.

The Americans on the islands had very few illusions left about their eventual fate by this time. Hopes of relief had long since faded, and once the Japanese had conquered Bataan most realized that their defeat was only a matter of time. Nevertheless, their morale was higher than might be expected, and most of the troops were prepared to give as good as they got. At that time, of course, the Americans were still thinking that they were fighting an enemy who respected the usual conventions on prisoners; the horrors of the Death March and the prison camps were in the future.

Within hours of the surrender on Bataan the first Japanese 75mm gun battery had moved down to the tip of the peninsula and had emplaced near Cabcaben, in view of Corregidor, and opened fire. It was immediately replied to by Battery Kysor, a four-gun battery of 155mm guns on the north shore of the island. This response was, however, soon stopped on the orders of General Wainwright, who had now located his HQ on Corregidor and assumed command; he feared that American guns firing into Bataan would be likely to hit some of the American hospitals still in place there, or upon US troops herded into prison compounds. It was not until 12 April, three days later, that he considered the danger to be past and authorised counter-battery fire to begin.

At the same time as the gun battery opened fire, the Japanese Army 22nd Air Brigade, with no targets remaining on Bataan, turned their attention to Corregidor and began regular bombing attacks. During the next few days 18 gun batteries were brought into position by the Japanese and a fire plan of sorts was worked out; this simply divided the island into three zones and allocated six batteries to each. A captive observation balloon (one of the very few used during World War Two) was brought into action and ascended above Mariveles so that the observer could oversee Corregidor and correct the gunfire. Flash and sound ranging equipment was also deployed, and the whole affair began to take on the air of technical exercise being carried out under textbook conditions.

At 0900 on 12 April the bombardment began in earnest, from 75mm and 105mm guns; 15cm howitzers were being emplaced and they joined in a few days later. The guns of the fortress returned the fire, but this was immediately the signal for all the Japanese to concentrate on the battery which had retaliated, and within a few days the results began to make themselves felt. Within two days all the emergency batteries emplaced on the north shore — three 155mm gun batteries and one battery of 3in AA guns — had been destroyed by intense bombardment. Most of the coast artillery rangefinders and position-finders, and the anti-aircraft height finders mounted on Topside were smashed, but by cannibalizing the remains the operators eventually managed to keep one of each instrument in working order until the last days of the siege. The coast defense searchlights were made a special target and most were soon shot out; it was made obvious that the Japanese had these registered when, as an experiment, the artillery commander ordered one light to be exposed for 15 seconds and then switched off. An exposure as brief as this would not allow a gun to take aim in the normal course of events, but in this case the operator switched off the light and ran for cover, and before he was 20 yards from the light, Japanese shells began to arrive.

In general, casualties from the shelling were low since men not concerned with firing back soon made for cover. On the 15th, 70 Philippine troops were trapped in a shelter when the intensity of the bombardment collapsed the cliff above them, burying them alive.

After 18 April, the terrible 24cm howitzers were moved down into firing positions and began to add their weight to the attack. These used high angle fire to drop their heavy shells into positions which the flat-trajectory guns could not reach, and, firing concrete-piercing shells, they soon began to do considerable damage. On 24 April their shells smashed into Battery Crockett, two 12in guns, wrecking the gun mountings, smashing the ammunition hoists, and starting fires which were fortunately extinguished before they could reach the magazines. On the next evening, one shell from a 24cm howitzer landed in a group of men who were standing outside the entrance to Malinta Tunnel, enjoying a last smoke in the cool of the evening before turning in for the night. The sudden detonation caused a rush of men to the tunnel gate, but the blast had blown

ANOTHER GRAINY JAPANESE PHOTOGRAPH, TAKEN BY SOME UNKNOWN SOLDIER IMMEDIATELY AFTER THE SURRENDER, SHOWING THE REMAINS OF BATTERY CROCKETT WHICH WAS EQUIPPED WITH TWO 12IN DISAPPEARING GUNS. THE MAJORITY OF THE DAMAGE SHOWN HERE WAS DONE BY THE BOMBARDMENT OF JAPANESE 24CM HOWITZERS, DROPPING CONCRETE-PIERCING 200KG SHELLS IN A NEAR-CONSTANT STREAM FROM POSITIONS ON BATAAN.

them shut and they could not be opened from the outside; as the crowd shouted to those inside, a second shell smashed down. Thirteen men were killed instantly, more died of wounds and at least fifty were wounded.

Unceasing attacks

By this time the Japanese had over one hundred guns in use, and the shelling never actually stopped. They set about destroying everything on Corregidor that could be seen with a single-minded intensity; they would open fire just before dawn and fire continuously until about noon; then there would be a lull until about 1500hrs, probably to bring up ammunition and allow the gunners a meal and a brief rest, after which the firing would recommence and continue until midnight. And while the guns fired, so the bombers came in as well, secure in the knowledge that the gunfire would prevent the Americans using the air defense weapons.

The combined attacks reached their zenith on 29 April, Emperor Hirohito's birthday. This began with an air raid warning at 0730, when two flights of bombers attacked Fort Hughes and three flights of dive bombers attacked the Corregidor south dock and the entrances to the Malinta Tunnel. While this raid was in progress the gun batteries opened fire on targets in the Bottomside area. Six more aircraft appeared and bombed Malinta Hill, while artillery fire concentrated on the tunnel entrance area. Then at 0820 the artillery shelling moved to Topside, to give the gun batteries their morning shelling. There was a short pause, and then more aircraft appeared and the shelling began on Middleside. At 1000hrs two ammunition dumps were hit and blew up.

The combined attacks continued in this manner throughout the day, without the customary lunchtime pause, and by late afternoon most of the island was wreathed in smoke and dust. Everything above ground on Malinta Hill was rubble; the searchlight power station was burned out, several observation posts were wrecked and three beach defense guns had been smashed.

By this time the remaining 155mm gun batteries had been withdrawn from their exposed positions and had become mobile single-gun units. Called 'roving guns' each would find a position and open fire; once the Japanese discovered it and began to shell the offender, the gunners hitched it to its tractor and departed, to find a position somewhere else. But with the rapidly worsening state of the roads and trails on Corregidor, and the gradual shearing away of all the island's vegetation by the constant rain of shells, these roving guns were beginning to find it difficult to pick a position from which they could fire for any length of time before being flushed out.

The two 12in mortar batteries, Way and Geary, now weighed in with their high explosive shells and began doing severe damage to the Japanese positions, though unfortunately the stock of these anti-personnel shells was no more than 400 rounds. Battery Way had, in fact, been in 'care and preservation' for many years, and it was not until 28 April that the four mortars were back in a serviceable condition. But as soon as the mortars began to have effect, the Japanese concentrated their artillery on to the two batteries and swamped them with shells. Two of the Battery Way mortars were soon put out of action, and on 2 May the worst disaster occurred when a 240mm shell pierced the roof of Battery Geary's shell magazine, located between the two mortar pits, and detonated the contents. There was colossal explosion which was heard and felt all over the island, and which blasted the eight mortars from their mountings. One 15-ton barrel landed 150 yards away from the battery pit and another was blown through a 3ft thick reinforced concrete wall and into the powder magazine. A slab of concrete weighing almost six tons was blown over a thousand yards away. Estimates of the casualties ranged from eight to 27 dead with more injured, several men being buried under the debris and never recovered. At the end of the day Fort Mills had two mortars left in working order.

By the end of April the garrison was in a sorry state. When the artillery bombardment began General Wainwright was urged to put the troops on full rations, so that they would build up their physical condition ready for the eventual Japanese assault and, also, in order that they might be better able to withstand the rigors of the bombardment. Wainwright called for a report on the supply situation and was advised that Corregidor held sufficient food to last the garrison until the end of June, provided it remained on half rations. Going over to full rations would mean that the food would run out by the end of May, and Wainwright, with no certainty that the Japanese attack would come by that time, decided to hold to the half ration. And so by the end of April the men were beginning to show the effects of this, with vitamin deficiency, the first symptoms of beri-beri, and an increased incidence of malaria for which there was little in the way of remedy in view of a shortage of quinine and atebrin. Surprisingly, in view of the constant strain of the Japanese bombardment, there were very few psychiatric cases; doctors reported no more than eight or ten men with shell-shock, battle fatigue or similar nervous complaints.

By this time, too, there were serious problems in materiel; the power station was beginning to break down more often and was becoming more difficult to maintain, particularly with the shelling, while the level of fuel was going down. Each gun battery had its own generator system for providing power to the guns, but these were severely rationed for fuel and guns were being operated on manual controls more and more often. The pumping stations which kept the water reservoirs topped up were also a problem, since the constant shelling punctured pipes and damaged pumps; during the entire month of April the pumps were able to work only one day, so that by the end of the month the men were rationed to one canteen of water per day for everything — drinking, washing, laundry.

The 'final bombardment'

As April came to an end, Homma issued orders for the final bombardment which, he said, would "overwhelmingly crush the island's defenses and exterminate its defenders." His invasion force was now ready, and once the remaining guns and searchlights had been located and destroyed and the beach defenses demolished, the assault would begin. On 1 May the final bombardment opened, with a saturation by shellfire of the areas of James Ravine (a gully running from a northern beach to the plateau of Topside) and on the narrow tail of the island north of Kindley Field. Since there were no military installations in either of these areas, the defenders reasoned that these must be potential landing areas and the Japanese fire was intended to scarify any defensive posts.

The bombardment on 1 May began shortly before dawn and continued until midnight, being interspersed with air attacks from time to time in the afternoon. The area around Batteries Geary and Crockett took no less than 3600 240mm shells in a five-hour period, plus innumerable shells of smaller caliber. On the following day the shelling followed the same pattern, with more bombardment of the north shore and concentrations on anything of military value on the rest of the island. It was during this bombardment that Battery Geary took the shell in its magazine, with the result already described. The intense shelling of Malinta Hill and the tail of the island sheared away the remaining trees and set fire to them, so that the troops in the vicinity had to set about trying to control the fire while being shelled.

Sunday 3 May saw more shelling, plus five air raids, which went entirely unopposed since by now there were no anti-aircraft guns or fire control equipment in working order. The remaining serviceable coast defense and field artillery attempted to fire at the Japanese, as, indeed, they had on every day of the siege, but the dust raised by the bombing was so bad that they could not even see the Bataan shore with sufficient clarity to correct fire. After dark, on that night, a US submarine managed to close up to Corregidor and take aboard a handful of passengers; one staff officer carried a complete nominal roll of all service personnel remaining alive, 13 nurses from the hospital were wisely evacuated, and other staff officers carried financial and other records and several bags of mail. It was to be the last communication with Corregidor other than by radio for three years.

Although the defenders doubted it to be possible, the Japanese bombardment on 4 May reached a level of intensity which was unparalleled; over 16,000 shells of all calibers landed on the island within the 24-hour period — a shell every five seconds on the average — and the explosions merged into a continuous drum-roll of noise. During the day observers spotted fifteen landing barges off Bataan moving to the north; they assumed that these were being moved out of range of the Corregidor artillery, but in fact they had seen the first sign of invasion; these barges were going to Lamao to load with troops.

The 5th saw the bombardment continue with the same intensity as on the previous day, with the Japanese appearing to concentrate their attention on the shoreline. The response from Corregidor was feeble; by this time only three 155mm roving guns were still serviceable. The remainder of the artillery — the roving guns, the 12in mortars and disappearing guns, the 6in and 10in disappearing guns, the 12in long-range barbette guns, the 3in anti-torpedo boat guns — almost all were smashed and silent. The task of attempting to silence the Japanese batteries was now being attempted by the 14in turrets on Fort Drum and the 14in disappearing guns and 12in mortars of Fort Frank, but they were operating at their maximum range and without the benefit of observation, so that their fire was mostly ineffective.

By the evening most of the beach defenses of the north shore were smashed, all communications had been severed, the road had been literally blown into the bay, cliffs had collapsed and a pall of dust lay over the shattered island. There was sufficient water for four days and no prospect of repairing the pumps and pipelines. And then, at 2100, sound locators on the tail of the island picked up the noise of motor vessels to the north. A warning order was passed ordering the beach defense troops to take post, and at 2200 barges were seen approaching in the light of the rising full moon. At midnight the artillery bombardment stopped, and its drum-roll was replaced by the clatter of small arms fire. The Japanese landings had begun.

The Japanese land

In fact the Japanese landing had begun with serious mishaps; the careful planning and reconnaissance had overlooked one important element, which was the set of the sea currents between Bataan and Corregidor. The outgoing tide caused a current to flow from east to west on the Bataan shore, and the Japanese assumed that this would be the case on the Corregidor shore as well. But due to the vagaries of the sea, the current was actually flowing from west to east off Corregidor, and the Japanese landing craft missed their assigned area by a thousand yards. Instead of striking the shore between Infantry Point and Cavalry Point, they actually landed between Cavalry Point and North Point. The fault appeared to lie with the Sea Operations Unit manning the boats who, having done some landings in the Singapore operation, were sure they knew all there was to be known about assault landings and neglected to reconnoiter or train properly. As a result not only did they land in the wrong place but they became mixed up and landed out of their proper order and at odd times. What was worse was that artillery barrages had been planned to protect the flank of the attack, and this was now falling a thousand yards to their right and doing them little or no good.

Nevertheless, the Japanese commanders on the ground were quick to sort out their problems, even though, devoid of artillery support, they found themselves engaged with the defenders more quickly than they had planned for. The defenders, though still shaken from the day's bombardment, soon had their machine guns in action, and a two-gun 75mm battery and a group of 37mm anti-tank guns close to North Point, which had never fired and had thus escaped discovery and bombardment, now opened fire at 300 yards range against the landing barges. Several of the barges were sunk and the Japanese took severe casualties. The last serviceable 12in mortar of Battery Way now came into action dropping massive shells among the landing fleet, while the guns and mortars on the other island forts joined in. Estimates of Japanese casualties, from Japanese sources, ranged from 50 to 75 percent, and one Japanese officer later claimed that of the 2000 men in the assaulting party only 800 reached the shore alive.

The landing appeared to have been beaten off, and those who had landed appeared to be contained, but at 0440 more barges were seen approaching Bottomside. All guns available were ordered to open fire on these new targets; again, the other forts joined in. The 14in turrets of Fort Drum attempted to fire but could see nothing for the pall of smoke and dust over the island. "Never mind that," the fire direction officer was told, "just fire anywhere into the smoke between you and Cabcaben and you can't miss." Once more the destruction of the Japanese force was terrible, between half and two-thirds of all the craft which had left Bataan having been sunk and hundreds of troops drowned.

In spite of this, though, the Japanese troops who had come ashore near North Point had managed to consolidate their foothold, had beaten off a force of defenders from the 4th Marines, had pushed forward, and by 0100 had crossed the island and reached the shore on the south side at Monkey Point. Thus the defenders on the eastern tip were isolated and kept at bay while the remainder of the landing parties turned right and began advancing along the island towards Malinta Hill. By 0130 they had formed a second line across the island cutting through Battery Denver (3in AA guns), and behind them a second relay of landing craft was already unloading infantry reinforcements, light artillery and three light tanks.

Due to the lack of communications, the American appreciation of the situation was faulty; several troops did not realize how far the Japanese had moved until they heard 'un-American' voices in the night. Reports reached headquarters in fragmentary form, and it was not until 0200 that it became obvious that the Japanese landing had succeeded and that there was nothing more than two platoons of infantry between the advancing Japanese and Malinta Tunnel. Artillerymen were quickly mustered from the silent gun batteries and ordered into action as infantry.

Getting this force into action was difficult; they had to make their way across Bottomside, which was under artillery bombardment, into Malinta Tunnel, through the tunnel and out of the eastern entrance, and by this time this entrance was under short-range artillery fire from the field guns which the Japanese had landed. Nevertheless, men got through, and three counter-attacks were thrown against the Japanese line without

AMERICAN TROOPS GATHERED OUTSIDE THE ENTRANCE GATES TO MALINTA TUNNEL IMMEDIATELY AFTER THE SURRENDER. THEY WERE THEN REMOVED BY THEIR GUARDS AND SET OUT TO MARCH INTO IMPRISONMENT, A JOURNEY WHICH MANY FAILED TO SURVIVE. ONE WONDERS WHETHER PVT STROBING IS AMONG THE FACES HERE AND WHETHER HE SURVIVED.

success. Their task was made more difficult by their physical weakness and by the fact that over half the men now manning the American line had little knowledge of the basic infantry tactics; one 'battalion' was described by one of its officers as '500 sailors with 500 rifles — nothing more.'

At 0430 the last American reserves were committed to battle; before the last of the column had left the safety of the tunnel, the head was suffering casualties from artillery and mortar fire. A counter-attack was launched at 0600 and gained ground, rolling the Japanese flanks back, but eventually the Japanese managed to anchor their position and prevent any further advance. They were, in their own view, in a difficult position, running short of ammunition. But their invariable tactical move of infiltrating began to pay off; small groups of Japanese infantry were able to make their way through the scattered American line, then turn about and take the defenders in the rear, a highly unnerving situation for even experienced troops. In addition, the three tanks which the Japanese had got ashore were now moving on the front and making their presence felt, while more artillery was being brought into action at short range.

By 1000 the position was critical; the Japanese were pressing hard, the Americans were pinned down and without hope of receiving more men, weapons or ammunition, and three tanks were loose in front of them. Casualties were mounting, and there was no way to get them out of the line and back to medical aid stations; between 600 and 800 men had already died and about 1000 were wounded. Prolonging the defense would merely mean more deaths, without altering the final outcome. There was no other answer than to surrender, and at 1000 General Wainwright took the most difficult decision of his career and ordered a surrender message to be broadcast to General Homma. Plans, already prepared, for the destruction of weapons went into effect, and at noon the American flag, which had flown defiantly on Topside throughout the siege, was lowered and replaced by a white flag. The surrender encompassed the other three island forts; the 14in guns of Fort Drum continued to fire until 1155. Indeed, the fort commander was in two minds whether to surrender at all, since he had ample stocks of food and ammunition for his 200-man garrison, but he was persuaded that to hold out might invite reprisals on American prisoners on Corregidor.

Sitting at the morse key of a radio set in Malinta Tunnel was a soldier who gave a moving commentary of events on that fateful morning:

> "They are not near yet. We are waiting for God only knows what. . . . Lots of heavy fighting going on. . . . We may have to give up by noon, we don't know yet. They are throwing men and shells at us and we may not be able to stand it. They have been shelling us faster than you can count. . . . We have got about fifty-five minutes and I feel sick at my stomach. . . . They are round now smashing rifles . . . They bring in the wounded every minute. . . . We will be waiting for you guys to help . . .

This is the only thing I guess can be done . . . General Wainwright is a right guy and we are willing to go on for him but shells were dropping all night, faster than hell. Damage terrific. Too much for us guys to take. . . . From here it looks like firing ceased on both sides. Men here all feeling bad because of terrific strain of the siege. Corregidor used to be a nice place, but it's haunted now. . . . Just made a broadcast to Manila to arrange a meeting for surrender. . . . The jig is up, everybody is bawling like a baby . . . They are piling dead and wounded in our tunnel. . . . My name Irving Strobing. Get this to my mother, Mrs Minnie Strobing, 605 Barbey Street Brooklyn NY. They are to get along OK. Get in touch with them as soon as possible. . . . My love to you all. God bless you and keep you . . . Stand by. . . .''

Nothing further was heard from Corregidor.

The lessons

Most of the lessons which emerged from study of the Siege of Corregidor were technical ones and they were soon assimilated. One of the most obvious was the nakedness of conventional coast artillery emplacements to aerial attack, and this led to a rash of concrete appearing over coastal guns from the Californian coast to the English Channel. Another was the vulnerability of communication lines unless they were buried.

Taken in conjunction with the fall of Singapore and of Hong Kong, Corregidor once again repeated the well-worn lesson that whilst a coast defense fort is primarily designed for coast defense, it must nevertheless be protected against an attack from the land. The Japanese had learned all about the weaknesses of the land side of coast defenses when they attacked and vanquished Port Arthur in 1904, and although the rest of the world saw and understood, few people managed to do anything useful. The location of Corregidor, close against the Bataan shore, ensured that once an enemy

with artillery reached that shore the island would be under serious attack, and it must be assessed as a failure of American staff appreciation that the guns of Fort Mills were not provided with an ample supply of anti-personnel ammunition for defense in this direction. Had they had something more than the 400 rounds of 12in mortar nose-fuzed shell, the Japanese artillery would not have been able to get close enough to do damage with impunity. According to an unconfirmed report, some Fort Mills officers wished to survey the foot of the Bataan peninsula in peacetime and prepare firing charts for landwards defense but were forbidden to do so on the grounds that it showed a defeatist attitude. It is doubtful if such a move would be forbidden in the more realistic climate of today.

On the lower levels, the siege led to an appreciation that no matter what a soldier's task was, he had to be an infantryman at bottom, and from then on the incoming recruit on all western armies was given a thorough grounding in the basic infantry skills before he went on to become a gunner, signaller, driver or cook. In later events rear echelon men would be called upon to fight, and after Corregidor care was taken to make sure that if and when this happened they had at least some knowledge of the rudiments. A frequently-quoted incident of the siege was when, during the last American counter-attack, a company of sailors acting as infantry found two Japanese assault boats full of troops grounded on rocks close to the shore. A platoon was sent down to the shore to deal with this helpless target; it took them half an hour and several thousand rounds of rifle ammunition before they completed their task, simply because half of them were unable to aim a rifle properly.

The strategic value of the Philippine Islands was, in spite of MacArthur's claims, small. The Japanese had already outflanked them and had swept to the Gilberts and almost to Australia. But the significance of Corregidor was that the spirited defense had held up the Japanese for six months; indeed, General Homma was recalled to Tokyo, relieved of active command and was in charge of a desk for the rest of his military career as a mark of Imperial disfavor over taking six months to do what he had promised to complete in 45 days. Corregidor showed that the Japanese could be stopped, even if the stopping was merely delaying the inevitable; it also focussed the attention of the USA on a valiant 'last stand' which will rank with Custer and the Alamo in the history books, and as such it had an enormous effect on morale. The 'Coast Artillery Journal', the 'house magazine' of the US Coast Artillery Corps had a section devoted to news from the various defense commands; from June 1942 until May 1945 when Corregidor was recaptured, its page devoted to news from the Harbor Defenses of Manila and Subic Bay consisted merely of a large empty page with 'I SHALL RETURN ! — MACARTHUR' emblazoned on it, a constant reminder to the CAC troops of their colleagues' brave stand and an incentive to them to live up to this conception of duty.

'I SHALL RETURN' SAID MACARTHUR, AND SO HE DID; HERE HE IS SEEN INSPECTING THE REMAINS OF THE MALINTA TUNNEL ENTRANCE IN 1945, IMMEDIATELY AFTER THE RECAPTURE, ACCOMPANIED BY HIS STAFF AND SOME OF THE AIRBORNE TROOPS WHO RE-TOOK THE FORT.

THE RAID ON DIEPPE

COMBINED OPERATIONS
AUGUST 1942

Overleaf

Canadian troops, accompanied by a Churchill tank, advance across the
open beach towards the Casino. The commanding headland, shrouded in smoke, is beyond.
(*Dieppe Raid* by C Comfort. Courtesy Canadian War Memorial, Ottawa)

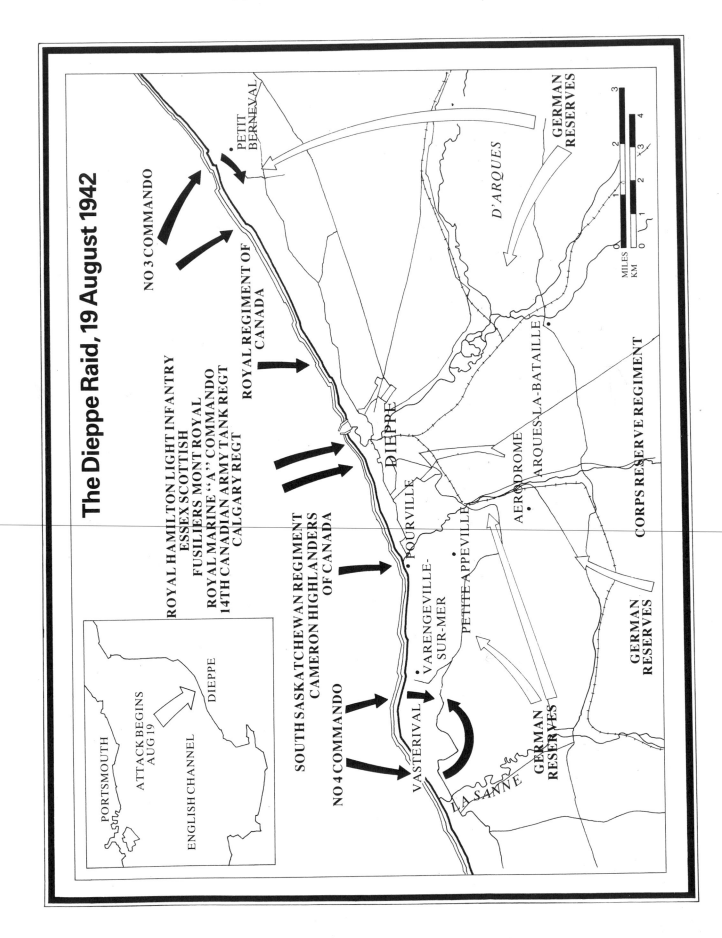

The Dieppe Raid, 19 August 1942

NO 3 COMMANDO

PETIT BERNEVAL

GERMAN RESERVES

D'ARQUES

ROYAL HAMILTON LIGHT INFANTRY
ESSEX SCOTTISH
FUSILIERS MONT ROYAL
ROYAL MARINE "A" COMMANDO
14TH CANADIAN ARMY TANK REGT
CALGARY REGT

ROYAL REGIMENT OF CANADA

DIEPPE

POURVILLE

AERODROME

ARQUES-LA-BATAILLE

CORPS RESERVE REGIMENT

SOUTH SASKATCHEWAN REGIMENT
CAMERON HIGHLANDERS
OF CANADA

VARENGEVILLE-SUR-MER

PETITE APPEVILLE

GERMAN RESERVES

NO 4 COMMANDO

VASTERIVAL

GERMAN RESERVES

LA SANNE

PORTSMOUTH

ATTACK BEGINS AUG 19

ENGLISH CHANNEL

DIEPPE

MILES
KM

72

In early 1942 the war was at a low ebb for the Allies — the German Army did not appear to be particularly inconvenienced by the Soviets; Rommel was rampaging through North Africa; Singapore, Hong Kong and the Philippine Islands had fallen to the Japanese; there was a threat to Australia and the British Army had been driven from Burma. And yet, in the face of all this, sooner or later the Allied armies were going to have to fight their way ashore on the continent of Europe and get to grips with the German Army, since in spite of high-flown theories, the war was only going to be won by engaging the enemy's forces and destroying them on the ground.

The prospect of making a landing in force on the shores of 'Fortress Europe' was a daunting one, and at the back of many minds must have been the disasters consequent upon the attempted landings on Gallipoli during the First World War. Although minor Commando raids on the French and Norwegian coasts had taught a few small lessons, there was by no means sufficient knowledge of techniques and tactics which would ensure a successful landing, and it became obvious that some large-scale operation would have to be launched in order, if nothing else, to settle some of the more debatable points which theorists and planners were raising.

Moreover there was the ever-present voice of Josef Stalin, furiously demanding to know what the Western Allies were going to do in order either to draw the Germans away from Russia or at least keep the forty-odd German divisions in France occupied, and thus relieve the pressure on his troops so that the Soviets could get their breath and begin organizing for a counterstroke. As detailed elsewhere, in an unguarded moment the Americans had been persuaded to promise a landing in force on the continent in 1942, even though this was totally impossible given the troops and equipment then available.

Taking all these things together, in late March 1942 the idea of a raid in strength on some selected Continental target was broached, and after some debate Dieppe was selected. This would, firstly, allow the planning staffs to test their theories, secondly, give the actual troops some experience, thirdly secure hard information on the nature of German defenses and their methods of operation, and fourthly give Stalin an assurance that at least the Allies were trying. Dieppe was selected after studies of air photographs of several comparably-sized French ports, all equally well defended; it had a harbor used extensively by the Germans for their coastal convoys, so that destruction would be an inconvenience, it had some worthwhile targets such as marshalling yards, fuel tanks, chemical factories and a power station which were valuable in themselves as well as being excellent examples for testing out destructive techniques; and the assault, in daylight, would bring out the Luftwaffe to be attacked by the Royal Air Force, something which mere air operations had failed to do for some months.

There was, though, one important difference between this operation and the ultimate target of an invasion. In an invasion you throw the troops ashore and keep them there at all costs; at Dieppe they were to be thrown ashore and then withdrawn after about eight or nine hours of stirring up the German hornet's nest, and during all this time the transporting ships would have to lie off shore under the threat of constant attack from coastal artillery and aircraft.

The target

Dieppe lies at the mouth of the River D'Arques, and is flanked by wide beaches for about five miles on either side, much of which are backed by high cliffs which are occasionally pierced by gullies. In 1942 these beaches, and the entrances to the port, were commanded by two powerful gun batteries, at Berneval to the east and Varengeville-sur-Mer to the west. The Dieppe beach, backed by promenades, gardens and the Casino, was flanked by two headlands which commanded the entire beach and the sea approaches. These had been put into a formidable state of defense by the Germans; the eastern headland, code-named 'Bismarck', was known by the British to have been driven through with tunnels and gun emplacements, even though the exact number, size and disposition of these guns was unknown. The western headland, 'Hindenburg', was similarly fortified, though this was believed to be of lesser strength. The 'worst case' envisaged by the planners was that both these headlands would turn out to be miniature Gibraltars, and it was extremely doubtful that either of them could be neutralized by air attack or by naval bombardment prior to the raid.

Dieppe itself was garrisoned by 572 Grenadier Regiment of the German 302 Infantry Division, supported by six batteries of medium artillery and with the remaining two regiments (570 and 571) a short distance inland and within call should the need arise. In addition the 332 Infantry Division was in reserve, and elements of 10 Panzer Division, recently returned from the Russian front for rest and refit, were only a few miles inland, acting as a mobile reserve for that stretch of coast.

The plan

Dieppe was obviously going to be a tough target, and the plans which evolved were elaborate. Among the first decisions was that two coast defense batteries at Berneval and Varengeville had to be put out of action early in the proceedings, otherwise nothing that floated would remain afloat for long. The first suggestion was to use airborne troops to neutralize these two positions, but upon careful examination, it was found that this was not practical; there was a shortage of suitable aircraft, there were difficulties in synchronizing the airborne and seaborne attacks, and parachuting was far too dependent upon wind and weather. Berneval would therefore be assaulted by No 3 Commando who would land on two beaches 'Yellow 1' and 'Yellow 2' and perform a pincer movement to attack the position from both sides. Varengeville would be similarly assaulted by No 4 Commando, part of which would land on 'Orange 1' beach and advance directly inland through the village of Vasterival, while the other part would land at 'Orange 2' just over a mile to the west and march in a looping arc to arrive at the rear of the battery (named 'Hess' by the planners) just as the element from Orange 1' arrived at the front.

The main assault was to be made by two battalions against the central Dieppe beach, and in order to protect this attempt the two headlands had to be dealt with. Two battalions were allocated for this task, one landing at Puys (Blue Beach) to the east of the town and moving in to take 'Bismarck' and the other landing at Pourville (Green Beach) to the west to take 'Hindenburg'. Once the headland-clearing battalion had landed on Green, a second battalion would land and pass through them to push straight inland with the intention of taking the airfield at St Aubin.

The main assault on the Dieppe beach (divided into 'White' on the west and 'Red' on the east) would be performed by infantry and a battalion of tanks; once the town itself was cleared, these tanks would push forward to the St Aubin airfield, assist the second battalion from Green Beach to clear the airfield and destroy whatever was on it, after which the combined force would push on to Arques-la-Bataille, a hamlet some four miles from the sea, in which the HQ of 302 Infantry Division was located. There they would do whatever damage they could, loot the HQ of secret documents and codes, and then make their way back to the beach. With their return the operation would be deemed to have been completed, and the troops would then fall back on the Dieppe beach, re-embark in their landing craft, and return to England.

The principal forces for 'Operation Jubilee' as the raid now came to be known, were Canadian; the Royal Regiment of Canada were to land on Blue Beach and attack the 'Bismarck' position, the South Saskatchewan Regiment and the Queen's Own Cameron Highlanders of Canada were to land on Green Beach and take 'Hindenburg', while the central beaches would be assaulted by the Essex Scottish Regiment (Red Beach) and the Royal Hamilton Light Infantry (White Beach), accompanied by tanks of the Calgary Regiment (14th Canadian Army Tank Regiment) and with the Fusiliers Mont-Royal in reserve. Nos 3 and 4 Commando were also to be accompanied by some fifty officers and men of the 1st US Ranger Battalion. There was also 'A' Commando, Royal Marines, who were to assist in the capture of the headlands, and a somewhat peculiar force of French light infantry carried on a naval gunboat who, while everyone was occupied on shore, were supposed to sail into Dieppe harbor, seize forty German landing barges anchored there, and tow them back to England. Just what this maneuver was supposed to accomplish is hard to see.

No less than 252 ships were needed for this force of some 6000 men: nine infantry landing ships, 24 tank landing ships, eight destroyers, a sloop, and a variety of landing craft, assault craft and small naval vessels, all preceded by minesweepers. Air cover was to be provided by sixty RAF squadrons, principally of fighters but including seven squadrons of fighter-bombers and bombers.

Conditions of time and tide governed the selection of a suitable date for the operation, and 18 August, 1942 was the last day in the year when conditions would be right. The operation was therefore planned for that date, but, in the event, the weather caused a postponement and it was not until the night of the 18th that the force eventually sailed from its ports in England, concentrated in the Channel, and set out for Dieppe.

The raid

At 0300 on the morning of 19 August the various elements of the fleet arrived at their stations off the coast and the troops began transferring into their landing craft. By 0330 the groups were moving off from their

A HERO OF DIEPPE

Lord Lovat is the 24th Chief of the Clan Fraser; after serving in the Brigade of Guards from 1934 to 1937, he returned to his estate in Scotland, but in 1939 took command of Lovat's Scouts. This unit had been raised during the South African war by the 14th Baron Lovat, Lord Lovat's father; it was composed of Highland stalkers and similar countrymen and earned a high reputation for scouting and mobile operations.

In 1942, at the suggestion of Winston

LORD LOVAT GIVING ORDERS TO HIS COMMANDO BEFORE THE RAID.

Churchill, Lovat's Scouts were converted into a Commando unit, and were sent to the Middle East. Lovat remained in Britain with the Commando force and led 4th Commando during the Dieppe raid. In 1944 he led the 1st Special Service Brigade, another Commando formation, during the Normandy landings and was severely wounded. He later joined a Military Mission to Moscow.

parent ships, silently and in good order, when the first check occurred; the group of landing craft carrying the Royal Regiment formed up behind the wrong escort gunboat, and almost half an hour was lost while this was corrected. This imposed a delay on the general run-in to the central beaches.

Meanwhile 3 Commando approached Berneval in 20 landing craft accompanied by a naval gunboat, and at 0347 they blundered into five German armed trawlers making a routine patrol. Within minutes the gunboat was shattered by the concentrated fire of the five trawlers, and the landing craft were scattered in the darkness. Two escorting destroyers, HMS *Brocklesby* and the Polish *Slazak* were about four miles away but failed to come to the support of the Commandos; the captain of the Polish ship was later to say that he thought the firing was coming from the shore batteries and that he thought it wiser to continue his patrolling.

One of the landing craft managed to maintain its correct course and landed in its appointed place on Yellow Beach 2 at the correct time, and its occupants — three officers and 17 men, with no heavier weapon than a 2in mortar — went ashore and with their small arms and mortar were able to keep the Berneval battery so occupied that the guns were unable to deliver any effective fire into the Dieppe area during the landings. This small party continued with their harassing until they began to run short of ammunition, whereupon they fell back to the beach and were removed by a landing craft which had, very bravely, stood off shore taking what shelter it could from smoke screens which were being laid to cover the main force movements.

Six more landing craft eventually reached Yellow 1 beach but by the time they did so it was daylight and they were immediately engaged by small arms fire. Eventually they were able to get off the beach but they were soon pinned down by fire from concealed strongpoints. They made no further progress and eventually the survivors, dragging and carrying the wounded, made their way back to the beach to find that there were no boats to take them off. They continued to fight until their ammunition ran out, and then surrendered. Of the 460 Rangers and Commandos who had left Newhaven on the previous night, 120 had been lost in this brief operation.

On the other flank of the operation, the 252 men of No 4 Commando performed a text-book maneuver. Batterie 813 — code-named 'Hess' by the planners — was on top of steep cliffs, about a kilometer from the sea, with an observation post in a lighthouse close to the cliff edge. The commandos, under Lt Col the Lord Lovat, were divided into two groups, one to provide covering fire while the other performed the actual assault. Group 1 landed on Orange 1 Beach at the foot of steep cliffs; at either flank of their landing point steep gullies ran up through the cliffs giving access to woodlands flanking the battery position. Their task was to ascend the cliffs, form a perimeter, and engage the battery with small arms and mortar fire so as to cover

the advance of Group 2, then to secure the line of retreat to the beach.

Group 2 was to land at Orange 2 Beach, beyond the cliffs and backed by relatively low land, but overlooked by higher ground which was studded with defensive posts. The Group were to land under covering fire from support landing craft, advance up the shallow valley of the River Saane, then leave the valley and move across country for almost 2km and into a small wood behind the battery. Here they would make their final dispositions and their assault.

Early successes

Both landings were successful, though the uproar over 3 Commando's melee with the trawlers further up the coast led the defenders of 'Hess' to fire a starshell just to check their own front. They appear not to have noticed the landing craft which were by then almost on the point of touch-down, and the landing of Group 1 went without incident. A quick reconnaissance showed that the western gully was passable, though it required the use of Bangalore Torpedoes to breach two bands of wire entanglement. This might have been expected to generate some response from the Germans, but it would seem that the gullies directed the noise upwards and by the time it was heard, it probably appeared to be part of the uproar going on further up the coast. In any event there was no response from any defensive posts, and the Commandos moved on.

Then the battery opened fire with its heavy guns, doubtless on the main assault fleet, and under the cover of this noise the Commandos were able to ignore any need for stealth and rush forward as fast as they could. Well up to their timetable they were able to take up positions overlooking the battery gunpits and opened fire

TWO LANDING CRAFT SEEN DURING THEIR LOADING, BEFORE THE RAID. NOTE THAT ONE CONTAINS A BREN GUN CARRIER, A VEHICLE WHICH APPEARS NEVER TO HAVE BEEN FORMALLY MENTIONED IN ANY HISTORIES OF THE RAID, AND THERE SEEMS TO BE SOME DOUBT AS TO WHETHER ANY WERE ACTUALLY LANDED.

against the gun detachments with good effect. Fire from an anti-tank rifle soon had effect against German machine gun posts, while the 2in mortar wreaked havoc with a lucky shot which struck a pile of heavy gun cartridges.

Group 2 reached its landing point at 0430, had some difficulty in getting past wire obstacles on the beach and were then hotly engaged by machine gun and mortar fire. Thanks to a sudden attack by three RAF bombers which drew the defenders' attention, the Group was able to get free of the defended zone and make its way up the river valley, hearing the firing and explosions due to Group 1's activities as they went. The wood was reached, a German machine gun post silenced, and the Commandos formed up for the assault. As they moved in they surprised a squad of German troops in a farmyard who appeared to be preparing to counter-attack Group 1. A stiff little battle developed and the Commando troop leader, his second-in-command and his troop serjeant were all killed within minutes. At this point Captain Porteous of the Royal Artillery, acting as the liaison link between the two groups, took over command of the troop; almost immediately he was shot through the hand, and, when the assault was ordered, he was the first to reach the German guns, being shot once again through the legs as he arrived. He was subsequently awarded the Victoria Cross for his actions.

The assault was a success, the German guns were rendered inoperative by charges of explosive placed on the breech blocks, the magazine was detonated and the Commandos then fell back, covered by Group 1, to the beach, their wounded being carried somewhat unwillingly by four German prisoners. The parties re-embarked and by 0730 were on their way back to England, having carried out their assigned task for the loss of two officers and 10 men killed, 3 officers and 17 men wounded and 13 men missing.

The most remarkable thing about this raid was that

LANDING CRAFT APPROACHING THE DIEPPE COASTLINE UNDER COVER OF A SMOKESCREEN LAID BY ESCORTING WARSHIPS. THE SMALL BOAT ON THE LEFT IS PROBABLY A NAVAL MARSHALLING CRAFT, RETURNING TO ITS PARENT VESSEL AFTER HAVING SHEPHERDED THE LANDING CRAFT.

COAST FORTIFICATIONS, DIEPPE

These drawings, from official plans, show examples of the fortifications constructed by the German Army on the Atlantic Coast. Below is a casemate for a 5cm anti-tank gun, little more than a reinforced concrete box into which the gun could be run and its trails spread. On the right is a far more complex emplacement for a 15cm gun. The gun is pivoted beneath the overhang of the casemate, designed to prevent attack from the air, and space is provided for the gun's crew to rest and eat. Notice the two machine gun posts covering the rear entrance, and the sentry-post in the top of the structure, allowing a watch to be kept all round the emplacement. The roof is about 2.5m thick, the walls about 2m, both adequate to stop all but the heaviest shells.

5CM ANTI-TANK GUN

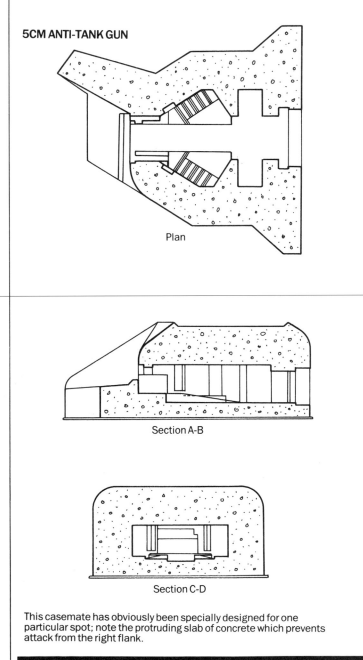

Plan

Section A-B

Section C-D

This casemate has obviously been specially designed for one particular spot; note the protruding slab of concrete which prevents attack from the right flank.

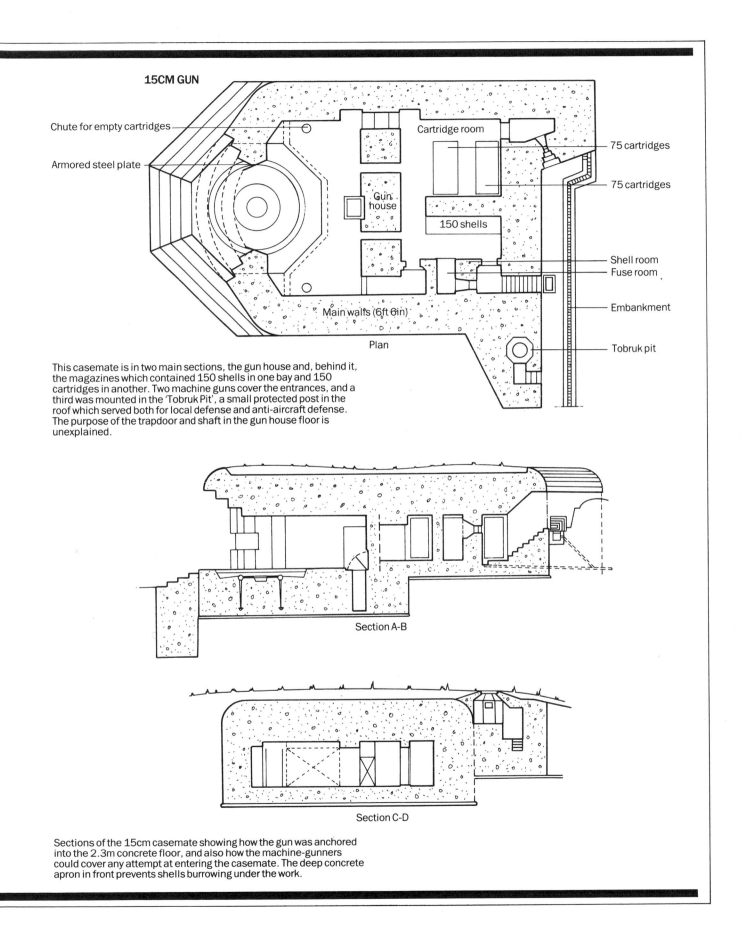

15CM GUN

Chute for empty cartridges

Armored steel plate

Cartridge room

Gun house

75 cartridges

75 cartridges

150 shells

Shell room

Fuse room

Embankment

Main walls (6ft 6in)

Tobruk pit

Plan

This casemate is in two main sections, the gun house and, behind it, the magazines which contained 150 shells in one bay and 150 cartridges in another. Two machine guns cover the entrances, and a third was mounted in the 'Tobruk Pit', a small protected post in the roof which served both for local defense and anti-aircraft defense. The purpose of the trapdoor and shaft in the gun house floor is unexplained.

Section A-B

Section C-D

Sections of the 15cm casemate showing how the gun was anchored into the 2.3m concrete floor, and also how the machine-gunners could cover any attempt at entering the casemate. The deep concrete apron in front prevents shells burrowing under the work.

the observation post of the battery, barely a mile away, knew nothing of the raid at all, their telephone communication having been cut by the Commandos, and it was not until some hours later that the German HQ realized that this vital battery was out of action.

Probably even more vital that the silencing of these batteries was the need to neutralize the two headlands, since they carried a far more immediate threat to the security of the landing. Blue Beach, on the eastern side of Dieppe, was defended by a formidable sea wall of ten to fifteen feet height, topped by barbed wire and surrounded by more wire obstacles. Two pillboxes with machine guns flanked the sea wall from each end.

The assault on this beach was carried out by the Royal Regiment of Canada, who, due to the setback during the launch, were now some 17 minutes late in arriving at their objective. This proved fatal; a German soldier sleeping in a house close to the beach was wakened by the noise of 3 Commando's engagement with the trawlers and, not waiting to find out what was going on, he ran down to his beach post in his night clothes and opened fire with his machine gun as being the best way to sound a general alarm. By the time the Royals began disembarking the entire beach defenses were manned and they opened fire, turning the landing into a disaster. A small party on the right flank, protected by an outcrop of cliff, managed to cut through some wire and make their way inland, to take one German defensive party from the rear, but they were soon driven back to the beach where, by this time, only a few men remained unscathed. Under the cover of RAF fighter attacks, landing craft made several attempts to return to the beach to remove the survivors, but of the 27 officers and 516 men who landed, only 3 officers and 57 men were saved, the rest being either killed or made prisoner. As a result, headland 'Bismarck' remained operational.

ORDER OF BATTLE

ALLIED

2nd Canadian Div (Commander: Gen Hamilton Roberts)

Royal Regt of Canada
Royal Hamilton lt Inf
Essex Scottish
South Saskatchewan Regt
Queen's Own Cameron Highlanders of Canada
Fusiliers Mont-Royal
14th Army Tk Bde

US Rangers (50 all ranks)

4Cdo (Commander: Lord Lovat)

3Cdo (Commander: Lt-Col Durnford Slater)

ALLIED cas: 3643 lost; killed, wounded and left or made prisoner

AXIS

302 Inf Div

Reserve: 332 Inf Div; elements 10 Panzer Div

AXIS cas: 597 KIA/WIA

On the other flank the attack against 'Hindenburg' headland began with more success. The South Saskatchewan Regiment landed on Green Beach achieving complete surprise and were across the sand and scaling the cliffs before the defenders realized what was happening. This, though, meant that they were in place and ready when the second wave of the assault came in, though their fire appeared to be on pre-set lines and once this was realized the Canadians were able to avoid the more dangerous areas.

'A' Company, whose objective was a radar station, were slowed by obstacles on their route and were finally brought to a stop some 200 metres from the station. 'C' Company went into the village of Pourville and within half an hour had taken the village and moved on to capture a fortified house overlooking the beach. 'B' and 'D' Companies pushed through Pourville, seized a small bridge to secure an exit, but were then stopped by a line of German pillboxes.

Now the follow-up troops, the Cameron Highlanders, landed and moved through Pourville, their task being to assault the airfield at St Aubin and then the German HQ at Arques in company with tanks landed on the main beach in Dieppe. The Camerons were able to reach a position in a wood, there to await the tanks; but by 0900, the scheduled time, the tanks had not made an appearance and since the assaulting troops were supposed to be back on their beach by 1000 in order to be removed by landing craft, further advance was abandoned and the Camerons began to move back.

On the beach the South Saskatchewans were holding valiantly in order to keep the beach for the return of the Camerons, though 'C' Company had been pushed from their fortified house, so allowing the Germans to occupy a position which commanded the whole embarkation area. The tide was ebbing fast, exposing more and more beach, and by the time the Camerons arrived there was an expanse of shingle some 200 yards wide which had to be crossed, after which a further 150 yards had to be waded through the sea since the landing craft could not come closer without risk of stranding.

The landing craft arrived at 1030, and attempts were made to cross the fire-swept beach with wounded in order to re-embark. Protected by gunfire and smoke screens from Royal Navy ships and by aircraft attacks, the Canadians gradually contracted into a ring on the beach, pressed inwards by advancing German troops. As the last landing craft pulled away Lt Col Merrit, CO of the South Saskatchewans, who had been severely wounded, and 100 men were left behind; they held out until their ammunition was gone and at about 1500 were made prisoner by the Germans. Merrit, too, was awarded the VC for his bravery in heading several attacks during the course of this brief action. Nevertheless, in spite of the gallantry and dash of these two Canadian regiments, they had failed to get within a kilometer of their principal objective, and the flanking headland on the west of the beaches was still operational.

The main assault against Red and White Beaches was to be a silent approach, with a last-minute air attack against the two headlands and the fortified buildings backing the promenade, accompanied by the laying of smoke screens. The air attack began at 0510 and the first landings on Red Beach were made at 0523.

Very few of the German defensive guns had been put out of action by the air attack, and as the Canadians left their landing craft a furious hail of fire swept the beach from end to end, machine guns, rifles, mortars, anti-tank guns and a lone 105mm howitzer all joining in. Snipers on the roof-tops of the fortified buildings concentrated on picking off officers and NCOs and within ten minutes the dead were lying strewn across the beach. A breach was made in the wire obstacles and six Churchill tanks came ashore from their special landing craft. This was the first time the Churchill tank was used in combat; five managed to clamber across the sea-wall backing the beach, while a sixth scrambled up a flight of steps in front of the Casino. Two, which had reached the promenade, began firing at machine gun posts and gun positions on the Hindenburg headland, while three moved off down the promenade behind the sea wall. The tank which had climbed the steps fell into a tank trap and the crew were killed. Four more tanks had now landed but were disabled; three were immobile but were able to use their guns to give some covering fire.

The tank breakthrough allowed small parties of infantry to follow them, one making for the Casino and others heading into the town. Smoke screens laid by aircraft were masking the headlands intermittently, but the last of this smoke blew away just as the second wave of tank landing tank were approaching the beaches at 0600; and in spite of covering fire from naval gunboats, heavy guns in the headlands now opened fire against the fresh wave.

The landing on White Beach was no more successful; the beach is narrower at this point, and the carefully-sited machine guns and mortars swept the area with lethal thoroughness. Seventeen tanks were landed but only six managed to get across the beach; some of the tank landing craft were hit and began to sink, taking their tanks with them. In desperation, the tank crews attempted to drive their vehicles through the water as the ships sank beneath them, but in spite of being waterproofed, they launched into water which was far too deep and the tanks were lost. Small groups of men managed to get clear of the beach in the wake of the successful tanks and made for the fortified buildings across the promenade.

Misjudgements offshore

Although little firm information had managed to get back to the command ship, HMS *Calpe*, the decision was taken to commit the reserve regiment, the Fusiliers Mont-Royal, shortly after 0700. Due to a change in the on-shore current, most of their landing craft were swept to the west and instead of landing on Red Beach they came ashore on White Beach close under the Hindenburg headland. There 300 men were trapped on a small stretch of shingle and rock beneath towering cliffs. They were pinned down by fire and were totally unable to move or intervene in the battle; they eventually surrendered about noon, after over one hundred had been wounded. Two other parties of Fusiliers managed to land in the right place and joined with the Royal Hamiltons in an attack against the Casino, capturing it by 0720. In other parts of the town small parties managed to fire a tobacco factory and destroy the gasworks.

For some reason, which has never been satisfactorily determined, the command on HMS *Calpe* now decided that things were improving and that the second reserve force, the Royal Marine Commandos, could be sent in to White Beach to reinforce. The landing craft set sail through smoke screens, and as they emerged from the screen close to the beach it became immediately appa-

TOP: TWO CHURCHILL TANKS STRANDED ON THE PRINCIPAL BEACH, WITH A BURNING LANDING CRAFT IN THE BACKGROUND. ABOVE: THE SAME SCENE, FROM A MORE DISTANT VIEWPOINT; NOTE THAT TWO MORE TANKS LIE STRANDED IN THE WATER, NEVER HAVING MADE IT AS FAR AS DRY LAND. THE ART OF WATERPROOFING TANKS FOR WADING THROUGH SURF WAS NOT WELL DEVELOPED AT THE TIME OF THE DIEPPE RAID.

rent to their commander, Lt Col Philips, that their landing was a forlorn hope; taking an immediate decision, he stood up in the front of his leading landing raft and, with white-gloved hands, signalled the remainder to turn about and leave the beach. Six craft got the message before Philips was shot down and killed, and they turned back for the sea, thus saving 200 men from almost certain death or captivity. The remainder landed but were able to do little more than scoop holes in the shingle and fight for their survival.

At about 0900 the Naval Force Commander, Captain Hughes-Hallett, came to the conclusion that the whole operation had failed, and he advised the military commander, Major-General Roberts, that the remaining troops should be evacuated as fast as possible, abandoning the tanks and other material which had been got ashore. Signals were sent to the shore, though with little hope of getting through to everyone, and plans were put in hand for the evacuation.

By this time, the German reaction had begun to spread. Units from the reserves had begun to move up to Dieppe; 1st Bn 571 Infanterie Regiment were moving in against the raiders at Pourville, an engineer battalion had been sent to deal with the raiders at Berneval — although by this time they were long gone — and the 676 and 570 Infanterie Regiments were closing up around the town. Elements of 10 Panzer Division had also been alerted and tanks were moving towards Dieppe, though this was more of an insurance since it seemed unlikely that the Canadians were even going to break into the town, much less break out of it. As the reserve troops arrived in Dieppe they were rapidly fed into the defenses, so strengthening the resistance to the landing and adding to the storm of fire sweeping every inch of the beaches.

The Luftwaffe now appeared in strength, but this was what the RAF had been waiting for, and the German aircraft were unable to make much impression on the ground battle, their principal concern being their survival against incessant RAF fighter attacks. At the same time, with the evacuation beginning, fighters and fighter-bombers of the RAF assaulted the Bismarck and Hindenburg headlands with non-stop fury. Fighters ranged far afield from Dieppe, catching the Luftwaffe flights on their way to the scene of battle, and many RAF fighter pilots flew three and four missions during that morning. By early afternoon the RAF could claim a complete victory; not one German bomber had managed to make an attack on the landing craft or the off-shore shipping. The RAF later calculated that they had flown 2617 sorties during the day, for the loss of 106 aircraft. The Luftwaffe lost 170 aircraft, and the half-day over Dieppe has since been assessed as the greatest air battle of the entire war.

Complex plans had been prepared for evacuation of the raiding force, plans which envisaged a careful relay of landing craft moving in and out over a three-hour period. In the circumstances, this was obviously no longer feasible and the plans were scrapped in favor of a simple dash into the beaches with every available craft to rescue as many men as possible. At 1022 the remaining destroyers formed a line and shepherded the remaining landing craft into the harbor, firing high explosive and smoke shells at the defenses in an attempt to deflect them from their task of slaughter. Even so, it was to take over two hours to collect as many men as possible, get them into the landing craft and ferry them back to safety. One destroyer, HMS *Berkeley,* was sunk by a chance bomb being jettisoned from a passing Ju 88 bomber which had been attacked by Spitfires. By ill chance the *Berkeley* was directly underneath as the bomb fell free and landed on the ship's bridge. By 1300 the last of the landing craft had left the beaches, and Operation Jubilee was at an end.

On the beaches were the remains of the assault; one Canadian history estimates that no more than 350 men were rescued from the town beach and about 600 from Pourville, while it is believed that less than ten men came off Blue Beach alive. Among those left was the Royal Hamilton Light Infantry chaplain, Captain JW Foote, who had spent the entire action moving along the beach giving succour to the wounded; he chose to remain with them instead of being evacuated, and was awarded the Victoria Cross in recognition of his selfless actions. The Germans now moved in to take prisoner those remaining, and at 1740 the signal was sent to HQ German C-in-C West: "No armed Englishman remains on the Continent."

The lessons

"What went wrong at Dieppe?" became a well-known heart-cry in the subsequent months, and, indeed, for many years after the war. The bill for the action was shocking; the Canadians lost 215 officers and 3164 men of whom about 1000 were dead on the beaches; the Commandos lost 24 officers and 223 men, the Royal Marines had 31 killed and 69 taken prisoner, and the Royal Navy lost 81 officers and 469 men together with

HMS *BERKELEY*, HER BRIDGE AND UPPER WORKS BADLY DAMAGED, ABANDONED AND SINKING. *BERKELEY* WAS THE VICTIM OF CHANCE, STRUCK BY BOMBS JETTISONED BY A GERMAN AIRCRAFT ESCAPING FROM THE RAF FIGHTERS.

ABOVE: CANADIAN PRISONERS BEING MARCHED THROUGH DIEPPE ON THEIR WAY TO TRANSPORT FOR THE PRISON CAMPS.
LEFT: GENERALFELDMARSCHALL VON RUNDSTEDT, GERMAN COMMANDER-IN-CHIEF WEST, DISCUSSING THE RAID WITH HIS STAFF DURING A VISIT HE MADE TO POURVILLE (GREEN BEACH) A FEW DAYS AFTER THE BATTLE. IN THE BACKGROUND IS A ROADBLOCK, PART OF A SERIES OF DEFENSES AND FORTIFICATIONS HURRIEDLY BUILT AFTER THE RAID IN CASE OF A REPEAT. SIMILAR DEFENSES WERE THROWN UP IN SEVERAL COASTAL TOWNS.

34 of the 252 ships involved. Of the 24 tank landing craft involved, only ten managed to close the beach and land 28 tanks, all of which were lost. On the defending side the Germans lost 345 killed, 268 wounded and the four prisoners taken by No 4 Commando.

After any military disaster there is a witch-hunt. The French Army invariably cry 'Treason' after any setback, since they cannot envisage their army ever making mistakes and therefore any failure can only be ascribed to treachery from some outside source. In similar vein, every army seeks to find a scapegoat since none can ever bring themselves to admit that they were at fault in any way. Seeking to mitigate the effects of the operation Winston Churchill, speaking in Parliament on 8 September, said:

> "The Dieppe Raid must be considered a reconnaissance in force . . . we had to get all the information necessary before landing operations on a much larger scale. This raid, apart from its reconnaissance value, brought about an extremely satisfactory air battle in the west which Fighter Command wish they could repeat every week."

The actual scale of the disaster was carefully concealed from the public at the time, the details only gradually becoming known over a long period, but within the military circles there was a careful enquiry into the causes of the failure.

Put bluntly, the operation failed because the defenses were too good for the attackers to defeat. The planners had poor information on the strength of these defenses, and even information on the physical features of the area was lacking. For example, the Camerons, landing on Green Beach, were told that the seawall was three feet high; when they got to it they found it to be seven feet high. Before that they had discovered that what they were told was a sand beach was in fact composed of large rock shingle, difficult to cross even on foot. The supposed German HQ at Arques, against which a raid was planned, was, in fact, no more than the local 'Kommandantur' — the garrison administrative office — the divisional HQ actually being at Envermeu, some miles away in a different direction.

There was, too, a great deal of optimism in respect of the damage which would be done to the defenses by naval gunfire and a short air bombardment. The naval forces capable of gunfire amounted to six destroyers with nothing larger than 4in guns, which had negligible effect on well-built defenses, and the air attack was too short and, by virtue of its direction, could expect to do little against defensive positions tunnelled into the face of cliffs. The need to neutralize the coast defense batteries was appreciated, and only ill-luck prevented No 3 Commando from destroying the Berneval battery as effectively as No 4 had destroyed that at Varengeville. But these two actions at least removed a threat which could well have sunk the six destroyers and left the flotilla of small craft without protectors and the rest of the assault without the little gunfire support it had.

Reviewing the plan one cannot help feeling that the whole thing was far too ambitious, trying to do too many things at once. In rebuttal, it can be claimed that once the decision had been taken to attack Dieppe, the plan could not be otherwise, since the five objectives were all vitally important; the two coastal batteries had to be silenced, and the two headlands were also vital targets if the frontal assault was to succeed. But one is entitled to ask whether the same 'information necessary before landing operations' could not have been obtained by raiding somewhere with a less involved defensive layout.

As a result of the raid, though, many important lessons were learned about the techniques necessary to make a successful landing. In the first place it became obvious that attacking a defended port was out of the question, and therefore when the invasion finally took place it would have to take place over open beaches in a relatively lightly defended sector. This then raised the question of how to get the necessary back-up supplies to the invasion force without port facilities, and this, in turn, led to the concept of pre-fabricated harbors, the 'Mulberries', which could be towed across and positioned as required.

The second vital point was brought out by the failure of the tanks to get off the beaches. Some were shot up as soon as they landed, but several simply scrabbled their way into the shingle and immobilized themselves. Others managed to get across the shingle but were stopped by the sea wall and the steep face of the promenade. Thinking about these defects gave rise to the 79th Armoured Division and the myriad of specialized tanks which are described elsewhere, tanks designed to overcome the various natural and artificial obstacles which could be expected on beaches.

Thirdly, the need for minute detail on every aspect of an invasion shore was revealed. Such apparently minor points as the nature and slope of a beach, the height of sea walls, the height of groynes between stretches of beach, the nature of the subsoil beneath the beach all assumed importance; and shortly after the Dieppe raid plans were drawn up for a broadcast appeal to the population of Britain to send to the War Office any pre-war photographs of continental beaches so that they could be analyzed. This appeal was duly made, in 1943, and from the thousands of pictures submitted the planners were able to extract an immense amount of simple but vital information. In addition to this, photo-interpretive techniques were devised which, for example, could determine the slope of a beach from the spacing of waves of surf as seen on a vertical air photograph.

Fourth, and very obvious, was the need to have the

most detailed information about the disposition of defenses. Agents of the French Resistance, skilled analysis of air photographs, and even surreptitious visits by members of the Special Boat Service and other Clandestine Organizations all helped to build up a picture of defenses at various places, and a special section of the War Office, the 'Martian' office, came into being in order to construct detailed lists and plans of every type of German defense structure from the North Cape to the Pyrenees.

In addition to these basic planning features, other factors were assessed and changed where necessary. The ineffective gunfire support was one such, and for the future it was decided to add the most powerful ships to an invasion force for no other reason than to provide the heaviest possible weight of shells. Special gunfire support vessels were constructed, as were landing craft weighed down with immense batteries of shore bombardment rockets. The air forces had done as well as they could, but in future their efforts would be increased a hundred-fold and the scale of pre-invasion bombardment a thousand-fold in order to do as much damage to the defenders as possible before the first soldier set his foot on the hostile shore.

Taking the long view, therefore, one can say that the Dieppe raid produced information and taught lessons which were, without any doubt, of vital importance for the successful planning of the Normandy invasion. As a stand-alone operation however, it was of negligible value. The casualty list of the Canadian Army soured relationships between the Canadians and British to some extent, which can be gauged by one commentator who wryly observed, after the war, that Dieppe was more costly to the Canadians that the eleven months of post-Normandy fighting. Against this, though, one must recognize that the British and Commonwealth forces had not, prior to 1942, had much in the way of casualties by which to compare the Dieppe raid, and the hard fact of the matter was that, after all, war means deaths and injury.

One strange aftermath of the raid was the effect upon the French citizens of Dieppe. The German Government offered 10 Million Francs (about £57,000) as compensation for the damage suffered, and the Mayor of Dieppe, an opportunist, whilst accepting this with thanks also pressed for the release of local men who had been made prisoner in 1940 and who were still in captivity in Germany. His request was backed by the commander of 302 Division, who pointed out that the conduct of the locals had been:

"... more than correct. Despite the losses suffered they aided the German troops in their combat, rendering services of all kinds. They put out fires, attended the wounded, and provided the combatants with food and drink ..."

As a result the prisoners of war were given their freedom; though how long they enjoyed it before being whisked back into forced labor battalions is another question.

CHAPTER FIVE

OPENING UP THE KOKODA TRAIL

JUNGLE WARFARE
AUGUST – NOVEMBER 1942

Overleaf

The hard fought battles on the Kokoda Trail finally opened up the
possibility of an attack on Buna, and the fierce action of Bobdabi Ridge, the subject of this painting.
(*Taking Old Vickers Position, Bobdabi Ridge* by I Hele. Courtesy Australian War Memorial)

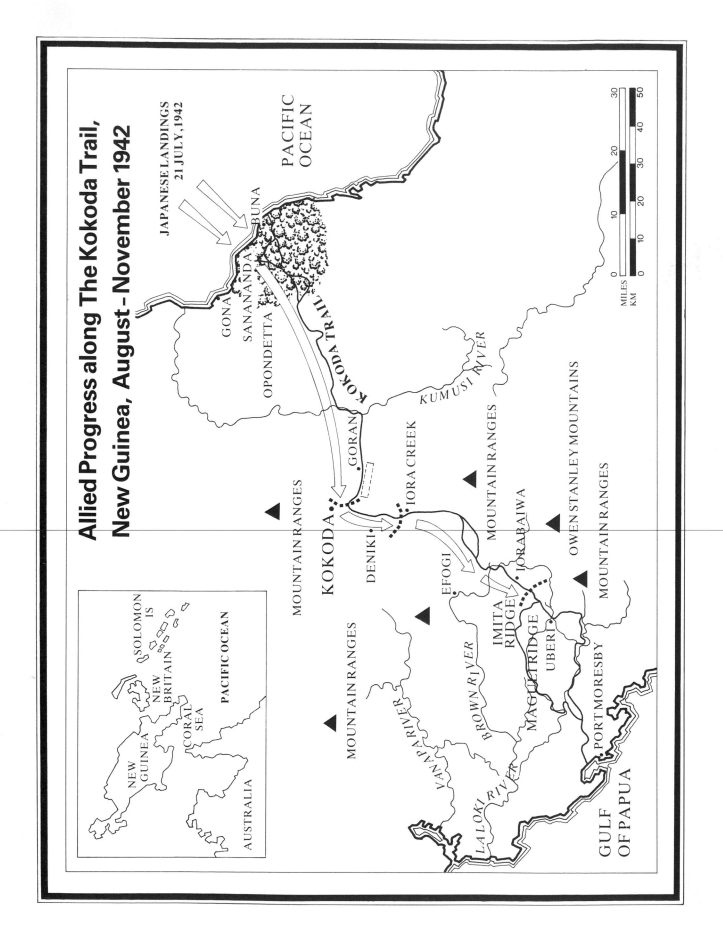

Allied Progress along The Kokoda Trail, New Guinea, August–November 1942

JAPANESE LANDINGS
21 JULY, 1942

PACIFIC OCEAN

BUNA

GONA
SANANANDA
OPONDETTA

KOKODA TRAIL

GORAN

KUMUSI RIVER

IORA CREEK

MOUNTAIN RANGES

KOKODA

DENIKI

MOUNTAIN RANGES

EFOGI

IORABAIWA

MOUNTAIN RANGES

OWEN STANLEY MOUNTAINS

IMITA RIDGE

MAGULI RIDGE

UBERI

MOUNTAIN RANGES

VANAPA RIVER

BROWN RIVER

LALOKI RIVER

PORT MORESBY

GULF OF PAPUA

MILES
KM

SOLOMON IS

NEW BRITAIN

NEW GUINEA

CORAL SEA

PACIFIC OCEAN

AUSTRALIA

Early in 1942 General MacArthur left his besieged headquarters in Corregidor and made for Australia, there to take command of the US troops that he confidently thought were awaiting his arrival and immediately begin his victorious return to the Philippines.

Unfortunately for the General, there were less than 25,000 US troops in Australia at that time, and most of them were either aviators, supply troops or anti-aircraft gunners. Quite simply, there were no forces available for any military adventure whatever. Nor were the Australians any better off; they had some 600,000 militiamen mustered and under training, and some elements of the Australian Independent Force which had been operating in North Africa were being shipped back to defend Australia, but they too had nothing with which to take the offensive.

While MacArthur and the Australian High Command debated what to do, the Japanese were moving. Their intention was to drive down through the islands of the Pacific and take New Guinea, then turn Port Moresby into an invasion base from which to attack Northern Australia. Unfortunately their major endeavor in this line was frustrated when a naval convoy bringing troops to capture Port Moresby was attacked and severely damaged in the Battle of the Coral Sea.

However landings were made on the north coast of New Guinea, supply bases were set up, and the Japanese decided upon a land advance, across the intervening mountains, to take Port Moresby from the rear, the tactic which had succeeded so brilliantly in Singapore and Hong Kong.

At much the same time, and once the fact of the Japanese landings had been made known, the American/Australian command decided on a similar maneuver in the opposite direction; an advance from Port Moresby northwards to take the Japanese in the rear.

The terrain

What neither side really understood was the type of fighting that was required in New Guinea. The maps — such as they were — marked a route from north to south over the Owen Stanley Mountains. The Japanese always referred to it as a 'route', the Australians as a 'road'. Neither was right; the line on the map was, on the ground, no more than a native track two to three feet wide at best, clinging to mountain sides, slithering down precipitous slopes and clambering up others, crossing streams by stepping stones or log bridges, and elbowing its way through undergrowth and head-high kunai grass.

The standard of knowledge about the area can be understood by this extract from an Encyclopedia published before the war:

"The Interior has not been fully explored but mountains have been named . . . the lower courses of the rivers . . . are known and Santani Lake has been visited. Much of the area is covered in primeval forest."

Primeval forest to a European probably conjures up romantic pictures of the great oaks of Sherwood as they might have been, or some of the old forests of Germany and Poland, but the New Guinea reality was far from this arboreal picture. Wet, with trees close together, with impenetrable undergrowth, with an innumerable variety of snakes and insects, the correct word in the English language was, simply, 'jungle'. Perhaps the best description of the jungle is this, from a British training pamphlet describing part of Burma:

"The hills are large, the valleys deep. Most of the hills are covered by dense growth. It is a country in which large formations of troops are quickly swallowed up. Vehicles, even tracked vehicles, are rarely able to move off a road or track until the engineers have got to work. Gun positions are difficult to find, and guns often have to be grouped in the few, small, suitable areas there are, or brought into action on the side of the road. Until tracks can be made, movement over any distance away from a road calls for mule or porter transport, and all movement off the road is slow and laborious. Good visibility can sometimes be had from ridge to ridge, but usually only with difficulty because of the jungle that covers most of the features."

The jungle posed a considerable problem in itself. In 1941 probably the only troops in the world with any experience of operations in jungle were the Japanese, and they did not have much. Their advance on Singapore, reputedly through jungle, was actually through forest far less daunting than that of New Guinea, but they had gained some jungle experience in parts of French Indo-China. Even so, it was relatively little; their advantage, so far as jungle warfare went, lay simply in that their troops were more hardy, their supply system more elastic and their support weapons both fewer and lighter than those of any other army.

One or two units of the British Army might have had some past experience in jungle fighting, since there were some comparable stands of forest in parts of India, but in truth both the British and their opponents tended to stay out of these areas when having their periodic differences. It is safe to say, therefore, that there was no jungle warfare knowledge whatever in the British, Australian, American or for that matter any other army of 1941. In one way this was advantageous since it meant that everybody began on an even footing; in another way it was disadvantageous to the western troops, since the Japanese showed a greater ability to adapt to the conditions rapidly and thus gave an impression of expertise and invincibility. Eventually the westerners did adapt and were able to outfight the Japanese in jungle, but this was to take time.

A western army fighting in jungle had to make some fairly massive readjustments on both the individual and the corporate levels. On the individual level the men had to learn to operate in stinking foetid conditions, in heat, and in the dubious ambience of leeches, snakes and mosquitoes. Once they had learned to live in this, they then had to learn to navigate, fight and operate as a coherent force in it. On the corporate level the basic tactics had to be rethought; here, for example, there was little scope for massive artillery support which relied, as it did in other theaters of war, on accurate survey and accurate knowledge of everybody's position on the battlefield.

It was unrealistic to depend upon wire communications and dubious to rely upon radio which, at that stage of its development, could easily fail to communicate from one valley to the next. There were no reliable maps, and even air photographs were of little value since they mostly showed the same vista of treetops no matter where they were taken. The troops operating in the jungle were liable to lose contact with each other very rapidly, and the terrain was ideal for ambushes. With the limited number of tracks available it was relatively easy to judge where an advance would come and make preparations for it; so much so that General Slim, commanding the British 14th Army in Burma was later to say that "to advance on a narrow front and attack the Jap frontally is to invite a bloody nose . . . use instead the broadest front possible and constant 'hooking' to get behind him . . ."

The background

After their highly successful beginning, capturing the Philippines, Singapore and Hong Kong, the Japanese moved southward, their eventual aim being Australia. On 3 May, 1942 their forces captured Tulagi, in the Solomon Islands, and on the following day a convoy of troop transports protected by warships and aircraft carriers moved southward to land at Port Moresby. The convoy was seen by Australian Coast Watchers and reported to base in Australia, and Japanese radio transmissions were intercepted and deciphered by US Naval Intelligence, with the result that the Allies knew as much about the convoy's movements as did the Japanese. As the convoy entered the Coral Sea it was attacked by aircraft from US naval forces.

The Battle of the Coral Sea was the first major naval battle in which neither side saw an enemy ship; all the damage was done by carrier-borne aircraft, and both sides suffered. But the Japanese suffered worst, and what was left of the convoy turned about and sailed back for the safety of Tulagi.

This saved Port Moresby from invasion and saved Townsville and other parts of Northern Australia from bombing attacks from the airfield which the Japanese intended to build around Port Moresby. But with this failure the Japanese decided that instead of risking another rebuff at sea they would, instead, take Port Moresby by an overland march.

Japanese troops had first landed in New Guinea on 8 March 1942, placing troops ashore at Lae and Salamaua. There was little or no opposition to these landings, and after getting ashore the invaders spent some weeks in building up their supply base and support facilities preparatory to extending their area of domination. With the failure of the seaborne convoy, it was now decided to put more troops into this beachhead and make this the springboard for the advance on Port Moresby.

The plan

The Allied plan, what there was of it, was relatively simple; the Australians would land at Port Moresby and march across the Owen Stanley Mountains to the northern coast of New Guinea. Once there they would attack and defeat the Japanese forces at Buna, Gona, and anywhere else they happened to be. The Japanese, however, had other ideas.

An Australian military presence in New Guinea had come into being well before the war in the Far East began. In mid-1941, as the war clouds gathered, Independent Companies — the Australian equivalent of the British Commandos — had been formed, given some jungle training and sent to various outposts, New Guinea among them. The New Guinea Volunteer Rifles, a part-time force made up of Australians living in New Guinea, had also been alerted and as soon as war broke out was mobilized. Both these forces were dispersed around Lae and Salamaua and kept watch on the Japanese, reporting their activities and dispositions to Australia by radio. In April 1941, the 5th Independent Company had arrived at Port Moresby and had forthwith marched across the Owen Stanley range to join these watchers and also to set up more observation teams in the Markham Valley north of the mountains and in the Huon Gulf in the south.

The knowledge that there were Japanese in New Guinea was all that MacArthur needed to spur him to planning an attack across the range, and he carried General Blamey with him. Blamey was commanding Australian Land Forces and had been in Greece and Libya but had been recalled to Australia in March 1942 to take charge of operations there. Popular with his troops, he was less popular with MacArthur since he had a certain lack of faith in some of MacArthur's wilder ideas and did not share MacArthur's high opinion of himself. Nevertheless he saw the need to make some move against the Japanese, although he was not prepared to fling troops hither and thither without giving the matter some thought beforehand.

Once the Battle of the Coral Sea was over and the immediate threat to Moresby dissolved, Blamey organized a new group called Kanga Force and had it flown into Wau, on the northern side of the Owen Stanleys. Kanga Force consisted of a headquarters, the NGVR, the 2/5 Independent Company and a mortar platoon, and it also absorbed a platoon of infantry already stationed at Wau.

Once inserted, Kanga Force began making probing patrols up to the edge of the Japanese positions in the area, making maps and reporting on the Japanese activities. In addition, once they had taken the measure of the Japanese, the force began guerilla operations, raiding outposts, blowing bridges, ambushing vehicles and generally taking every advantage they could.

At much the same time as Kanga Force was enjoying itself, the Japanese High Command decided that it was time for the big push in New Guinea. Lt Gen Hyakutake was ordered to assemble the component formations of the 17th Army, which was then scattered across the Pacific, with elements in the Philippines, Java and the Solomon Islands, concentrate them, and make a two-pronged attack on Port Moresby. One prong would begin with a seaborne assault on Milne Bay, followed by an overland advance along the coast to Port Moresby, while the other prong would be an overland attack across the Owen Stanleys from their bases at Buna and Gona.

The Milne Bay landing is little remembered today, but it marked a very significant point in the war. The Japanese force had been reduced by removing one regiment of infantry to reinforce Guadalcanal, which had been invaded a short time before by the US Marines, but the Japanese commander, Kawaguchi, had no qualms since he knew that the Milne Bay area was lightly held by no more than two or three companies of Australian infantry, kept there to guard a small airfield with a handful of elderly aircraft.

For once the Japanese intelligence was at fault. Milne Bay held two full infantry brigades, one a regular brigade which had fought in the desert, and the other a militia brigade, while the airfield contained two squadrons of Kittyhawk fighter-bombers.

On the morning of 26 August, 1942 the Japanese landed at Milne Bay and immediately ran into fierce opposition. The untried militia proved capable of

AN AUSTRALIAN MILITIA OFFICER SITS ON THE REMAINS OF A JAPANESE TYPE 95 LIGHT TANK, KNOCKED OUT IN THE FIGHTING FOR MILNE BAY. THE 37MM GUN HAS ALREADY BEEN REMOVED FROM THE TURRET AND PROBABLY PRESSED INTO AUSTRALIAN SERVICE AS AN ANTI-TANK GUN.

fighting as well as the regulars, and the Kittyhawk fighters came out and pounded every Japanese they could see, sinking a supply ship with 300 troops on board, shooting up movement on roads and jungle trails, bombing and strafing the landing area. The Japanese managed to land a handful of tanks, and the Australians were completely without anti-tank guns, but in fact these tanks were of little value and most of the fighting was a simple matter of infantry section against infantry section at short range.

The Japanese mounted several night attacks in an attempt to get among the Australians and confuse them, though with little success, and during the hours of darkness Japanese naval ships would enter the bay and bombard the Australian positions. But the Japanese made very little progress and took severe casualties, so much so that on the night of September 6, under cover of a naval bombardment, the surviving invaders were taken off the beach and the force withdrew.

This was the first time that Western troops had bested a Japanese force, which is what makes Milne Bay significant. MacArthur, in a display of picque which put paid to his chance of ever being respected by the Australians, said that "The enemy's defeat at Milne Bay must not be accepted as a measure of the relative fighting capacity of the troops involved." In truth it could be accepted as nothing else; the Japanese had put a combat-wise force up against a defense composed half of untried militia and had been soundly beaten, and that could only be taken as a very good indicator of the relative quality of the troops involved. Whatever MacArthur said, the Australian Army knew that they had proved their worth and that henceforth the Japanese were not quite the supermen they had previously been thought. Shortly afterwards the US forces on Guadalcanal vanquished the Japanese defenders there, but MacArthur made no sour remarks about that effort.

But it was the Kokoda Trail, from Buna and Gona to Port Moresby, which was to be the testing ground for the Australians.

The opening battles

The Japanese landed their advanced parties on the north coast on 21 July and immediately began pushing patrols along the track leading to the Owen Stanleys. On the track were elements of Kanga Force, in small patrols, and these were gradually pushed back by the weight of the Japanese advance. The Japanese patrols which made contact with the Australians rapidly called up reinforcements with mortars and heavy machine guns, and this firepower was enough to drive the Australians back step by step. As the Japanese strengthened their attacking force, so they were able to use elements to pin down the Australians by fire while other elements circled round in the jungle and continued up the trail. In this way the Australians, falling back to what they thought would be fresh defensive lines, frequently found that the Japanese were there before them and they, in their turn, had to take to the jungle and leapfrog round to await the next Japanese attack. Thus the two sides fought and maneuvered their way up the trail, reaching Kokoda on 28 July and eventually digging in at a small village called Isurava on 13 August. Short of ammunition, food and everything else, the remains of Kanga Force prepared to make a stand there and deny the Kokoda Trail to the Japanese.

On that same day a reinforcement convoy arrived at Buna with more Japanese troops, and a further reinforcement appeared a few days later. By mid-August the Japanese commander, General Horii, had 8000 soldiers, 3000 naval construction troops and 450 marines under his command. The entire coastal strip between the sea and the foothills of the Owen Stanleys was securely under Japanese control and almost every Australian, military or civilian, in the area had been hunted down and killed.

While all this had been going on the Australians were preparing their expedition to Buna-Gona. The 7th Division, returned from its campaigns on Libya, was sent to Port Moresby in the first week of August; one brigade went to Milne Bay and was part of the successful force there, the other two brigades were earmarked for the Kokoda Trail. But as the two brigades prepared to set out into what was virtually the unknown, a problem arose. There was a shortage of native carriers, who would be required to porter the army's supplies forward. It was eventually decided to fly the bulk of the supplies to a forward base which would be set up in a small valley near the summit of the range which had been named Myola. Rations and ammunition for the journey up would be carried by the troops themselves, and they would then be resupplied when they reached Myola. And on 16 August the march began.

THE DATE IS 17 AUGUST, 1942 AND THE SMOKE RISES OVER PORT MORESBY AIRFIELD AS THE 78TH JAPANESE AIR RAID IS IN PROGRESS. THE MITCHELL BOMBER IN THE DISTANCE APPEARS TO HAVE ESCAPED DAMAGE.

Each man was carrying 70lb of equipment; this is not considered an excessive amount by practical soldiers. In spite of the long-repeated story of the 60lb loads carried by British soldiers on the Somme in 1916, and their effect on the speed of advance, the fact remains that Australian troops operating in Vietnam in the 1960s carried 100lb and often more, British Marines in the Falklands Campaign of 1982 carried 140lb, and a careful physiological study in the USA in 1983 concluded that a soldier could carry — and fight with — a load of 90lb. But in 1942, soldiers who had been accustomed, in the Middle East, to carrying the minimum load on their backs and having motor transport to do the portering found that 70lb loads, in the conditions of the Owen Stanley mountains, were too great. Moreover the terrain made the load-carrying even more difficult; what might be carried successfully on a smooth flat surface cannot necessarily be carried easily on a slippery trail which climbs and drops, tilts, and is surrounded by jungle greenery which cuts and slashes as you go by.

Before the day was out the men were exhausted. The next day saw men dropping out of the line to lie panting for breath, whey-faced, in the mud; men hacking branches from trees to act as staves which would help support them and their loads; men whose legs shook and trembled with muscular fatigue with every step they painfully took.

A lightly-laden advance party forged ahead up the track to prepare the supply dump at Myola. But when they reached the area they discovered that nothing was awaiting them; MacArthur's promised 40,000 tons of rations and ammunition had not arrived, because a Japanese air raid on Port Moresby had destroyed the transport aircraft scheduled to fly in the supplies. A sortie of bombers was promised, but these carried far less than the transport aircraft and would require correspondingly longer to build up the 30-day supply which was necessary. So that when, eventually, the tired troops reached Myola they would have to remain there, awaiting the build-up, and further advance would have to wait until that had been completed.

The officer in charge of the advance party then went forward to Isurava, to find that the small party who had dug in there on 13 August were still manning their posts; they were ragged, they were starving, they were mostly sick from malaria, but they were still holding their position. It was decided to replace them with the first battalion of troops to arrive at Myola, and this took place on 26 August, just as the Japanese began a concerted attack. Radio calls for reinforcements to be sent up from Port Moresby were greeted with the news that no reinforcements could be spared; Port Moresby was being put into a state of defense because the Japanese had just landed at Milne Bay.

At dawn on 27 August the Japanese attacked the post at Isurava from the flank. On the previous afternoon some Australian reinforcements had arrived, and more were expected during the 27th. The Australians held the Japanese off, and the addition of more troops

JAPANESE WEAPONS IN NEW GUINEA

Type 92 Howitzer
The Type 92 70mm infantry Howitzer seen in the firing position.

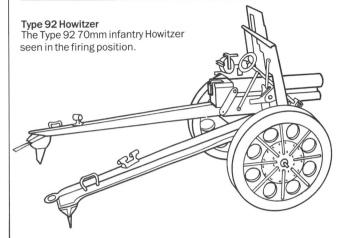

The Japanese Army was a highly mobile force which did not burden itself with heavy equipment unless there was a need for it, and this need was not apparent in New Guinea. Consequently their artillery never exceeded 105mm in caliber, and the most common infantry support weapon was the small 70mm Infantry Howitzer Type 92. Issued two to each battalion, it could be easily moved by two or three men, and it could also be rapidly dismantled into its separate parts for carriage by mules or manpower through narrow jungle trails. Robust, simple to operate and maintain, it could fire either a 3.75kg high explosive shell or a 3.3kg shaped-charge anti-tank shell to a maximum range of 3000m. With a maximum elevation of 75° it could fill the role of battalion heavy mortar as well as that of a direct-firing support gun.

Heavier support came from the 75mm Regimental Gun Type 94 (not shown) which was a mountain gun capable of being carried in 11 loads of 95kg or less. It fired a 5.6kg shell to a range of 10,900m and had a crew of five men.

Japanese Type 95
The Type 95 Light Tank weighed 7.5 tonnes and had a speed of 40km/hr on hard roads.

The Type 95 Light Tank was perhaps the best Japanese design, developed for use in China and Manchuria and fitted with a six-cylinder air-cooled diesel engine so that it operated well in any climate. The inside of the tank was padded with asbestos to try and keep the interior cool in hot climates, and this also gave the crew some protection over rough country. Armed with a 37mm gun in the revolving turret, a 7.7mm machine gun in the hull front and another 7.7mm machine gun in the rear of the turret, it had a three-man crew. The commander had not only to command but also operate the turret main gun and machine gun when necessary. The armor was no more than 12mm thick, with parts of the hull only 8mm thick, but it was unlikely to meet much opposition in China or Manchuria, and even the Australian Army had little in the way of anti-tank guns in the first part of the New Guinea campaign. The Type 95 was, of course, never used on the Kokoda Trail, but it did see employment later around Buna and Salamaua and a small number were sent ashore in the abortive Milne Bay landing.

---

in the latter part of the day turned the tide and finally the Japanese broke off and slid back into the jungle. A further attack was thrown in next day, but, again, more reinforcements had arrived for the Australian line, bringing with them a 3in mortar which proved to be very effective in breaking up the Japanese attacks.

This sudden stiffening of Australian resistance upset the plans of General Horii, who was watching the battle from a nearby ridge. He had allowed two days to march from Kokoda to Myola, and a further five days to move down the southern slopes of the range to Port Moresby, and this interruption at Isurava was disrupting his time-table. He therefore called up reserves and artillery and put in a full-scale attack.

This broke on the Australians on 29 August and in spite of strenuous fighting the position had to be given up and the Australians fell back steadily through the jungle to Alola. This was soon engaged by Japanese artillery and the remaining Australians fell back once

more, this time to Eora Creek village. Reaching there on 31 August, Brigadier Potts, the commander of the small force, received orders to hold a line in that position. Potts knew that he had no hope of holding there, since the Japanese were moving parallel with him on his flanks and were he to stop they would rapidly surround him. Moreover he had no more than 600 men, most of them exhausted; Potts fell back on his base at Myola.

Myola is lost
Once arrived at the base the tired men were able to enjoy a hot meal and the luxury of fresh, clean clothes while they snatched a little rest, but on 4 September a runner arrived with the news that the Japanese had broken through the outpost line and were moving towards Myola at a rapid rate. The defense of the large area of Myola was clearly impossible with the men available, and so, destroying the supply dump, Potts and his men fell back once more to Efogi, the next mountain spur

behind them. It was here that the long-awaited reinforcements from Port Moresby found them; and no sooner had they taken up positions around Efogi than the news came that the Japanese had passed through Myola and were on the track for Efogi and the ustralian position.

During the following night the Australians at Efogi watched the twinkling lanterns of Japanese soldiers moving down the jungle tracks, out of range of their weapons. The movement continued all night, promising a strong body of Japanese to mount an attack, and Potts managed to call Port Moresby and bring down an air strike just after dawn. The strike was duly performed, and looked most impressive, but it appears that most of the Japanese melted into the jungle and few casualties were actually incurred. No further action took part that day, because Horii was busy receiving reinforcements and making his dispositions for the attack, which finally broke on the morning of 8 September. Horii now had about 5000 troops and two

mountain howitzers, and his attack began with a storm of small arms, mortar and howitzer fire against the Australian positions. Flanking movements through the jungle soon cut the Australian position into segments and Potts and his headquarters were cut off from the rest of the force. Under constant attack the Australians melted into the jungle, fell back, and reformed at nightfall in Menari, where they were re-joined by Potts who had managed to break out under cover of darkness.

On the following day patrols moved forward once more, but they were soon in contact with Japanese probing forward and Menari soon came under mortar and howitzer fire. The retreat continued to the next fall-back line, that of Ioribaiwa Ridge, where the positions were so close to Port Moresby that the sound of aircraft on the airstrip could be heard at night. There the Australians finally managed to stabilize their line and they were holding when, on 13 September, they were relieved by fresh troops of 25th Brigade.

The new commander, Brigadier Eather, immediately

ANTAGONISTS IN NEW GUINEA

General Sir Thomas Blamey (1884–1951)

Blamey served as Chief of Staff to Monash during the First World War, retiring after the war to become Commissioner of Police for Victoria state in Australia. In February 1940 he was recalled to take command of the Australian Independent Force in the Middle East. Arriving in Greece in 1941 he was just in time to supervise the withdrawal of ANZAC forces from Greece and Crete, after which he became Deputy Commander-in-Chief Middle East.

He returned to Australia in 1942 to become Commander-in-Chief of Allied Land Forces under General MacArthur. He then took personal command of Australian forces in New Guinea, recaptured Buna, and remained in command of Australian troops in that country. He also retained the post of CinC

ALF SWPAC until the end of the war. A good fighting soldier and a sound administrator, he was popular with his troops but less popular with MacArthur since he did not always agree with the latter's strategic concepts.

Lieut-General Robert L Eichelberger (1886–1961)

Eichelberger was the Commandant of the US Military Academy West Point on the outbreak of war and was rapidly posted to command the 1st US Corps in the Pacific. He fought a successful campaign in New Guinea, defeating the Japanese at Buna in 1943. In September 1944 he was given command of the 8th Army and led it in the re-capture of the Philippine Islands.

A highly competent soldier, it is generally conceded that Eichelberger was capable of greater

GENERALS BLAMEY (LEFT) AND EICHELBERGER INSPECTING A JAPANESE DEFENSIVE BUNKER IN NEW GUINEA.

things but never had a command commensurate with his abilities.

Lieut-General Tomitaro Horii (1890–1942)

Horii was a graduate of the Japanese Military Academy, having been commissioned in 1911. After service in China and Manchuria, in

August 1940 he was appointed Colonel, commanding the 55th Infantry Corps. Shortly after this he was given command of the South Sea Detachment (which had 55th Corps as its foundation) and led this force in the attack of Guam. In January 1942 he was ordered to take Rabaul, and in August 1942 was given the task of attacking Port Moresby by way of Buna and Gona. After his death, he was posthumously promoted to Lieut-General.

began planning to advance, intending to regain control of the trail at least as far as Kokoda. Leaving the original defenders in place, now backed by a fresh battalion, Eather moved his other two battalions around the blocking position, one on the right to make an advance up the trail and one on the left to take Nauro. This was immediately stopped by the Japanese who retaliated with fierce mortar and gunfire, concentrating their fire against the defensive line held by the original troops who had been chased down the trail. By this time these men were worn out and in no condition to withstand very much more, and when the Japanese counter-attacked, Eather requested permission from Port Moresby to fall back to the final ridge before the town, Imita Ridge, which offered him a better position and a better start line for subsequent operations. He was given permission, but was plainly told that there would be no further move back; if necessary he and his troops would die on Imita Ridge. By midday on 17 September a position on Imita Ridge was being set up.

While this retirement had been in progress, other activity had been going on. On 5 September, when the news of the Australians' loss of Myola was given to MacArthur, he had immediately sent his Chief of Staff, General Sutherland, across to Port Moresby to bring back an eyewitness account of what was going on. He returned with news of the Australian countermoves, which appeared to mollify MacArthur who then began planning what he called a 'wide turning movement' over the Owen Stanleys to the east of the Kokoda Trail so as to outflank the Japanese. The 32nd and 41st US Infantry Divisions had arrived in Australia in May and were now fully trained and awaiting assignment, and it was decided to take a regiment from one of these divisions to carry out MacArthur's plan.

General Eichelberger, commanding I Corps, was told to select the regiment; he chose the 126th from 32nd Division, since they seemed no better and no worse than the others, and on September 15 the leading elements were air-lifted into Port Moresby. Ready for the fray, they were somewhat disappointed to find that their first task was to be road-building.

MacArthur intervenes

MacArthur's planners had organized the plan of campaign straight off the map. A coastal road ran part of the way from Port Moresby to a village called Kapa Kapa, from where a road, and then a track ran about 16 miles to the top of the mountains. From there it dropped down and then split into two tracks, both of which offered routes for getting behind the Japanese. The men of the 126th Regiment would have to begin by extending the road all the way to Kapa Kapa but after that they would merely have to march over the trail. Merely! Neither the planners nor the soldiers knew what they were about to experience.

It was while these soldiers were performing their road-building task that the news arrived of the Australian fall back to the Imita Ridge. MacArthur

GENERAL EICHELBERGER ACTING AS CHAUFFEUR TO GENERAL MACARTHUR DURING THE LATTER'S VISIT TO NEW GUINEA IN OCTOBER 1942. HE WENT AS FAR AS THE START OF THE KOKODA TRAIL AND THEN RETURNED TO AUSTRALIA.

immediately rang John Curtin, the Australian Prime Minister, complaining that although the Australians out-numbered the Japanese (nobody knew where he got that tit-bit of information from) they were still retreating and what did Curtin propose to do about his inefficient troops? Since the Australians appeared to be in difficulties, MacArthur said, he would send 40,000 US troops into New Guinea to stem the Japanese attack, and would Curtin kindly send General Blamey to New Guinea to take charge of the situation there?

The remainder of the 126th Regiment was already moving towards New Guinea, and now the 128th Regiment was to move out from its camp near Brisbane as well. Military and civil aircraft, rounded up from all over Australia were standing by at Townsville to fly them all across to Port Moresby in the biggest airlift of troops so far in the war. By September 23 the two regiments were in New Guinea, and on the same day General Blamey arrived.

General Lowell, commanding the Australian troops, felt that Blamey's arrival indicated a lack of confidence in his ability. For his part he had no faith in MacArthur's flanking move across the mountains. But Blamey tended to MacArthur's views, and, in arranging for Australian troops to be flown across the mountains to prepare an airstrip, he went behind Lowell's back, which brought about a flaming row and Lowell's return to Australia, replaced by General Herring.

Since 17 September the Australians on Imita Ridge had been awaiting a Japanese attack, but nothing had happened. Even after bombarding the Japanese positions with artillery, there had been no reaction. On the 27th, a probing attack was launched against the Japanese positions on Ioribaiwa, which soon discovered that the positions were deserted; the Japanese had silently pulled out, nobody knew when.

(LEFT) A COMPANY OF TIRED AUSTRALIAN TROOPS ABOUT TO LEAVE THE IMITA RIDGE POSITION FOR A SHORT REST, SEPTEMBER 1942. NOTICE THAT EACH MAN CARRIES A STICK AS WELL AS A RIFLE, FOR HELPING HIM THROUGH THE MUD. (ABOVE) AUSTRALIAN INFANTRY PLOUGH THROUGH MUD ON THE KOKODA TRAIL. THE COMBINATION OF MUD AND SLOPE WAS UNIQUELY EXHAUSTING TO MARCH IN, LET ALONE FIGHT IN, AND CAUSED MORE CASUALTIES THAN DID THE JAPANESE.

In fact the Japanese had withdrawn on orders from Tokyo. They had halted at Ioribaiwa as planned, to rest and reorganize ready for a two-pronged attack on Port Moresby. They were to form the land prong while the other half was to come in by sea once the Milne Bay position had been dealt with. But since the Milne Bay operation had failed, and since, too, there was bad news from Guadalcanal, where the Americans had taken the island, and since there was a shortage of rations and little or nothing to be garnered from the surrounding countryside, things began to take on a different air in the Japanese camp. Finally, on 24 September, came a radio message from Rabaul, ordering General Horii and his force to withdraw back up the Kokoda Trail, pick a good defensive position near the crest of the mountains, and take up his stand there. Barely had Horii assimilated this than a second order came, cancelling the first and ordering him to withdraw from the mountains completely and concentrate his force at Buna. And this was followed by another, this time from Imperial HQ in Tokyo, confirming his second order.

It appears that Imperial HQ had received intelligence of MacArthur's intention to attack Buna, but without details of his plan. They assumed it would be an amphibious landing, and after seeing what the US Marines had done on Guadalcanal, they wanted all the troops they could muster around Buna to repel the attack. In any event, and in spite of misgivings, the Japanese withdrawal began on the morning of 25 September and the troops melted away into the jungle and began their climb back up to the summit. But when they reached Myola, Horii detached a battalion of infantry with supporting engineers and artillery, and detailed it off as a rearguard. This, the 'Stanley Shitai', was to take up its positions around a ravine beyond Myola, prepare an ambush position, and cause as much delay as possible to the Australians, so as to allow the bulk of Horii's force to get over the ridge and well on their way down the other side.

The Australians, having debated the matter, finally moved out from Ioribaiwa on 1 October and began slogging their way back up the trail. As they progressed, so they had to detach burial parties to deal with the bodies of Australians which they found along the track, relics of their earlier passage in the opposite direction. They also found plenty to show that the Japanese were in a worse state than themselves; emaciated Japanese bodies were found with no wounds or signs of injury, village gardens were cleaned of every scrap of vegetation, and there were even indications that men had been trying to eat twigs and grass.

By 7 October the first Australian patrols were entering Myola, to find it abandoned. And then came

ORDER OF BATTLE

ALLIED	JAPANESE
7th Australian Div:	17th Army (Commander: Hyakutaki)
7th Inf Bde (Mil) 18th Inf Bde (AIF) 21st Inf Bde 25th Inf Bde 2/14th AIF Bn 2/16th AIF Bn Papuan Inf Bn	41st Inf Rgt 144th Inf Rgt Bn Mountain Arty Engr Bn Engr Bn
32nd US Inf Div	Japanese cas (estimated; 13 000 KIA)
Australian cas: 2165 KIA; 4335 M/WIA (64% of cas occurred at Milne Bay)	
US cas: 930 KIA; 1070 M/WIA	

natives from the jungle to say that the Japanese had fallen back all the way to Kokoda. Things were looking good.

On the previous day the first US troops had begun their move up the road from Kapa Kapa; an advance squad which had gone ahead had reported that the track was 'practicable for marching', so the GIs were expecting a slightly strenuous hike through the forest. In fact it turned out to be worse than the Kokoda Trail. The first troops to move out were the support companies of 2 Bn 126 Infantry under the command of Capt Menendorp, from which they became known as 'Menendorp Force'. At the end of their third day of marching they reached the foothills of the Owen Stanleys, and already they were beginning to feel the strain. Haversacks were being lightened by throwing out unessential — and some essential — items, and the trail was already littered with socks, underwear and bars of soap. At every stream the men rushed forward to drink, without thought of possible diseases, while stragglers lined the track and were rounded up and brought in by the battalion medical officer bringing up the rear. There was no problem in persuading the stragglers to plod on into camp — they were scared that if they stayed out on the trail the Japanese would get them. And on the fourth day of marching their native carriers deserted them, leaving the soldiers to carry their own heavy equipment.

Arriving at Laruni, where an air-drop area was planned, Menendorp detached a squad to prepare the drop zone and pushed ahead with the rest of his men, heading for the summit of the divide, a lonely area of stifling days and cold nights, where festoons of moss shrouded the trees, where daylight rarely penetrated and no birds sang. The track was so narrow that single file was the rule, and so steep in places that the men had to crawl and claw their way on hands and knees. It was not until 20 October that they reached their objective, Jaure, on the far side of the mountains and where the track split into two. It had taken them 14 days to march approximately 30 miles.

Pursuing the Japanese

The remainder of the two battalions, some 900 strong, had begun following Menendorp Force on 14 October; on the second day of their march tropical rains began and continued for five days and nights. This was bad; but the first day of marching had seen many men discard their raincoats, shelter halves and blankets, so that when the rain came they had no protection during the day and nothing to shelter or comfort them at night. The rains turned the track into a glissade of mud into which, after the churning of marching feet, men were sinking up to their knees. Instead of their standard 'C' rations, they were supplied with Australian army rations consisting of rice, corned beef and tea; because of the downpour they were unable to light fires for cooking and so threw away their rations or ate them cold. Many suffered from dysentery. Ragged, filthy,

hungry, diseased, they managed to crawl into Jaure on 28 October, and although they advanced down the trail and were resupplied with clothing, rations and even helmets by air, it was of little avail; the men were in no shape to advance or fight — the terrible ordeal of the Trail had virtually destroyed two battalions.

What made it worse was the realization that the entire exercise had been unnecessary; when they finally reached the flatlands beyond the mountains they found stretches of grass in which airfields could be constructed with the minimum of effort, and the remainder of 126 Regiment, together with the whole of 132 Regiment, were flown in to an improvized strip at Pagnani, about 30 miles south of Buna.

Meanwhile MacArthur, chafing at the bit as usual, decided that the Australians were not doing enough to get across the mountains, and had, on 21 October, fired a peremptory signal off to Blamey that the Australian progress was 'Not, Repeat Not, satisfactory.'

The reason for their slowness was that they had just come up against Horii's surprise in Eora Creek, the ravine where the Stanley Shitai were carefully placed in excellent positions to entrap them. The advancing Australians had met the first signs of Japanese defense as they entered the ravine on 20 October but the leading companies of 16 Brigade were fresh and in good condition, and they smartly brushed the outposts from their path. The next day, however, as they attempted to move through the ravine to the high ground beyond, they were struck by heavy machine gun fire from above them and were driven to dig in.

Horii's men had virtually constructed a fortress in the jungle from logs and earth. A central redoubt some

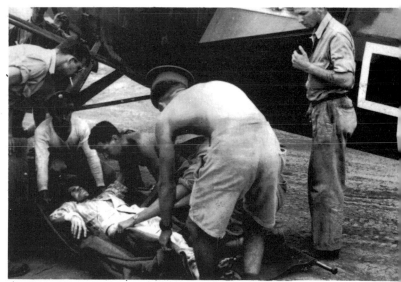

AUSTRALIAN SOLDIERS AND AMERICAN AIRMEN WORKED TOGETHER TO FLY WOUNDED OUT OF NEW GUINEA AND INTO HOSPITALS IN AUSTRALIA. HERE A WOUNDED SOLDIER IS LIFTED FROM THE AIRCRAFT LITTER TO A STRETCHER FOR THE AMBULANCE RIDE TO HOSPITAL.

(LEFT) THERE WERE NO BRIDGES ON THE TRAIL; EVERY RIVER AND STREAM HAD TO BE CROSSED BY FORDING OR BY ROPE BRIDGES OF THE SORT SHOWN HERE OVER THE KUMUSI RIVER. ONCE THE INITIAL ADVANCE WAS ACROSS, ENGINEERS WOULD THEN BUILD SOMEWHAT MORE SUBSTANTIAL CROSSINGS, THOUGH NONE SUPPORTED MORE THAN A MAN AND A MULE. (ABOVE) MANHANDLING A 25-POUNDER FIELD GUN INTO A FIRING POSITION ALONGSIDE THE KOKODA TRAIL. THE 25-PR GUN WEIGHED 1800KG AND HAD TO BE TAKEN ALMOST EVERY INCH OF THE WAY FROM MORESBY TO BUNA BY MANPOWER, USING ROPES AND PULLEYS, AS DID THE AMMUNITION SUPPLY.

300 yards broad was the focus, and from this radiated trenches to machine gun posts, direct-fire artillery and mortar positions. Most of the posts had thick overhead cover and they were all sited so as to cover each other with fire. They were in a superior position; all they had to do was shoot downhill and the Australians were at their mercy, trapped into two-man foxholes which they deepened as fast as they could. Once in these, they could not move by day; they could not light fires and were reduced to eating iron rations, and they had no water other than the rainwater they could collect. The Australians could do very little except attempt to scrabble up the muddy slopes towards the Japanese. MacArthur became upset once more and General Allen, commanding at Myola, was fired, and replaced by a new face, General Vasey.

In the event he was able to do little, because on 28 October, as Vasey was on his way to take command, the Japanese decided that it was time to pull back, and they set about making preparations for their departure by grenading and machine-gunning every inch of the forest below them. This was enough to anchor the Australians firmly into their defenses, and during the night which followed the Stanley Shitai disengaged and slipped away. The Australians, realizing what might be happening, were quick to take up the pursuit and were right behind Horii's men, so close that on reaching Alola on 30 October they found warm cooking pots.

At Alola the pursuing force split into two; 25th Brigade went on toward Kokoda, while 16th Brigade were sent east to capture Oivi. The troops were in good heart, having managed to get their first hot meal for almost a week, the weather had cleared up, there was plenty of fruit for the taking along the trail and, most welcome of all, they had left the wretched mountains behind and were marching on flat grassland. On 2 November, Eather's 25th Brigade entered Kokoda to find that the Japanese were two days ahead of them. On the following days work began on an airstrip and air dropping of supplies began. General Vasey arrived to hoist the Australian flag, but the edge was taken from his day when a message arrived telling him that two destroyers and two transports had been seen off Buna. He immediately sent a runner to 16th Brigade ordering them to move fast and take Oivi.

16th Brigade had already run into Japanese rearguards, but they pressed them closely, and on 5 November mounted a full-scale two-battalion attack on Oivi while the third battalion was out to a flank, probing towards a village called Gorari. But the attack stalled in the face of a very fierce defense; as well it might be. For unknown to the Australians Horii's main force was no more than ten miles away, delayed by the crossing of the Kumuri River, and the rearguard at Oivi was determined that the Australians were not going to interfere.

On hearing of the failed attack, General Vasey immediately sent 25th Brigade on a lateral march to take Gorari and the Japanese position from the rear. Horii had foreseen this as a possible move and he had put a battalion into Gorari; they had picked sound defensive positions and they stopped 25th Brigade in its tracks and even counter-attacked. But one battalion, even in a defensive position, is poor odds against a brigade and by the evening of 10 November the Australians were in possession of Gorari and the rearguard were running back to report to Horii. Moreover the fall of Gorari threatened the rear of the Oivi position, and this force now withdrew. Since the road through Gorari was blocked, the Japanese commander, Colonel Yazawa, was forced to move through the jungle using a track leading to the Kumusi River. From here he hoped to march along the bank of the river to gain the coast some 12 miles north of Gona.

Added to Yazawa's problems was the fact that he had his commanding general in his care, since Horii happened to be inspecting the positions at Oivi when the withdrawal became necessary. Horii was impatient to get to Gona; and when the marching column reached the river, instead of following its bank, a winding trail through marshes, he elected to cross the river and make for a track on the far side which would lead them direct to Gona. A log raft was constructed and General Horii and four of his staff set off across the river. The current was far swifter than they had anticipated, the raft overturned, and in spite of several soldiers jumping into the water to save them, Horii and his aide Colonel Tanaka were swept away; they were never seen again.

The remains of Horii's force, starved, ragged, some mad, most suffering from malaria and other diseases, eventually arrived at the coast where they were later taken off by transports which brought Japanese reinforcements. On 17 November one thousand fresh troops disembarked and were sent to reinforce Buna, while more arrived to flesh out the defenses of Gona and Sanananda. Along the 11-mile front from Gona to beyond Buna the Japanese had now constructed a powerful defensive line behind which they awaited the combined American and Australian assault. But that is another story; so far as the Allied troops were concerned they were finished with the horrors of the Kokoda Trail.

The lessons

The lessons which came out of the US and Australian experiences on the Kokoda Trail were to be of considerable value later in the war when jungle operations got into their stride. Probably the most vital lesson, at least for the planners, was that it was unwise to plan operations off a map. In the first place the map was likely to be unreliable, and in the second place no map could give the faintest impression of what the terrain was actually like on the ground. Map plans had to be amended in the light of reconnaissance reports and reports by people who had some experience of the terrain in question. This was a difficult lesson for many planning staffs to hoist on board, and even a year later it was not uncommon to find men with practical knowledge of a particular area being ignored when their observations did not agree with the preconceived notions of the planners.

New Guinea taught a great deal about Japanese tactics and operational methods. It also taught the Allies a great deal about their own tactics, and about the particular equipment requirements which the jungle environment imposed. Clothing, rations, medical supplies and treatment, all had special demands when the jungle

AUSTRALIAN INFANTRY FIRING THEIR 3IN MORTAR NEAR BUNA. THIS COMPANY SUPPORT WEAPON FIRED A 4.4KG BOMB TO 2550M RANGE AND ITS HIGH TRAJECTORY MADE IT PARTICULARLY VALUABLE IN JUNGLE OPERATIONS.

BY THE TIME THE AUSTRALIANS REACHED BUNA, ON THE NORTH COAST, THEY WERE BEING SUPPORTED BY TANKS, WHICH COULD OPERATE ON THE COASTAL PLAIN. THIS M3 LIGHT TANK IS BOMBARDING JAPANESE PILLBOXES WHILE THE INFANTRYMEN WAIT TO PICK OFF ANY ESCAPEES.

was in view, and in course of time all these were met. There was also an obvious need to train men in living and surviving in the jungle, training them to overcome their natural fear and revulsion at the filthy conditions, the insects, the malaises which were endemic to the surroundings. To do so with absolute success would demand far more time than the Allies were able to afford, but at least some measure of training was enough to give troops some pointers to jungle life and help them come to terms with their surroundings. The US troops in New Guinea were thrown straight from camp life in Australia into the worst jungle in the world, and it was hardly surprising that they soon fell victims to the terrible conditions.

The initial advance of the Australians and their aborted air-supply at Myola pointed up the fact that operations in jungle must be well supported by a cast-iron supply system if the troops are not to carry everything on their backs. Whilst the Myola drop was well planned, the simple matter of a single air raid on Port Moresby completely wrecked the plan and had a knock-on effect on the remainder of the operation. The later operations of Wingate's Chindit force in Burma, wholly supplied by air, showed that such a system was feasible but it also showed that even supplying a small force of men on the ground demanded a massive strength in transport aircraft and a complicated network of organization to make sure that the supplies arrived in spite of the occasional spanner being thrown

into the works by the Japanese.

So far as tactics went, the basic infantry maneuvers had to be rethought in a jungle context; even a simple fire and movement maneuver of a rifle platoon became a major problem when visibility was measured in feet and once a section moved off a trail it was virtually lost to its companions. The infiltration tactics of the Japanese un-nerved troops who would probably have been quite steady under a similar attack in European meadowland, and it was some time before Allied troops could be made to understand, as General Slim said, that if the enemy are behind you, you are automatically behind him and should proceed accordingly.

But in the long run, the important thing which came out of the Kokoda Trail and Milne Bay was that the Japanese were not supermen; that they could be defeated by determined troops, and that all that was needed was to familiarize Allied troops with the peculiar conditions. Except for some stretches of Burma, it is doubtful if the Allies ever again came up against conditions as tough as those on the Kokoda Trail, and the message was that if the Japanese could be beaten there, they could be beaten anywhere.

CHAPTER SIX

THE BATTLE FOR TARAWA

AMPHIBIOUS ASSAULT
NOVEMBER 1943

Overleaf

The grim scene on Red Beach in the first hour of landing with the first
wave pinned down behind the log barricade, from which individuals and handfuls of Marines eventually
managed to break out to complete their task.
(*Tarawa* by Colonel C H Waterhouse, USMCR. Courtesy US Marine Corps Museum's Art Collection)

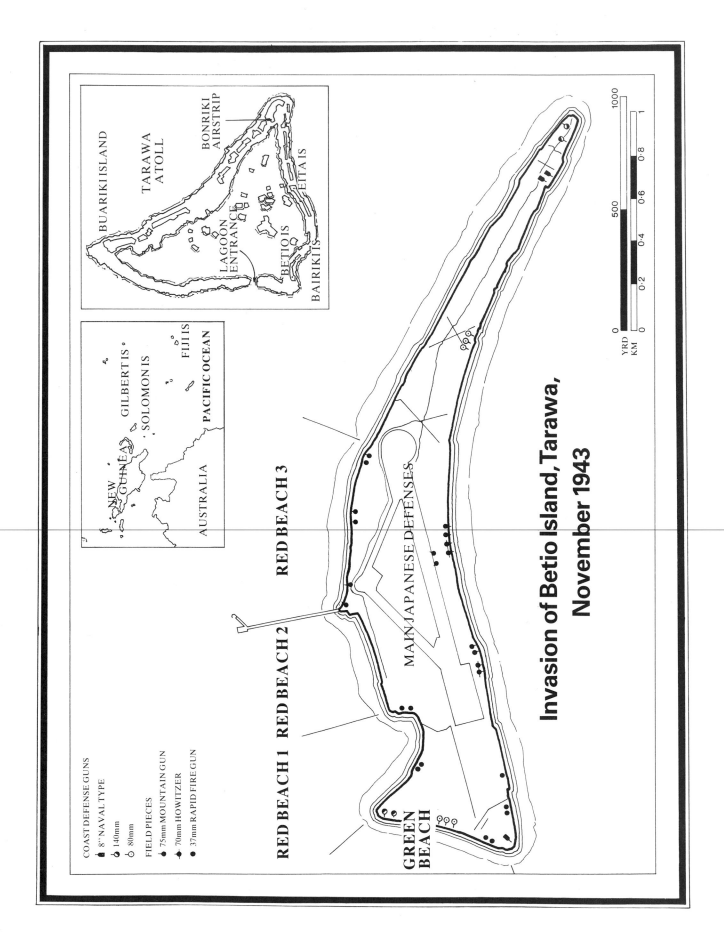

Invasion of Betio Island, Tarawa, November 1943

COAST DEFENSE GUNS

◣ 8" NAVAL TYPE
◔ 140mm
◒ 80mm

FIELD PIECES

◆ 75mm MOUNTAIN GUN
◆ 70mm HOWITZER
● 37mm RAPID FIRE GUN

RED BEACH 1   RED BEACH 2   RED BEACH 3

GREEN BEACH

MAIN JAPANESE DEFENSES

BUARIKI ISLAND

TARAWA ATOLL

BONRIKI AIRSTRIP

EITA IS

LAGOON ENTRANCE

BETIO IS

BAIRIKI IS

NEW GUINEA

GILBERT IS

SOLOMON IS

FIJI IS

PACIFIC OCEAN

AUSTRALIA

By the latter end of 1943 the US forces in the Pacific Theater had acquired some stock of knowledge of how to perform an amphibious landing, but there was a world of difference between an amphibious landing — an uncomfortable disembarkation across a beach — and an amphibious assault — doing the same thing in the face of an enemy determined to prevent it. Tarawa was to be the first major amphibious assault; it proved to be a bloody affray and one which, for the first time, brought home to American citizens just what was the price of all-out warfare against a tenacious enemy on his own ground. In retrospect, it was seen that the price, stiff as it was, was cheap for the strategic gain and for the lessons which the operation taught, lessons which led to improvements in every facet of amphibious warfare, lessons which were still valid almost ten years later when MacArthur assaulted Inchon with the aid of men who had learned their trade on the beach at Tarawa.

The background

Tarawa is an atoll in the Gilbert Archipelago, and its principal island is called Betio. The Gilberts, sixteen atolls, straddle the Equator, and their closest neighbors are the Marshall Islands, a group of 36 atolls some 400 miles or so to the northwest. The Marshalls were a major Japanese stronghold which, sooner or later, were going to have to be attacked. Seizure of the Gilberts was a necessary preliminary step, since only this would provide airfields for land-based reconnaissance aircraft which could then obtain the information on Japanese positions which was vital to a successful attack. Moreover such airfields would provide a base for aircraft which could support such an attack, a necessary augmentation to carrier-borne aircraft. After the capture of the Gilberts and Marshalls, the assault would then swing southwest to take the principal Japanese base at Truk; this course of action had been on the US Naval plans since the early 1920s, designed in peace against the possible requirements of war, but the early Japanese successes had caused the plans to be shelved until the middle of 1943.

The Casablanca Conference, early in 1943, allowed Admiral King, American C-in-C in the Pacific, to put forward his views on keeping the pot boiling in his parish. He wanted about thirty percent of the Allied war effort in order to keep pressure on the Japanese and prevent them consolidating their gains. His principal aims were the re-opening of the Burma Road, the recapture of the Aleutians, the seizure of Rabaul and the opening up of the Central Pacific with the ultimate aim of recapturing the Philippines.

King advocated the Central Pacific route, via the Gilberts and Marshalls; MacArthur wanted the effort to come in the South-West Pacific, his theater of operations, stepping off from New Guinea. It would be pointless to rehearse all the arguments which flew between King, MacArthur, Nimitz and the Joint Planners in Washington through the summer of 1943,

but eventually Nimitz was given the task of assaulting the Gilberts with the Second Marine Division, who were at that time resting and training in New Zealand, and the Army's 27th Infantry Division from Hawaii. He was also given three marine defense battalions and three army engineer and construction battalions; his naval force was to comprise five new battleships, seven escort carriers, eight heavy and four light cruisers, 66 destroyers, 27 attack transport and cargo ships, and nine merchant ships for additional cargo and transport work. All this naval force was contingent upon the hope that the anti-submarine campaign in the Atlantic proceeded smoothly and there was no unexpected rash of sinkings which would demand some of this shipping back.

The plan

In order to conduct the Gilberts campaign with unity of control, Nimitz created a new command, the Central Pacific Force, commanded by Vice-Admiral Raymond A Spruance. Spruance, from the very beginning, had one over-riding factor in front of his eyes; the ability of the Japanese to respond violently by sea and air from their nearby bases in the Marshalls. Therefore the whole attack had to proceed with the utmost speed once it was launched, so that the objectives could be taken and placed in a state of defense before the anticipated counter-stroke developed. In the event this counter-stroke never happened; unknown to the planners, the Japanese had decided that their principal danger was coming from the South-West and they had withdrawn much of their mobile force from the Marshalls and repositioned it at Truk. An assault on Bougainville by MacArthur on 1 November, 1943 strengthened the Japanese belief that this was from where the main American thrust would start, and thus much of the Japanese naval and air support which might have proved critical at Tarawa was absent, watching Bougainville and Rabaul. When Tarawa erupted, in the words of one American writer, the Japanese naval commander at Truk "was turning his head faster than a man watching a tennis match."

One minor difficulty for historians of this campaign is that the US Marine commander was Major General Holland M Smith, USMC, while the 27th Army Division's commander was Major General Ralph C Smith, USA, and the Marine Divisional commander was Major General Julian C Smith, USMC. The top Marine General was a sharp-tongued martinet, familiarly known to his troops as 'Howling Mad Smith'; the Army general was something of a lightweight who was later relieved of his command, though much of this may have been a personality clash with HM Smith; while the junior Marine General was an unassuming but highly competent professional.

The division of forces, since the Tarawa operation was to take place as a concerted assault on three separate islands, was a problem. HM Smith had little confidence in RC Smith and his 27th Division, and therefore allocated them to the capture of Makin Island, the Japanese garrison of which was thought to number no more than 250 men. On studying his available shipping, HM Smith discovered he could not lift the entire division, and so decided that the assault would be made by the 165th Regimental Combat Team, the best-trained divisional unit.

He then removed the 6th Marine Regiment from 2nd Marine Division to be the Corps Reserve, leaving him with only two reinforced rifle regiments, the 2nd and 8th Marine Regiments, with which to assault Betio, the garrison of which was conservatively estimated to be some 2500 strong. JC Smith was also given the task of assaulting Apamama, a lightly-held atoll some 80 miles SSE of Tarawa, for which he was given three platoons of the 5th Amphibious Corps Reconnaissance Company, the fourth platoon being attached to the Army troops taking Makin.

In order to speed up the assault and not to give away their intentions to the Japanese, the American commanders decided to reduce the amount of preliminary bombardment. The Marine force was, after all, being launched straight into the center of a Japanese enclave, and ideally the attack would have gone forward by picking off the lightly held atolls on the perimeter and gradually subjecting Tarawa to greater and greater aerial and naval bombardment. But doing it this way would have signalled the forthcoming moves and given the Japanese ample time to move on their counterattack. So the preliminary bombardment was reduced to about three hours of naval gunfire and air attacks on the morning before the landing.

JC Smith therefore had little or no freedom of action. His forces were just about twice the expected strength of the defenders — and most thinking of that (or any other) time reckoned that a three-to-one superiority was mandatory. Conventional thinking also

recommended diversionary and supplementary attacks to keep the defenders guessing and their strength spread out, but had JC Smith done any of these things his main assault force would have been even more reduced. Furthermore the Navy were apprehensive about possible Japanese reaction and were unwilling to hang about while complex plans were put into effect; they wanted it quick and simple so that they could put the troops ashore and then get out to sea so that they could feel safe with some sea-room around them.

The Second Marine Regiment, commanded by Col David M Shoup, was to make the assault on Betio Island, the principal Japanese base in the Tarawa Atoll. A battalion of the 8th Marines was attached, giving Shoup four reinforced rifle battalions. The plan was to land three battalions abreast, keeping one in regimental reserve. Reinforcing the rifle battalions would be a company of medium tanks, the Special Weapons Group of the 2nd Marine Defense Battalion, units of combat engineers, eight shore-based fire control and air liaison parties, medical and service units, and a battalion of 75mm pack howitzers.

The divisional reserve consisted of the 8th Marine Regiment, less one battalion and its attached components, plus a support group with a battalion of artillery and miscellaneous personnel. Not under JC Smith's control, but ordered close to Tarawa was the 6th Marine Regimental Combat Team with three reinforced infantry battalions.

Preparations

Tarawa Atoll is in the north center of the Gilberts group; it is shaped like a triangle, the hypotenuse forming the north-east side and consisting of a string of long and thin islets; the southern leg is similar, while the western side is largely a reef sheltering the lagoon. There is only one navigable entrance to the lagoon, close to the island of Betio which is at the southwestern corner. Betio, like all the other islands, is surrounded by a coral reef. Before the war it had been the British administrative headquarters for the area and was thus provided with a jetty and a wharf which was capable of taking small boats at high tide.

The Japanese had adopted Betio as their principal base; in September 1942 they had built an airfield capable of operating medium bombers and surrounded it with formidable ground defenses. The island was flat, nowhere rising more than ten feet above sea level, covered with palm trees and scrub undergrowth. There was absolutely no cover, no natural features which would admit of enfilade fire or maneuver; the assault would have to hit the beach fighting, its only hope of cover being to capture man-made defenses and turn them to its own advantage.

Although photographic reconnaissance had managed to pinpoint about 90 percent of the Japanese defensive positions, there was little or no hydrographic information available; the only charts were a century old, and such matters as currents and tides were a

ONE OF THE 203MM COAST DEFENSE GUNS ON BETIO ISLAND, PHOTOGRAPHED SHORTLY AFTER THE ISLAND HAD BEEN SECURED. THESE WEAPONS, WITH A RANGE OF ALMOST 20KM, WERE A MAJOR THREAT TO THE AMERICAN INVASION FLEET.

REAR-ADMIRAL KEIJI SHIBASAKI, COMMANDER OF THE
TARAWA GARRISON. LITTLE IS KNOWN OF SHIBASAKI'S CAREER,
WHICH ENDED MYSTERIOUSLY AFTER A FINAL STIRRING MESSAGE
TO HIS TROOPS; IT IS ASSUMED THAT HE WENT OUT TO SEEK DEATH
AT THE HEAD OF HIS COMMAND, BUT HIS BODY WAS NEVER
IDENTIFIED.

matter of conjecture. As a result, 2nd Marine Division
decided to use amphibious tractors tactically. This was
an innovation. Amtracs had previously been used only
in logistic roles, taking supplies onto beaches after the
beach had been secured and they were neither armed
nor armored. 2nd Division acquired 75 of these
machines and proceeded to armor them with boilerplate
and mount machine guns on them, and to train their
drivers in maneuvering over coral reefs while loaded
with men and equipment. A further 50 Amtracs, an
improved model with armament and partial armor,
were located in San Diego and these were hurriedly
shipped out to join up with the assault on the day before
it took place, giving the drivers no time for rehearsals or
training.

But even 125 tractors were not enough. JC Smith's
plan called for the use of 100 tractors to carry the first
three assault waves, with 25 tractors in reserve. But
since only the Amtrac could cross the reefs surrounding
Betio, it meant that after the first three waves got ashore
the assault would grind to a halt unless the tides allowed
the remaining two waves to be boated ashore in landing
craft. These demanded at least four feet of water over
the reef.

The tides were a considerable problem; as noted
above, there was little firm information. Moreover, for
a variety of logistical and strategic reasons, the assault
had to go in during the neap-tide period. Critics have
said it might have been better to wait seven days for the

spring tide period, but the high tides would then have
come during the hours of darkness, which was unac-
ceptable. Only by delaying for well over a month would
the high tide have come at a practical time of day, and
this amount of waiting was out of the question.

With the best available information collected and
studied, the planners decided that the optimum time for
the assault would be 0830hrs on 20 November 1943, and
planning was therefore based upon this key time. The
concensus of opinion from those acquainted with the
area was that at that moment there would be five feet of
water over the critical reef, a foot more than the draft of
the Amtracs.

The next decision to be taken was where to land, and
there appeared to be little choice. Wherever the landing
took place the result was going to be bloody, since the
Japanese had some 200 pieces of artillery on Betio,
ranging from 20mm cannon to 8in guns, and most of
these were able to engage targets on the beaches. The
first line of defense for Betio had been provided by
nature; it was the reef, which ran between 800 and 1200
yards out to sea from the beaches and prevented all but
the most shallow-draught vessels approaching. At the
inshore edge of the beach, all around the island, a
barricade of coconut palm logs, three to five feet high
and reinforced with wire, had been built, behind which
a myriad of rifle pits and machine gun emplacements
were excavated. Backing these were more permanent
machine gun posts, of reinforced concrete, log and
coral construction, covered in sand, difficult to see and
extremely difficult to silence. Backing these were some
25 pillboxes and concrete emplacements in which were
installed 37mm anti-tank guns and 75mm field guns,
covering most of the shore.

The Japanese, not unnaturally, expected any attack
to come from the open sea to the east: at each corner
of the island, and dotted around the shore, were fourteen coast defense guns ranging from 80mm to 203mm
in caliber. These covered the beaches and the sea
approaches, and were backed by concrete bombproof
shelters for their crews and magazines for their
ammunition. In order to present these guns with the
optimum target opportunities, concrete obstacles were
planted in the sea so as to shepherd any invasion force
into the fields of fire of these heavy guns. It was
undoubtedly the intention of the Japanese commander
to stop, contain and destroy any invasion on the beach.

(It might be noted here that the commonly-held
belief that the heavy guns on Tarawa came from the
captured British defenses of Singapore is incorrect;
none of the Singapore guns were captured in a workable
condition, and their repair was considered uneconomic
by the Japanese.)

The commander of the Japanese forces was Rear-
Admiral Keiji Shibasaki, who had at his disposal 1122
sailors from the 3rd Special Base Force and 1497 sailors
from the 7th Special Naval Landing Force. In addition
there were some 1200 Korean labourers from the 111th
Construction Unit and another 970 from the 4th Fleet

THE 16IN MAIN BATTERY OF THE USS *MARYLAND* OPENS FIRE AGAINST THE BEACH DEFENSES ON TARAWA. THE CONCUSSION OF THESE ENORMOUS WEAPONS CAUSED IMMENSE PROBLEMS WITH COMMUNICATIONS.

Construction Department Detachment. And to act as his mobile reserve, there were seven Type 95 light tanks, each with a 37mm gun and two machine guns.

However, careful study of aerial photographs indicated that the south or west coasts were more heavily defended than the rest, since they offered an invader the easiest landing. Moreover these shores tended to a series of concave beaches, so that a landing on any one would attract fire from both sides as well as ahead. On the other hand the northern shore tended to the convex, so that enfilading fire was more difficult; and therefore the northwestern lagoon beach was selected as the landing area. It was far from ideal, but it was the best of the available choices. It also had the slight bonus of having the pier in the middle of it, which, once secured, would be of use for resupply and evacuation of wounded.

The eventual plan was to send a scouting platoon to clear the pier, and then to land three reinforced battalions abreast on three beaches, two to the right of the pier and one to the left. The left beach was now 'Red 3', the beach to the right of the pier subdivided into 'Red 1' and 'Red 2', and the westernmost beach, the 'blunt' end of the island, became 'Green Beach'. Preliminary air and naval bombardments would be conducted, to destroy as much of the defenses as possible, and particular emphasis was laid on dealing with the 8in and 5in coast defense guns located on the three corners of Betio; unless these were put out of action the entire naval force would be at risk.

The Second Marine Division left New Zealand on 1 November and arrived in time to make some practice landings at Efate in the New Hebrides; these were principally useful in allowing the troops to gain experience in working with the Amtracs. What was not sufficiently stressed, it seems, was the fact that this was to be an assault, and not merely a landing. The Second Division had some experience of jungle fighting in Guadalcanal, and appear to have been of the opinion that Betio was to be a walk ashore, followed by more jungle operations. Another area of deficiency which was to show up in operations was a general lack of communication between the various elements of the attacking force. The infantry practised their skills, the engineers and armor practised theirs, but there was little collaboration between them.

The Army troops of the 27th Division had been given some training in amphibious landings under HM Smith's supervision in the Hawaii area. On 18 November the Army force from Hawaii and the Marine force from the New Hebrides met each other at sea, and the final preparations for the assaults were made. During the night of 19/20 November the assault force began closing on Tarawa. And that was when things began to go wrong.

The assault
The first sign of problems came with the transports. These had reached their assigned area, ready to load the Marines into their tractors and landing craft, but unknown to the planners this area of the ocean held strong currents, and instead of the ships lying idly in formation they rapidly began to drift in all directions in the darkness, causing chaos as Amtracs and boats milled round trying to find their assigned transport.

Then as dawn began to lighten the sky the coast guns on Betio, which were supposed to have been silenced by air bombardment during the previous days, opened fire on the assembled fleet. Their aim was poor, and no ship was hit, probably because their fire control system had been damaged during the air attacks. Nevertheless, a few near-misses splashing in the already crowded water did little to cheer the Marines as they waited. Rear-Admiral Harry Hill ordered his naval ships to open fire and silence the shore batteries, which they promptly did, but the vibration due to the heavy guns firing immediately silenced the communications equipment on the command ship USS *Maryland*. This meant that there was no communication with the carrier-borne aircraft which were scheduled to come in and attack the beaches.

In the event, however, the carrier-borne bombers failed to appear on schedule at 0545. Just why this happened has been the subject of long debate, but it appears probable that because the aircraft involved were absent during a vital part of the planning phase, the commander had not been properly briefed and was under the impression that his services were required at 0615. The shore bombardment had stopped to allow the bombers a free run; but when they failed to appear, it was resumed. The *Maryland*'s guns remained silent and repairs were made to the communications, so that when the bombers finally appeared at 0615 there was communication. But the renewed shore bombardment had kicked up such a cloud of dust on the targets that the bombers were unable to make out their designated targets and, since the shore bombardment programme was due to commence at 0630, they had a scant ten minutes in which to make their attack and then clear the area to allow the shelling to begin. As a result the aerial attack achieved very little of practical value.

The whole operation, of course, had to revolve around the moment the first Marine put his foot on shore. This, as we have said, was supposed to be at 0830, and the prior bombardment was timed to suit this. However, even at this early stage in the technique of amphibious warfare, it was recognized that things could go awry and that the landing might not take place at the precise minute ordained. Therefore there was supposed to be the capability to move events around so that whatever time the landing occurred, things would work at the right time intervals.

The next phase of the operation, the shore bombardment was therefore scheduled to take place in two phases. The first, opening at 0630 and lasting for 75 minutes. At the end of this period it was assumed that the Marines would be on their way in to the beach and would be in a position to be able to say with some certainty what time they would make their landing. The gunfire would therefore slacken while adjustments were made to the remaining gunfire and air support timings so that they would henceforth be in synchrony with the actual landing. Then an intense gunfire bombardment, coupled with aerial strafing of the beach areas, would

commence 45 minutes before the predicted landing time; this would stop as soon as the Amtracs reached the shore and would be immediately replaced by bombing attacks inland for a further 15 minutes. At the end of this time both the naval guns and the air element would be 'on call' from the ground commanders to deal with whatever targets the ground troops required silencing.

The preliminary bombardment got under way a few minutes late, and began saturating the entire island. While this continued, the Marines began embarking into their Amtracs and landing craft. At 0615 two minesweepers steamed into the lagoon channel to clear any mines which might have been planted there. After them sailed two destroyers, laying smoke screens to conceal the activity of the minesweepers and bombarding the beach area at short range with good effect.

At 0730 the gunfire slackened as the first phase came to an end; now was the time to decide what the actual landing time was going to be. And now came the news that the Amtracs were moving far slower than had been planned and were nowhere near their line of departure. There was, apparently, an offshore wind causing a current which flowed against the tractors, and, moreover, they appear not to have been capable of the four-and-a-half knots the planners insisted was their speed. Actually checks done during the run-in to Betio showed that they were averaging just under four knots. And to add to the confusion, one of the minesweepers, which was supposed to be marking the line of departure, got so engrossed in bombarding the shore that it had steamed out of position and when the Amtracs reached it, they found that they were still not on the imaginary line across the lagoon. R-Adm Hill weighed all the factors and made his estimate; the landing would take

ORDER OF BATTLE
ALLIED
Joint Expeditionary Force (Commander: Vice Adm Kelly Turner)
5th Amphibious Corps (Commander: Maj-Gen Holland M Smith)
2nd Marine Div (Tarawa) (Commander: Julian C Smith), comprised of:
2nd Marine Regt 6th Marine Regt (Reserved) 8th Marine Regt
165th Inf Div (Makin) (Commander: Ralph C Smith)
US cas: 1000 KIA; 2072 WIA
JAPANESE
III Special Base Force (Commander: Rear Adm Shibasaki)
Sasebo VII Special Naval Landing Force
Construction Troops
7 Lt Tanks
50 guns
Japanese cas: 4700 KIA; 146 POW

place at 0845. Phase two of the bombardment was to be delayed but would be delivered as ordered, commencing at 0800.

This duly happened, but at 0823 Hill learned that the tractors were just crossing their line of departure; no reasons were given at that time for their slowness, but Hill knew that careful calculations had shown that from the line to the beach would require forty minutes. He therefore re-set the landing time to 0900. The naval gunfire support was ordered to continue past its scheduled time. At exactly 0855 Hill ordered the gunfire bombardment of the beaches to stop, for fear of hitting the marines who would now be closing on their target, and move inland.

Unfortunately, at 0855 the Amtracs were still a long way off the beaches; they were running fifteen minutes behind the revised schedule. This would not have been too serious had communications with the air been working properly, but the persistent gunfire had, once more, ruined the Maryland's transmitters and Hill had been unable to advise the airmen of the change in landing time. In theory this should not have been critical, since during their initial briefings the airmen had been instructed that although the strafing of the beaches was to begin (under the original timings) at 0825, this was a moveable timing and the governing factor was the distance of the craft from the beach.

Everyone in the fleet could see the Amtracs were late; the minesweepers and destroyers had deliberately abandoned their smokescreen so that the assault wave would be visible from the air. Admiral Hill's liaison aircraft, flying above the lagoon, and reporting on progress had a perfect picture of precisely where the Amtracs were. But the carrier pilots apparently failed to see all this and began their attack on the beach precisely at 0825. The naval gunfire was stopped, in case a shell struck an airplane, Maryland's radio was persuaded to work, and the air strike was called off. Gunfire began once again and continued until 0855, whereupon the carrier planes were ordered back to complete their strafing.

Some of them did; some did not. Those which did return did so in a desultory and disorganized manner and, instead of, as their orders laid down, waiting and continuing to make attacks until the Amtracs were within 100 yards of the beach, the last aircraft left almost ten minutes before the first Amtracs reached the shore. They returned to their carriers assuring their debriefing officers that all targets had been thoroughly saturated and that there was nothing left of the defenses of Betio; what with this and 3000 tons of shells dumped on the island, the Marines, it was said, would walk ashore with no opposition.

The landings begin

Finally, at 0910, 0917 and 0922 the three battalions reached their assigned beaches and began to land. Lieut William D Hawkins, USMC, and his scout and sniper platoon had reached the end of the pier in advance of

MAIN TYPES OF ARMOR ON TARAWA

JAPANESE

The Japanese on Tarawa were more concerned with defense than offense, and therefore had but a handful of Type 95 light tanks. In spite of their spindly appearance these were probably the best Japanese tanks of the war, using a light and powerful air-cooled engine to give high speed and armed with a 37mm turret gun and two 7.7mm machine guns. Their armor was no thicker than 12mm, which was average for their period — they had been designed in 1933.

Since their campaign in China met little or no armor, the Japanese had neglected the development of anti-tank guns, and their standard pre-war gun, the 37mm Model 97, was simply a license-built copy of the 37mm German PAK 36, adequate to deal with anything the Chinese might produce. But the prospect of war with the United States led them to demand something more powerful, and to short-cut the development time they simply took a Soviet 45mm design, captured during one of the pre-war border incidents, modified it to 47mm caliber, and put it into production as the 47mm Model 01. Although still below western standards of the time, it could defeat 70mm of armor at 500m range, so that in the short ranges involved in the fighting on Tarawa it was quite good enough to deal with the 64mm maximum armor of the Sherman tank or the thinner plating on the landing craft.

AMERICAN

There is no evidence of American anti-tank guns being put ashore on Tarawa; at that time the only such gun was the 37mm, which, like the Japanese gun, was more or less a copy of the German 3.7cm PAK and had similar performance. Reliance for anti-tank work was placed on the shaped charge shell fired from the 75mm howitzer, the standard Marine support weapon, and it is supposed that this and the 2.36in Bazooka dealt with the few Japanese tanks which were met.

The US armor consisted of the well-known Sherman M4 medium tank, plus numbers of the Howitzer Motor Carriage M8, a variation of the Light M5 tank mounting a 75mm howitzer in the turret. This was intended to act in the assault gun role, accompanying infantry in the attack and dealing with obstacles at point-blank range, which might have been a better idea with a heavier piece of artillery mounted. Moreover the armor protection of the M8, with a maximum hull thickness of 45mm, was not really good enough for something in the forefront of the attack.

The Roebling-designed Landing Vehicle Tracked (LVT-1), more commonly called the Amtrac, was not armored, the body being made of common sheet steel. It had a rigid suspension system, the tracks being designed to paddle the vehicle through the water and over-ground performance being considered secondary. This was overcome in the second model, the LVT-2, of which a small number were used in the Tarawa landing.

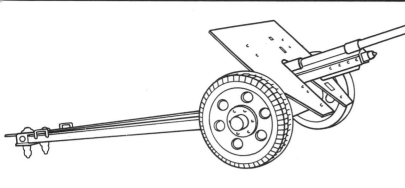

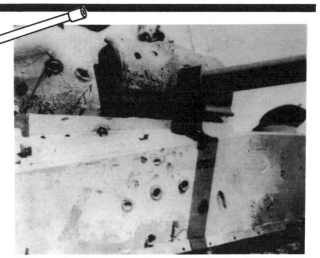

Japanese 47mm Gun Type 01
Based on the Russian 45mm ZIK, this weighed 750kg and fired a 1.4kg shot at 823m/sec or a 1.5kg shell to a range of 7680m when used in a general support role.

Holes punched by Japanese 47mm armor-piercing shells in the side of a Sherman tank on Red Beach One. The turret is gouged but not penetrated.

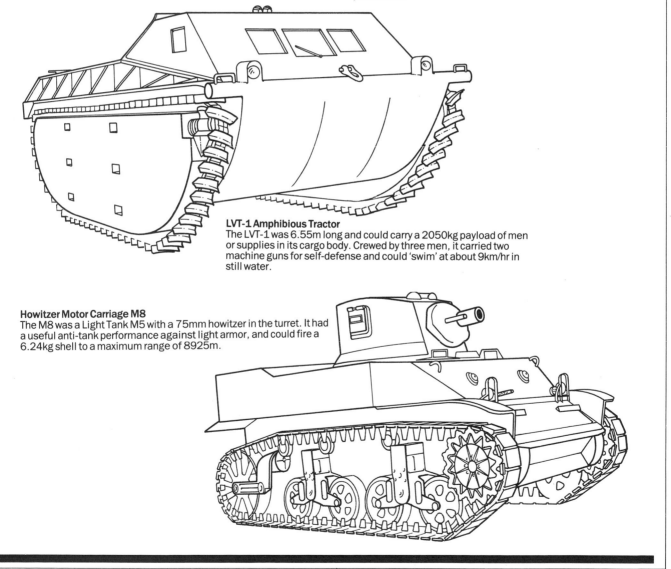

LVT-1 Amphibious Tractor
The LVT-1 was 6.55m long and could carry a 2050kg payload of men or supplies in its cargo body. Crewed by three men, it carried two machine guns for self-defense and could 'swim' at about 9km/hr in still water.

Howitzer Motor Carriage M8
The M8 was a Light Tank M5 with a 75mm howitzer in the turret. It had a useful anti-tank performance against light armor, and could fire a 6.24kg shell to a maximum range of 8925m.

the first waves and had cleared it of Japanese snipers, so that there was no enfilading fire across the beaches from there. There was relatively little opposition fire from the beaches, the Japanese defenders being well and truly subdued by the preliminary bombardments and strafing, and in spite of some half-hearted artillery fire which burst over the heads of the approaching Amtracs, the first three waves debarked on to the beach. The original plan had been to drive the Amtracs well ashore before disembarking the Marines, but the beach barricades stopped this idea; two tractors did, in fact, find an opening in the barricade close to the pier and drove through it to unload their cargo inshore, but the remaining tractors all halted at the water's edge to unload. The Marines ran up the beach to the barricade and there they halted. And at about that time the Japanese regained their senses and began putting up a stiffer and stiffer defense as every minute went by. A few bold leaders managed to persuade their men to get across the barricade, but the majority of the force which had landed stayed there, becoming pinned down by the increasing fire.

The fourth wave, approaching in landing craft, now ran into trouble. Instead of the forecast five feet of water over the reef, there was no more than three feet at the best and only a few inches at the worst. The landing craft all grounded on the reef, and the only course open to the fourth wave was to jump out of the boats and wade ashore. And as soon as they did this the defensive fire of the Japanese switched from the beach to these new, exposed, and tempting targets. Casualties in the third wave amounted to about ten percent of the force; and most of the officers and senior NCOs, who were, inevitably, the first to leap from the landing craft, were shot down. As a result, those men who eventually struggled ashore were leaderless; either their officers and NCOs were dead or wounded, or they became separated from them during the long trudge through the water. Only one of the battalion commanders reached the shore alive. A further hazard was that the bottom of the lagoon was not regular; many men vanished from sight into deep coral holes and were drowned under the weight of their equipment.

The fifth wave, which arrived about noon, carried tanks, and these, too, were forced to disembark at the reef and drive ashore through the water. One platoon of tanks (four medium tanks) moved to Red 3 beach where the Second Battalion, 8th Marines under Major Henry P Crowe was firmly ashore. With the aid of these tanks Crowe managed to consolidate his hold on the beach and directed the tanks to attack southward; by the end of the day one tank had been destroyed by a 'friendly' bomber, one by Japanese gunfire, and a third by a combined attack by Japanese guns and US bombs. Nevertheless, he had managed to force a way through and was in contact with the Marines on his right. On the left, though, the Japanese were dug in strength, and in order to clear this area JM Smith released the Third Battalion 8th Marines from the reserve to rein force Crowe.

Under the command of Major Robert H Ruud, the battalion moved in on landing craft and was forced to debark on the reef and wade ashore under intense fire from the Japanese position. It was not until late in the afternoon that Ruud himself managed to get ashore, and he found most of his force disorganized, with many officers and NCOs missing.

A head count revealed that the reinforcements were already weaker than the men they had come to support, and there was no hope of any attack against the Japanese before night fell. At the end of the day Crowe and Ruud controlled their sector of beach from the pier to a distance east of some 300 yards, and they had penetrated about 250 yards from the water's edge.

TWO VIEWS OF THE RED BEACHES; (TOP) RED BEACH 1 SEEN AFTER THE LANDING, WITH DAMAGED AND STRANDED ARMOR AND OTHER DEBRIS OF WAR. NOTE THE TANK CREW AWAITING RESCUE. (ABOVE) A PICTURE TAKEN DURING THE ACTUAL BATTLE, SHOWING ONE OF THE FOUR SHERMAN M3 MEDIUM TANKS TO COME ASHORE ON RED BEACH 3. OF THE FOUR ONLY ONE SURVIVED FOR ANY LENGTH OF TIME.

Red 2 beach had been assaulted by the Second Battalion, 2nd Marines, and intense fire during their landing had caused them to be dispersed, their commander being landed far to the right of his designated spot. The senior ranking officer on the beach, Lt Col Walter I Jordan, was actually there as a liaison and observing officer from Corps Headquarters, but he stepped in and took command of the men to the best of his ability.

The trouble, as he later said, was that the men 'didn't know him from Adam' and were not inclined to accept orders from strangers. The Marines had moved some 75 yards from the water and were there pinned down by machine gun and sniper fire.

Fortunately, Col Shoup, commanding 2nd Marines, was in a boat at the line of departure and was able to see what was going on, to some extent, and was also in radio communication with various elements of the assault force. He soon saw that the center beach was in trouble and forthwith committed his regimental reserve, the Third Battalion. They were fortunate in being able to use a number of Amtracs which, having dropped the first waves, had now returned to the line of departure. In truth, many of them never made it, being shot and sunk as they drove slowly back; only sufficient to lift two-thirds of the reinforcement battalion were available, and one company had to wait for them to take the first companies in and make yet another hazardous return before they could take their place.

The first two companies of the Third Battalion, in their Amtracs, approached the beach at about 1130, and in doing so passed across the mouth of a small valley which ran inshore. This valley was well stocked with Japanese, who opened a withering fire on the tractors as they passed. The battalion took 200 casualties before the tractors reached the shore, and a proportion of the force was driven off to the right, landing out of position and on the wrong beach. The remainder managed to reach their proper destination but came ashore disorganized, demoralized, and having lost much of their equipment.

With his reinforcements ashore, Shoup decided that it was now time that he went ashore and took control of affairs, and he landed about noon. Shortly afterwards four 75mm pack howitzers were landed. Shoup set up his command post, managed to get in contact with Crowe on his left, but was unable to make contact with Red 1 beach since there was a sizeable force of Japanese dug in between Red 1 and Red 2 beaches. Since there was little radio communication working (most of the landing force sets had been soaked during the landing and were out of action) Shoup was unable to speak to JM Smith, Smith had no idea of what was going on ashore, and neither of them knew what was happening on Green Beach.

Progress on Green Beach

In fact, things on Green Beach were going far better than anyone knew or expected. The landing had begun badly, since there was a considerable Japanese force — the same force which prevented Shoup from knowing what was happening on his right — occupying four-fifths of the beach area, but troops of the Third Battalion under Maj Michael P Ryan got ashore, as well as a number of stragglers from the other battalions who had been driven from their course and finished up here. With these men Ryan consolidated his position and cleared the northwestern tip of the island. Then, about noon, two medium tanks waded ashore from the reef; Ryan's engineers blew a hole in the beach barricade and with the tanks in the lead Ryan's men advanced about 500 yards southwards before the tanks were knocked out and he came to a halt. Unfortunately he was unable to hold this position overnight; he had bypassed a number of Japanese positions and did not have the heavy weapons to deal with them, and so as night drew closer he fell back and set up a defensive position on the northwestern tip.

At much the same time one of his radios dried out and began to work, so that he was at least able to inform Shoup and JM Smith of his position and also find out what was going on with the remainder of the force. Unfortunately, the communication was poor and neither end of the conversation was completely clear as to what was going on. Ryan, not knowing what lay ahead of him and conscious of his lack of heavy weapons, could not promise to clear the entire beach on the following day. Smith, for his part, was under the impression that Ryan was closely beset and unable to move at all. In fact it would have been possible to land reinforcements under Ryan's protection, across the northwestern tip of the island, during the night, but the opportunity was lost.

But long before this Julian Smith had realized that the outcome of the battle was on a knife edge and that he needed reinforcements, and at 1330 he requested the use of the Corps reserve, which was approved very quickly. He now had another four battalions at his call, but the problem was that he had not, by that time, received any hard information from the shore and had no idea where best to put these reserves. Assessing the battle to the best of his ability, and conscious that the 'tail' of the island was relatively untouched and might contain a Japanese force which would roll over the beaches in a counter-attack, he decided to send the First Battalion 8th Marines, who were already in boats and waiting at the line of departure, to land at the eastern end of Crowe's beach, to divert any Japanese attack which might come from that direction.

As it happened this maneuver, which would undoubtedly have massacred the First Battalion, never took place. Just as Smith was about to issue the orders, a Marine liaison aircraft flying across the lagoon saw a number of boats leave the line of departure and head for the beach. It was, in fact, a battery of 75mm howitzers, but in the confusion of boats and Amtracs in the water beneath him the pilot assumed that this must be the First Battalion, and he duly reported by radio that the First Battalion was now landing on the center beach. Smith assumed the pilot knew what he was talking about, wondered why the First Battalion had taken matters into their own hands, plotted them on his map as being ashore in the center, and turned to other things. As a result the First Battalion spent most of the night floating about on the line of departure, wondering what they were supposed to be doing.

During the night things were relatively quiet on shore, though the Marines were alert for a counterattack. JM Smith had decided that by this time, with, as he thought, two regiments ashore, he should now send a general officer in to take command and he sent orders for Brigadier General Leo D Hermle to land on Red 2 beach and take over. Communications failed yet again and Hermle heard nothing of this. Nevertheless, during the night Hermle decided he had had enough waiting and on his own initiative made his way to the shore, landing on the pier in an attempt to get some radio sets ashore so that Smith might be able to find out what was going on. Here he met runners from Shoup and was informed that Shoup was demanding reinforcements. Knowing that the First Battalion were still on the line of departure, Hermle made his way to a destroyer in the

lagoon and managed to get in touch with Smith, as a result of which the First Battalion at last received some orders — to land on the center beach at dawn.

Shoup had told his runners to impress upon whoever they met that there was a safe and sure way into the beach, a 'corridor' of deep water which ran from the pier; this they failed to pass across to Hermle, with the result that the First Battalion landed on the reef and began the long wade ashore at sunrise. They suffered heavy casualties in the process, since there was an old hulk on the shore which had been occupied by Japanese machine gunners and snipers. Air attacks were called in on this hulk, and it was struck with bombs, but during the attack the aircraft also managed to fire into a group of Marine wounded awaiting evacuation on the beach.

The First Battalion reached the shore in a disorganized manner, having lost much of their equipment and many of their officers and NCOs. Those who made it were taken by Shoup and fed into his defenses, facing the Japanese pocket to the right, but the reinforcement did little to improve Shoup's ability to mount any sort of an attack. Nevertheless, whilst holding on the right, the Marines managed to move forward, and by the end of the second day elements from Red 2 beach had gone

---

LEADING THE MEN ON TARAWA

Major-General Holland M Smith (1882–1967)

'Howling Mad' Smith was one of those generals who becomes a legend in his own lifetime.

A tough and unforgiving man, he believed in hard training, and he was also not deterred by casualty figures, maintaining simply that people got killed in wars. He is often called the 'father of amphibious warfare' which is perhaps stretching things a little, but there is no doubt that he was responsible for developing much of the amphibious tactical doctrine of the US Marines, and he was also the architect of much of the tri-service cooperation without which most amphibian landings would have foundered.

He led his men

against Attu and Kiska in the Aleutians, against Tarawa and Makin in the Gilberts, Kwajalien and Eniwetok in the Marshalls, and Saipan and Tinian in the Marianas, so he had some warrant to be considered an expert in the business.

After the losses at Tarawa he modified his attitude about casualties somewhat and maintained that much of the Pacific island-hopping was a waste of time, the islands being open to by-passing, but this was not considered official doctrine.

As was seen at Tarawa, he frequently had a chip on his shoulder when it came to dealing with the US Army, and this came to a head later in the war when the Okinawa invasion was being put together. Nevertheless, he

never lost sight of the overall picture, and his disagreements were usually able to be mended by higher echelons. Put bluntly, had Smith not been on the spot at the right time, it is difficult to see who would have hammered the US Marines into the formidable force they very rapidly became in the Pacific.

Vice Admiral Richard Kelly Turner (1885–1961)

Turner, a career Naval officer, was more familiar with the enemy than most of his contemporaries, since he had served in the War Plans Division of the US Navy before the war and had been involved in various political negotiations with the Japanese. In July 1942 he was sent to the South Pacific to take command of the Amphibious Force, since he had long been a student of amphibious operations and had a considerable reputation as

a theorist in that field.

With instructions to command transportation, escort and bombardment forces accompanying such operations, Turner's first practical experience came with his support of the Guadalcanal invasion in August 1942. Due to tactical mishaps, the US Fleet suffered in the Battle of Savo Island and Turner was forced to withdraw his unprotected amphibious fleet from its supporting role, an unavoidable move but one which, in the circumstances, did his reputation no good with the Marines. However, he was to overcome this setback by his work at Tarawa, and his subsequent commanding of the attacks in the Marshalls and Marianas. Late in 1944 he was sent to Saipan to set up the airbase there from which B29 bombers attacked the Philippines and Japan, and in February 1945 he commanded the expeditionary force which assaulted Iwo Jima.

through the Japanese and reached the far coastline, cutting the Japanese defense in two.

During the night Ryan, on the northwestern tip of the island had received some reinforcements, among them flame-throwers and two more medium tanks. Aided by two air strikes, which destroyed some Japanese artillery, he was able to move out of his position at 1000 and found little opposition; in a surprisingly short time he cleared the entire western beach and had reached the coast south of the pier.

Smith immediately ordered the Sixth RCT under Col Maurice Holmes to land in two battalions on the cleared western Green Beach in the evening and attack at first light due east towards the airfield. At the same time Shoup was to devote his energies to destroying the Japanese pocket which was sitting between the Red and Green beaches, and Ruud and Crowe were to use two battalions of the Eighth Marines to attack the Japanese force located to the left flank of Red 3 beach.

Information also reached Smith that Japanese had been seen moving off Betio and in the direction of Bairiki, a smaller island. The eventual task of Smith's force was to clear the entire atoll, and there seemed to be a danger that the Japanese would pull clear of the fight on Betio to set up shop on Bairiki and there make another determined stand which would be difficult to overcome. A battalion of the Sixth Marines, together with a battalion of 75mm howitzers, was therefore sent post-haste to Bairiki. Smith hoped that once the artillery was in position and capable of stopping any refugees from Betio occupying the islet, the infantry element could return to Betio and add to the weight for the final clearance.

The assault on Bairiki was something of an anti-climax. The garrison consisted of about 15 Japanese with two heavy machine guns, and for reasons which no doubt seemed good to them, they had a large can of fuel in the vicinity. A preliminary air strike found this can with a .50 incendiary bullet and the subsequent explosion burned out both machine gun positions. The entry of the Sixth Marines was unopposed, the howitzers were installed and promptly began registering targets on the southern end of Betio, and the infantry returned to the main battle.

In the late afternoon the First Battalion, 6th Marines under Major William K Jones landed on Green Beach under Ryan's guidance, the first unit to reach Betio in an organized condition. During the night they reinforced Ryan's position, preparatory to making a morning assault, and they helped repulse a number of Japanese counter-attacks.

On the morning of 22 November, the third day, Jones began his attack, fighting his way along the south coast between the beach and the airstrip until he reached the handful of marines who had crossed the island on the previous day. Assisted by gunfire from Naval destroyers, and with the aid of flame-throwers, seven light tanks and his one remaining medium tank, Jones later reported that his force had little trouble in

TOP: MARINES TAKING A PILLBOX ON BETIO ISLAND BETWEEN RED BEACH 1 AND RED BEACH 2; THIS PARTICULAR STRONGPOINT HELD OUT FOR TWO DAYS BEFORE BEING TAKEN.
ABOVE: ADMIRAL SHIBASAKI'S COMMAND BUNKER, BEHIND RED BEACH 3, WITH KNOCKED-OUT TYPE 95 LIGHT TANK IN FRONT OF THE ENTRANCE.

clearing the strip and had covered about 2.5km and made contact with the outlying marines by noon. The attack continued, Jones being instructed to carry on with his clearance until the end of the day and then side-step left to make contact with the Eighth Marines to secure a perimeter for the night.

But the rate of progress slowed during the afternoon; it was now becoming apparent that the light tank was of very little use in this sort of battle. Its 37mm gun lacked the penetration to deal with Japanese defensive positions, fashioned from layers of palm tree trunks and coral rock, and the tank had insufficient weight to damage such defensive structures by crushing them.

The medium M4 tank, with a potent 75mm gun and twice the weight, was the only practical vehicle, and Jones's single tank worked overtime. By the end of the day Jones' force had reached the end of the airstrip and made contact with the Eighth Marines. They, under Crowe and Ruud, had pushed eastward and fought their way to the end of the airstrip.

By early evening there was a line of marines across the island east of the airstrip, and the area behind them, though not entirely cleared of small pockets of resistance, was being thoroughly checked out by Shoup's men. With the major Japanese force now penned up on the end of the island, Smith called in naval gunfire support to bombard the Japanese positions while the battalion of 75mm howitzers which had landed on Bairiki added to the shelling. The line of marines sat quiet, not disclosing their positions by indiscriminate firing, and let the artillery break up any Japanese formation which showed an inclination to counter-attack.

On the morning of the 23rd the Third Battalion 6th Marines under Col Kenneth F MacLeod passed through the line and advanced on the remaining Japanese positions. At the same time, Shoup began his final assault on the Japanese pocket of resistance in the valley leading from the northwestern beach. Shortly after noon on 23 November the 6th reached the southern tip of the island and Shoup finally cleared the ravine; at 1312hrs Smith announced Betio was secured. The remainder of the atoll was cleared in a relatively easy operation and by 28 November the operation was over and Tarawa firmly in American hands.

The lessons

Tarawa cost the Marines just over 1000 killed and 2100 wounded; it cost the Japanese 4690 killed and 146 prisoners, only 17 of whom were Japanese soldiers, the remainder being Korean laborers. Reviewed with hindsight, the Marines got off lightly, largely because the Japanese commander had pinned his faith on stopping any invasion on the beach, and had made no contingency plans for fighting inshore. Moreover he was killed by a naval shell which struck his command bunker during the initial bombardment. As a result the Japanese tactics were poor, little more than fanatic bayonet charges which were easily repulsed. Had the Japanese been better organized for their defense the Marine casualty list would have been larger, and when one compares the Tarawa operation with later operations in the South Pacific the percentage of killed and wounded is seen to be less on Tarawa. Nevertheless, it was the first battle in the Pacific which produced a large number of casualties in a short time, and its effect on the American public was little short of traumatic.

It also shocked some of the services into realizing that they had better do something about improving their supporting techniques, otherwise future operations were likely to be even bloodier. There was a noticeable improvement in the dedication of naval aviation after Tarawa; studies into the effectiveness of shore bombing and strafing were made, and training in these vital techniques improved immensely. They were carefully instructed in the principles of amphibious landings so that they appreciated the significance of keeping up their preliminary attacks until the approaching marines actually reached their objectives. In future operations naval pilots were at pains to bomb as precisely and as frequently as they could, and never again was a wreck or hulk or building which could shelter snipers neglected.

Naval gunfire support was also improved; there was little to fault so far as the navy's willingness to support its marines was concerned, but the type of ammunition necessary to demolish shore installations was carefully studied, as well as techniques of bombardment and barrage fires and the observation and reporting of fire.

The biggest improvement was demanded in communications; firstly the troops needed radios which would withstand the soaking they would inevitably get during the run in to the beach, and secondly the control side had to be capable of working to the various levels without being silenced by vibration from gunfire. The eventual solution was to have dedicated communication and control ships from which the commanders of operations could control their men and run their battle without the ship being required to attend to naval affairs at the same time.

The advantage of the Amtrac in crossing the reef was obvious, and instructions for stepping up production of Amtracs went out forthwith; at the same time the development of an armed and armored version, which was under way, was stepped up and the design put into production. In future landings these not only delivered marines to the beaches but then drove ashore and acted as armor screens and support until tanks could be put ashore. The light tank was deleted from future operations, but since the flame-thrower had shown itself an extremely useful weapon, a number of light tanks were modified to become mobile flame-throwers and were subsequently of great value in reducing stubborn defensive positions.

And the final thing which came out of Tarawa was the need for closely integrated training. No longer did a rifleman perfect himself on the rifle and leave demolitions or mortar firing to somebody else. It had become apparent than men needed a range of skills so that holdups would not ensue whilst waiting for the right man to appear. Closer integration between rifle squads, flame-thrower teams, tanks, combat engineers, every element of the landed force, was now realized to lie at the heart of a successful operation.

It is greatly to the credit of the officers and men of the US Marines that in the aftermath of Tarawa they were their own most fierce critics. They dissected the entire operation, and their training policies, and then set about ensuring that the various mistakes would not be repeated. The subsequent course of the South and South-West Pacific campaigns is the proof that they learned their lessons well.

CHAPTER SEVEN

D-DAY IN NORMANDY

INVASION
JUNE 1944

Overleaf

The controlled chaos of an opposed invasion landing is well conveyed by
this painting, which also manages to depict almost all the various types of equipment employed on
the Normandy Beaches. (*D-Day* by T Cuneo, OBE)

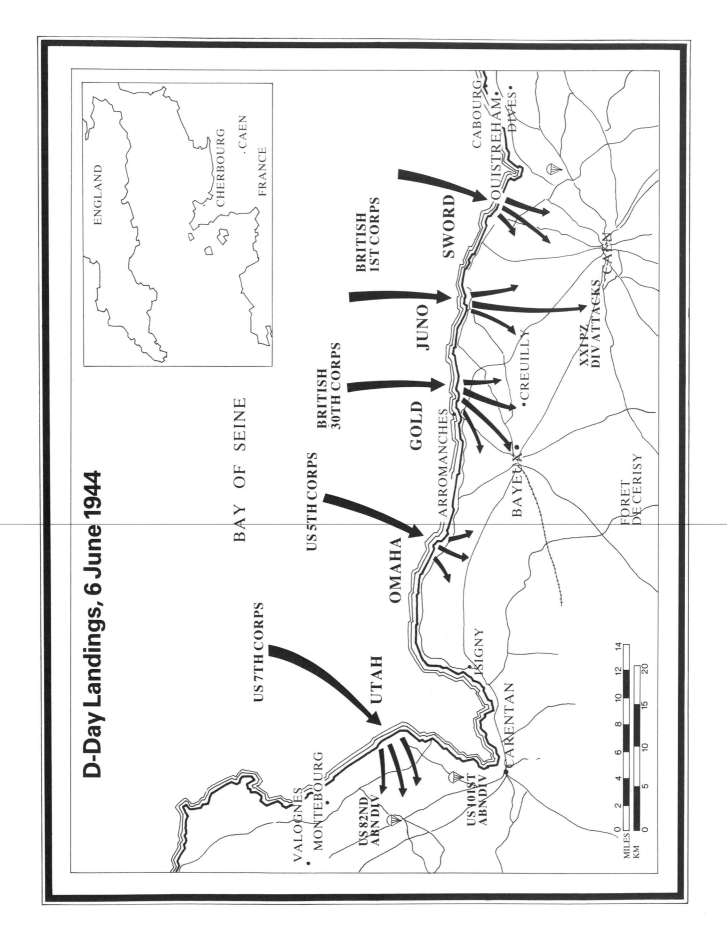

D-Day Landings, 6 June 1944

ENGLAND

CHERBOURG

· CAEN

FRANCE

BAY OF SEINE

US 7TH CORPS

UTAH

US 5TH CORPS

OMAHA

BRITISH 30TH CORPS

GOLD

JUNO

BRITISH 1ST CORPS

SWORD

CABOURG·

OUISTREHAM·

DIVES·

ARROMANCHES

·CREUILLY

BAYEUX

CAEN

XXIPZ DIV ATTACKS

FORET DE CERISY

ISIGNY

CARENTAN

VALOGNES

MONTEBOURG

·

US 82ND ABN DIV

US 101ST ABN DIV

MILES

KM

0 2 4 6 8 10 12 14

0 5 10 15 20

In spite of the siren voices which urged Allied military action in theaters removed from Europe — the policy known during the First World War as 'knocking away the props' and as ineffective then — the inescapable fact was that in order to come to grips with the German Army and destroy it, sooner or later it would be necessary to invade the mainland of Europe. The enthusiasm with which this concept was embraced varied in proportion to the distance of the embracer from the potential invasion coast.

The background

When the British Army took stock after Dunkirk, re-invasion of the continent was not among its most immediate concerns. More important were the basics of re-equipping the existing forces and amassing and training an enlarged army for the future — whatever that might entail. That an invasion would have to take place was not doubted, but that was some considerable distance in the future. In the meantime, there was a campaign in Africa pending, and there were Commando raids which could pinprick the German garrisons, and these, it was felt, would suffice to keep the war ticking over.

In December 1941, when the Japanese joined the war, more diversions pressed in upon the planners, and European invasion appeared further away than ever. But even before this, the US Army had begun making their own plans for the future shape of the war, even before they were properly in it.

In July 1941, Lt Col Albert C Wedemeyer of the War Plans Division reviewed the then situation and drew up a paper for President Roosevelt, a 'strategical concept of how to defeat our potential enemies.' Wedemeyer had a considerable advantage over most Allied planners in that he had attended the German Army Staff College from 1936 to 1938 and was therefore entirely familiar with German military thinking and with European concepts of warfare. His concept was to amass a force of 61 armored divisions and throw these on to the European shore in the middle of 1943. His date was arrived at by simple logistics; it would require that long to build up an 8 million strong army, equip it, train it, and build the 10 million tons of shipping necessary to transport it to its chosen invasion point.

In December 1941, after America's entry into the war, General Eisenhower became chief of the War Plans Division. After reviewing the situation in the Pacific he adopted Wedemeyer's plans and passed them up to General Marshall, Chief of Staff, who in turn put them before President Roosevelt. Roosevelt approved, and the plans were slightly polished until they became a firm proposal for placing 30 US and 18 British divisions on the Continent of Europe on 1 April, 1943. This 'Marshall Memorandum' was then taken to Britain and put before Winston Churchill.

The Memorandum contained two contingency plans; the first, code-named 'Roundup', concerned the full-scale invasion on 1 April, 1943; the second, code-named 'Sledgehammer', was to take place if Russia should suddenly show signs of collapse or if Germany's military position should suddenly deteriorate, in which case five British and American divisions would invade no later than October 1942. Both plans were dissected and discussed by the British Chiefs of Staff, and they were quick to show that Sledgehammer was totally impractical, since five divisions would be flung back into the sea with very little trouble. Roundup was slightly more practical, even though it relied on the provision of some ten thousand landing craft, none of which had even been designed, let alone built. Nevertheless, by the end of April 1942 there was broad agreement on action 'possibly in 1942, certainly in 1943'.

This would have been enough to be going on with, but President Roosevelt, in a typically 'frank and free' gesture, informed Molotov, Soviet Foreign Minister, of the decision and was then pressured by Molotov to make a firm commitment to the 'Second Front' in 1942.

This jovial assurance was somewhat wrecked a few days later when Lord Mountbatten arrived in the USA to explain quite precisely why an invasion in 1942 was impossible. In plain figures, he showed that Britain had but 13 fully-trained divisions, America would have no more than three divisions in Britain by September 1942, and that in any case there were only sufficient small craft to lift 4000 men, less than one-third of a division. And when they landed they would be faced with 27 German divisions backed up by a Luftwaffe with more first-line aircraft in the skies over Britain and France than the British and Americans put together could muster.

As a result, Allied operations in 1942 were directed against North Africa; and after that, against Sicily and then Italy. And the success there tended to draw British attention away from the projected invasion, with a particular emphasis on clearing Italy and the Balkans. We need not detain ourselves with this, but the eventual result was that the US Chiefs of Staff agreed to assist in the Mediterranean war on condition that Britain was ready to invade the continent across the English Channel by late spring 1944.

By this time it had become apparent to the Americans that no matter what their enthusiasm might be, the plain facts were against them; as Eisenhower himself put it, on the first page of his 'Report to the Combined Chiefs of Staff on the Operations in Europe';

> "Some consideration was given to the possibility that a return to the Continent in force might take place late in 1943, but a review of the build-up figures of United States forces in the United Kingdom indicated that this would be impossible and that no large-scale attack could be undertaken until 1944."

On November 30, 1943 the decision was finally taken: to launch Operation Overlord in May 1944.

The plans

In fact planning had begun some time before; by July 1943 the Outline Plan for Overlord had been drawn up by Lt Gen FE Morgan, Chief of Staff to the Supreme Allied Commander (Designate) or COSSAC. The title of this post was deliberately chosen; at the time of Morgan's appointment no-one knew who the eventual commander would be, nor when the invasion would take place, but this was no bar to getting down to the initial planning.

The COSSAC plan had been drawn up in response to guidelines which indicated that there would be sufficient landing craft to put five infantry divisions ashore, three in the initial assault and two as immediate backup. In addition two airborne divisions would be dropped, and two more infantry divisions would be ready to move across as soon as landing craft were available. After this initial lodgement, a further 20 divisions would be ready to reinforce as quickly as possible.

Since there were only sufficient landing craft for five divisions, it was necessary that the assault be a concentrated one; and since some 20-odd divisions had to be fed into the beachhead, it was likewise imperative that the assault should capture a port facility. Finally, the selected assault area had to be within fighter cover from air bases in England, which put a limit of about 200 miles radius from central southern England. All this pointed to the Pas de Calais, and this area had the additional advantage that good roads ran into northern France and Belgium, facilitating the subsequent advance. Unfortunately, what was apparent to Allied planners was equally apparent to the Germans, and the Pas de Calais was probably the most heavily defended stretch of coastline between the North Cape and the Pyrenees. An attack on this area with five divisions would be suicide.

The only feasible alternative was the coast of Normandy, between the mouth of the Seine and Cherbourg. This was less well defended, had reasonably good beaches, but was without port facilities and was difficult of exit because of marshes and flooded areas behind the beaches. But in spite of its drawbacks it offered better prospects than did the Pas de Calais, and therefore Normandy was chosen as the assault area. Again, similar thoughts entered the heads of the Germans, particularly after Rommel had taken command of the area, and while the planners worked, so the Germans strengthened their defenses, though not to the degree which obtained around Calais.

In December 1943 General Eisenhower was officially appointed Supreme Commander of the Allied Expeditionary Force, and General BL Montgomery commander of 21st Army Group, the combined Allied force which was to make the assault. They were introduced to the COSSAC plan, and after a very short amount of study Montgomery objected to it and carried Eisenhower with him. The objection was simply that the scale of the assault was too small, both in manpower and area. Instead of landing three divisions on a 20-mile front, five divisions across a 50-mile front would offer a better chance of success. Extending to the east would

place the assault units in a better position to take Caen, an important road and rail junction, and airfields in its vicinity; extending westwards would give the assault a strong foothold on the Cotentin Peninsula and a head start on securing Cherbourg and its port facilities.

The airborne contribution was also to be stepped up, two divisions landing on the right flank and one on the left in order to secure vital road junctions, bridges and beach exits. This latter demand ran into instant opposition from the Air Forces, who foresaw casualties of 75 percent or more, but in spite of this gloom, Eisenhower persisted and obtained the necessary aircraft.

The increase in manpower demanded more landing craft, and this had its effect on the planned date. Initially it was decided to make the assault on May 1, and there was little hope that the extra landing craft to carry the two additional divisions could be ready by that date, whereas postponement for one month would give time for these extra craft to be provided. Moreover an additional month would permit a very thorough aerial bombardment of the target area and other parts of France in order to destroy defenses, and it would also allow more time for the navies to train their landing craft crews. Since early June also offered favorable tides, after much discussion June 5 was eventually set as the date for the assault.

With this as the frame, the planners now began to work on the details. One of the first requirements was to set up a deception plan which would direct the Germans' attention to the Pas de Calais as being the primary invasion area and Normandy as being no more than a diversion; if this was believed, then there would be a delay in reinforcing Normandy because the German reserves would be held back in readiness to deal with the attack on Calais. An advantage in this idea of deception was the weakness of the Luftwaffe and the absolute Allied air superiority which obtained by this time, which meant that air reconnaissance by German aircraft was at a minimum and was unlikely to uncover anything which argued against the deception plan.

Gradually, over a period of months, spurious radio traffic, carefully crafted snippets of information fed into the German secret agent network (which was totally controlled by British intelligence by that time), deliberate 'leaks' and 'careless talk' in neutral embassies provided a jigsaw to the German intelligence which, when assembled with a little imagination, soon began to build up a picture of immense troop concentrations in East Anglia and South-eastern England which were obviously threatening the Pas de Calais.

The air plan consisted of two parts, the preparatory phase and the assault phase. The preparatory phase was to be mounted by both Strategic and Tactical Air Forces and would involve attacks on targets in the invasion area and on targets outside it; in order that the direction of the attack should not be deduced from assessment of the bombers' targets, two targets outside the invasion area were to be attacked for every one inside it. Heavy bombers would deal with road and rail junctions, supply dumps, bridges and similar targets over an area extending well into France, the object being to cut the lines of communication so as to prevent the ready supply of reinforcements and stores to the German forces in the invasion area.

The Tactical Air Forces would direct their attacks against tactical targets; gun positions, command and communication centers, bridges, airfields, coastal batteries, radar stations and similar objectives in and around the invasion coast and also in the Pas de Calais and other coastal areas. Within a 130-mile radius of the landing beaches all enemy airfields and radar installations were to be attacked, and all the Seine and Loire bridges below Paris and Orleans were to be cut prior to D-Day to isolate the invasion area from the rest of France.

This air effort was not to be mounted without severe opposition from the Allied air force leaders. Their sole purpose in life, according to them, was the ending of the war by strategic bombing, irrespective of what the land and sea forces might be doing, and they were less than agreeable to interrupting this crusade for such a mundane purpose as assisting an invasion. Left to themselves the bombing forces would end the war before any foot soldier ever reached the borders of Germany, and therefore to take them from this divine mission was tantamount to treason and a waste of time into the bargain. Harris of the Royal Air Force and Eaker of the 8th US Army Air Force were united in their belief in strategic bombing, and it took a great deal of hard argument and the eventual issuing of explicit orders before they could be brought to heel and persuaded to agree to Eisenhower's master plan.

In the event, this pre-invasion campaign by the Strategic Air Forces was to be to their benefit; one of their designated target areas was fuel supply, the attack

A TETRARCH LIGHT TANK BEING MANEUVERED INTO A HAMILCAR GLIDER PREPARATORY TO THE AIRBORNE OPERATION. THE TETRARCH WAS BUILT SPECIFICALLY TO CARRY IT. ALTHOUGH THE IDEA WAS APPEALING, THE TETRARCH WAS A THIN TARGET AND WAS RARELY USED.

of refineries and oil stores so as to deprive the German armored forces of the power to move their tanks. When the Air Forces returned to their strategic bombing of Germany they were to find that German fighter opposition had dwindled, simply because there was insufficient fuel to allow them to fly all the missions necessary to defend against the bombers.

Another task which fell to the Royal Air Force was to mount a vital part of the deception plan. 617 Squadron (the famous 'Dam-Busters') were given the task of flying in precise formation and at a regulated speed on a course leading towards the Pas de Calais, scattering 'Window' — strips of metallized paper — as they went. Their progress consisted of a few minutes of forward flight scattering Window, then a turn, a flight back along their track, another turn and another forward flight scattering more Window, so that the German radars would see a slowly advancing mass on their radar screens, a mass moving at the speed of seaborne convoy and thus giving the impression of an enormous armada sailing towards the Pas de Calais.

To give direct support and protection to the actual invasion force, 171 squadrons of fighters and fighter-bombers were allotted. There would be a sustained density of ten squadrons covering the beaches, with six more in support, demanding a total of 54 squadrons to give reliefs; a further 15 squadrons would protect shipping, 36 would be available on call for direct support against ground targets, 33 squadrons were earmarked for offensive operations and escorting bombers, and 33 squadrons formed a 'striking force' to be held in reserve for use as the air situation might require.

Finally, of course, the air forces were responsible for aerial reconnaissance of the invasion area and Europe in general, and the photographs they brought back, over a period of about a year prior to the invasion, gave the planners some indication of what sort of defenses they were going to have to breach.

The preparations

So far as men were concerned the problem of landing in Europe resolved itself into using one of two methods; either they ran ashore from a landing craft, or they jumped out of an aeroplane. But men alone would not suffice to penetrate the defenses; tanks were necessary. The only tanks which could be flown in were too small to be of any practical value, which left the prospect of tanks driving ashore from landing craft. But to do this in safety required the beach to be secured, which meant that the infantry had to go in first, clear the beach, deal with the defenses, and silence the enemy guns. This was putting the cart before the horse, since the purpose of the tank was to go ahead of the infantry and support *them* on to their objective.

Moreover an abortive raid on Dieppe in 1942 had revealed the hazards of simply dumping tanks onto a hostile beach. This had been the first time the British Churchill tank had been used in action, and it ended in disaster with every tank either shot to pieces or abandoned. Most of the tanks were unable to scramble off the beach on to the esplanade behind, and the others simply scrabbled their way down into the shingle and sand and stuck there. It followed from this that some serious thought had to be put into the question of tanks and how to ensure that they landed successfully and then got off the beaches so as to be able to fight onwards.

Examination of the air photographs and reports from agents soon enabled the planners to build up a picture of the defenses, and they were able to break them down into categories; artificial obstacles, with or without mines attached; mines; soft sand; concrete walls; ditches; heavily armed pillboxes and strong-points. Since most of these obstacles had been designed with the idea of stopping tanks, then it would be neces-sary to develop some special tanks in order to overcome them. And thus, in late 1943, the British 79th Armoured Division came into existence, probably the only armored division in the world which consisted of nothing but armored vehicles — no supporting infan-try, no artillery, just highly specialized tanks.

Allied ingenuity

The underwater obstacles on the beaches were to be dealt with by frogmen, leaving the foreshore relatively clear, and so the first requirement was a tank which could be launched from a ship some distance from the beach and then swim ashore. Amphibious tanks had been developed before, but these had all been small tanks enclosed in buoyancy tanks and intended for crossing a river, and they were unsuitable for this task. What was needed was a method of swimming a full-sized 30-ton combat tank in the sea. And in the strange way that brings questions and answers together, an

A LOW-LEVEL RAF RECONNAISSANCE PHOTO OF THE MANY DIFFERENT OBSTACLES STREWN ACROSS THE D-DAY BEACHES.

inventor was ready with a solution.

Nicholas Straussler, an Hungarian engineer working in Britain, had developed a number of armored vehicles in prewar days and he now produced a simple method of making any tank float. An impervious canvas screen was attached to the hull of the tank and erected like a wall around the upper hull and turret. This increased its displacement sufficiently to make it float. The tank's hull was, in fact, below water level but the commander, standing in his turret, could see over the screen and could steer the tank by means of a tiller. A propeller was driven from the tank's drive sprocket, and it could make about 4 knots through the water and survive in seas of Force 5. This became known as the 'DD' tank, for 'Duplex Drive', a name which was accurate enough, since the tank drove by propeller or tracks, but was sufficiently vague to conceal the significant floating feature.

The next problem was that of mines which might be buried in the sand of the beach and thus wreck the swimming tanks as they came ashore and shed their flotation screens. This had been solved in 1942, in the Western Desert, where a Major AS du Toit of the South African Army had devised a 'flail' tank. A rotating drum was carried on arms ahead of the tank hull and driven by means of a shaft from a truck engine mounted on the tank hull. Chains were attached loosely to the drum, so that as it revolved so the free ends of the chains 'flailed' the ground beneath, ahead of the advancing tank, with sufficient force to detonate any mines. When the mine went off, the worst that could happen was that one or two links of the flail chain might be snapped off, damage which could be rapidly repaired. This idea was now taken and improved, adapting it so that the drum was driven by the tank's main engine, so doing away with the vulnerable truck engine outside the hull. This became the Sherman 'Crab'.

Another method of dealing with a minefield was to subject the surface of the ground to the pressure of a sudden explosive blast, the problem being how to dis-tribute the explosive. But if the requirement was reduced to one of merely clearing a strip through a minefield, sufficiently wide to admit one tank, then the answer became more practical. Two devices were developed; the 'Conger' and the 'Snake'. The 'Snake' was a 20ft long 3in steel pipe packed with TNT; several of these could be connected end-to-end and then pushed ahead of a Sherman tank into a minefield. Once it had been positioned, the tank backed away, laying a cable as it did so, and the Snake was electrically detonated. The blast cleared a strip about 20 feet wide. Snake proved very useful, and it was also in demand for removing wire entanglements.

The 'Conger' was rather more ambitious; it con-sisted of several hundred feet of empty canvas hose attached to a rocket and carried in a trailer behind the tank. On arrival at the minefield the rocket was fired, so pulling out the hose and dropping it flat on the ground in the desired direction. Now came the difficult part;

ORDER OF BATTLE

ALLIED

21st Army Group: (Commander: Gen Montgomery)
1st US Army
5th Corps 7th Corps 8th Corps 12th Corps 15th Corps 19th Corps 20th Corps
Armored Divisions: 12th,3rd,4th,5th,6th,7th and 2nd French
Infantry Divisions: 1st,2nd,4th,5th,8th,9th,28th,29th,30th,35th,79th, 80th,83rd,90th
2nd Ranger Bn
5th Ranger Bn
Airborne Divisions: 82nd, 101st
2nd Brit Army
GHQ & Army Troops 79th Armd Div Armored Brigades: 4th,6th (Guards), 8th,27th,33rd, 2nd Canadian Tank Brigades: 31st, 34th 56th Infantry Brigade Special Service Brigades (Commando): 1st,4th
1st Corps 8th Corps 12th Corps 30th Corps   Guards, 7th, 11th Armd Divs 47th RM Cdo 6th Brit AB Div
1st Canadian Army
2nd Cdn Corps
1st Polish Armd Div

AXIS

Army Group B (Commander: Fld-Marshal Rommel)
5th Panzer Army (Formerly Panzer Group West) 1st Army 7th Army 15th Army
Panzer Corps: 1SS, 2SS, 47, 48
Infantry Corps: 2 Parachute, 25, 67, 74, 80, 81, 82, 84, 86
Panzer Divisions: 1SS, 2, 2SS, 9, 9SS, 10SS, 12SS, 21, 116, Lehr
Infantry Divisions: 2,3,4,5, 6 Parachute, 16, 17, 18 Luftwaffe Field, 47, 48, 49, 77, 84, 85, 89, 91 Airlanding, 226, 243, 245, 265, 266, 271, 272, 275, 276, 277, 326, 331, 343, 344, 346, 348, 352, 353, 363, 708, 709, 711, 716

use, though it should be said that an improved version, with a less nervous explosive filling, is in use today by the British Army and is highly effective.

To deal with the soft sand and shingle found on many beaches, and also to overcome wire entanglements, 'Carpet Laying' machines were developed. These carried a large roller on the front of the tank, around which a 100-foot length of 'carpet' — a strong cloth reinforced with strips of wood — was wrapped. The free end of the roll was weighted, and when the tank reached the soft area or the wire obstacle this free end was released to fall under the advancing tracks of the tank. The tracks ran on to the 'carpet', and as the tank went forward so the 'carpet' was unrolled and laid on the ground beneath, being pressed into place by the weight of the tank. As the end came off the roll, so the tank continued on its way and discarded the empty roller, leaving a pathway ten feet wide which could be used by other tanks or by wheeled vehicles.

After the sand came the beach walls and esplanades, or possibly ditches, and to deal with these the Churchill 'ARK' (an acronym derived from 'Armoured Ramp Carrier') was devised. This was a turret-less Churchill tank carrying two timber trackways on top of the hull. At each end of these trackways were hinged extension ramps which were pulled up and secured by cables. After landing, the ARK drove to the foot of the wall, scrabbled as far up as it could, and then applied its brakes and released the ramps; the front ramps reached the top of the wall, the rear ramps fell to the ground behind the tank. Now a following combat tank could drive up the ramp, across the top of the ARK on the trackway, off the front ramps and was on top of the wall.

If, as was generally the case, the top of the wall was the boundary of a road or esplanade, then the combat tank simply drove on. If, as sometimes happened, the wall was a wall, and there was a drop behind it, then the second tank was to carry a 'fascine', a bundle of wooden stakes wrapped together with wire. This was balanced on the nose of the tank and secured by cables with explosive links. On arriving on top of the wall the explosive was fired and the fascine dropped off the tank to rest against the reverse face of the wall and thus form an artificial ramp down which the tank could slide to reach the ground.

If the obstacle at the end of the beach was a ditch, then a fascine tank merely drove up and dropped its fascine into the ditch to fill it, then drove across. But if the ditch was too big for the fascine, then an ARK tank drove into the ditch, settled itself in the middle, and then unfolded its ramps so that following tanks could drive down the ramp, across the ARK, up the ramp the other side and so cross the ditch. If the ditch was really deep, then a second ARK would drive on top of the first and unfold its ramps.

Alternatively, it might be simpler to simply blast the wall away, and for this the 'Goat' was prepared. This was a tank carrying a huge framework loaded with

the hose was pumped full of liquid nitro-glycerin, the tank withdrew, and the explosive was then fired electrically. The system worked on trials, but it was generally agreed that asking men to sit on the forward edge of a defended minefield under enemy fire and gently pump several hundred gallons of liquid dynamite into a hose-pipe before lighting the blue touch paper and retiring was asking a little too much! Conger was rarely put to

THE SPECIALIZED ARMOR OF D-DAY

The British 79th Armoured Division was expressly conceived as a specialized formation to operate armor capable of overcoming every conceivable obstacle on the Normandy beaches. It manned vehicles carrying fascines for filling ditches, bridges for spanning them, flamethrowers for dealing with pillboxes, explosive charges for more difficult obstacles, and the AVRE (Armoured Vehicle, Royal Engineers) which carried a 7.5in mortar firing an enormous explosive bomb over short ranges against strongpoints.

The Duplex Drive tank took its name from the propellors which drove it through water, the name concealing the important fact that it swam. Buoyancy was given by means of a flexible screen which extended upwards from the hull and was locked in the vertical position by struts. When swimming the screen was about a foot above the water level and the propellors, driven from the tank engine, gave it a speed of about four knots. On arriving on shore the struts were broken by explosive charges and the screen collapsed, leaving the turret free to fire in any direction. Although other designs were used during development, all service DD tanks were American M4 Shermans.

Duplex Drive tank
The Sherman Duplex Drive tank, showing the screen lowered prior to launching. This particular tank is probably an experimental model, since it has a protective plate across the suspension, something never seen in service. Once in the water the driver was blind (right), and the tank was steered by the commander, standing on the turret and operating a simple tiller connected to the rudder and propellors.

explosives. It drove up to the wall, then, by hydraulic arms, lifted the framework and placed it upright, in contact with the wall. The tank then backed away and fired the explosive by electric cable, blowing a hole in the wall through which subsequent tanks could drive.

These various machines were for dealing with inanimate obstacles; but sooner or later there would be an obstacle containing men and guns, and they would have been built with the intention of resisting the usual sort of projectiles fired by tanks. Moreover, there might be obstacles such as walls or concrete structures incapable of being overcome by the ARK or fascine, perhaps protected by gunfire so that 'Goat' could not get close enough. For all these contingencies, a tank carrying a very powerful demolition weapon was required, and this led to some very odd suggestions.

Perhaps the most fearsome was 'Conkernut', a tank festooned with rockets carrying powerful explosive warheads which it would fire at any obstacle. The idea

The flail tank (left) was first developed in the desert but was used more in Europe after the invasion. The Sherman tank carried a rotating drum at the front, with free lengths of chain. This was revolved at high speed by a truck engine, and the chains were kept at the correct height automatically. As they lashed the ground, so they would set off any mines, well ahead of the tank. The fascine tank (below) carried a bundle of wooden stakes bound with wire and held by a quick-release. The difficulty was steering it, particularly under fire, when the driver could barely see beneath the bundle and the commander could not see over the top. Once in position the fascine was released, to drop into the ditch, the tank being free to use its gun from then on.

The Fascine tank

The Churchill Fascine tank was really a revival of one of the earliest tank tactics, since tanks carried bundles of wood in 1916 to fill in trenches and ease their crossing. Preparation of the fascines required machinery in order to compress the bundle so that it would not contract further under the weight of the tank once it was in position, and a fascine which burst on being dropped was a dangerous device.

was tried and then turned down, partly because a single rocket could not guarantee efficient demolition, and a subsequent rocket could not guarantee to land in the same hole to improve matters, and partly because it was felt unwise to drive into hostile fire inside a metal box encased in high explosive.

The weapon eventually selected was the 'Mortar, Recoiling Spigot', or 'Petard', a short-range launcher which fired a 40lb high explosive bomb to a distance of about 75 yards. The heavy frontal protection of the

THE CROCODILE FLAME-THROWING TANK DEMONSTRATING ITS ABILITY. THIS WAS A MODIFIED CHURCHILL TANK WITH THE FLAME GUN MOUNTED IN THE HULL FRONT, AND WITH AN ARMORED TRAILER CARRYING THE FLAME FLUID. ONCE THE FLUID WAS SPENT, THE TRAILER COULD BE SEPARATED BY AN EXPLOSIVE CHARGE AND JETTISONED, AFTER WHICH THE TANK COULD OPERATE WITH ITS GUN IN A NORMAL ROLE.

Churchill tank meant that it was usually possible to get within that range before firing, and very few obstacles withstood the impact of the 'Flying Dustbin' as the troops called the bomb.

The final specialized tank was the Churchill 'Crocodile' which carried a flamethrower in the hull, alongside the driver. The fuel, a thickened gasoline mixture, and the nitrogen which provided the pressure to eject the fuel, were carried in an armored trailer behind the tank, feeding through armored pipes, and the connection between the tank and the trailer was via an explosive link. The flamethrower had a range of about 100 yards and a duration of 80 seconds, usually fired in short bursts. Once the fluid had been exhausted, or if the trailer was damaged, the explosive link was fired, severing the connection.

The armor was thus arranged; the infantry were practised and repractised at leaving their landing craft and dashing up beaches. The air support was arranged.

AN AMERICAN AIRBORNE OFFICER BOARDS HIS AIRCRAFT ON THE EVE OF D-DAY. ARMED WITH A THOMSON SUBMACHINE GUN AND PROBABLY CARRYING A PISTOL AND DAGGER AS WELL, HE WEARS TWO PARACHUTES AND CARRIES AN ENORMOUS BURDEN OF EQUIPMENT WHICH WILL DOUBTLESS HELP HIS DROPPING SPEED.

What remained now was to ensure adequate gunfire on the beaches prior to the actual landing, so that the defenders were either disposed of or at least kept their heads down and their fingers away from firearms until the first waves were ashore, and then to ensure an adequate supply system to keep the invasion force well provided with ammunition, food, fuel and all the thousand-and-one other things which they thought they needed.

Gunfire support was provided by the Royal Navy and US Navy, who mustered as many gun-bearing warships as they could and then practised naval and army officers in the technique of spotting and calling for gunfire support. In addition, special craft were provided to thicken up the fire. The 'Landing Craft, Rocket' was a landing craft modified by the bolting-on of a steel launcher frame so that it could discharge 1098 rockets with 5in explosive warheads in a series of 'ripples' or volleys. The backblast of the rockets being launched was thought likely to be detrimental to the structure of the craft, and arrangements had to be made to flood the decks with water prior to firing to avoid accidental ignition of the ship. Other landing craft,

detailed to ferry artillery ashore, were loaded so that the field guns could be fired from the ship towards the shore during the run-in, adding to the mass of explosive landing on the beaches, though, to be honest, the accuracy to be expected from this arrangement was not of a high order.

Some tank landing craft, which were taking Royal Marine 'Centaur' tanks armed with 95mm howitzers, were loaded so that the tanks could fire their guns against targets which they might spot on the beaches during their run in. Altogether, anything which could float and shoot at the same time was expected to do just that; even if its precision was suspect, the weight of explosive added up to a fearsome bombardment, and every little helped.

In the absence of a suitable harbor capable of receiving freight, the only prospect in view was to supply the invasion force across the beaches it captured, a somewhat daunting prospect at the best of times and one which could only be viewed with dismay in the circumstances of an invasion. This would involve transporting supplies by seagoing ships to the coast of Normandy, then transferring them to lighters which could move closer inshore, and then perhaps even transferring them once more to amphibious trucks which could actually get the loads on to the beach. Such a performance would be considered difficult in smooth water and in peacetime, but in the usually choppy English Channel and with the prospect of interruptions from the enemy, it was obvious that such a system would be slow and inefficient.

Churchill, in a now-famous memorandum, had suggested 'piers which float up and down with the tide'. From this suggestion grew the 'Mulberry Harbour' project. Two complete harbor installations were constructed in Britain, consisting of 'Bombardon' breakwater units, 'Caissons' — massive concrete structures weighing up to 6000 tons to form the outer breakwaters, floating piers and pierheads and floating roadways to connect the piers with the land. Each harbor enclosed an area of about two square miles and was capable of handling tens of thousands of tons of stores daily. One was to supply the British at Arromanches, the other to supply the US forces at St Laurent. The harbors were built, and most of the components then towed out from their construction sites and sunk in the coastal waters around Britain so that they would be invisible.

The landing

As finally planned, the landing would be spread across five beaches. On the Allied right flank — the western end of the invasion area — the 4th Infantry Division of 7th US Corps under Lt-Gen Lawton Collins would assault 'Utah' beach around the village of La Madeleine. Next, moving eastward, came 'Omaha' beach near St Laurent, to be taken by the 1st Infantry Division of 5th US Corps under General Gerow. 5th and 7th Corps collectively formed the US 1st Army under General Omar N Bradley.

Moving east again, in the vicinity of Arromanches was 'Gold' beach, to be assaulted by the British 50th Infantry Division and 8th Armoured Brigade, both of XXX Corps under General Bucknall. Adjoining 'Gold' beach was 'Juno', around Courseulles, which was the target of the Canadian 3rd Infantry Division and 2nd Armoured Brigade, part of the British I Corps under General Crocker. And finally, around Ouistreham was 'Sword' beach, the objective of the British 3rd Infantry Division and 22nd Armoured Brigade, also part of I Corps. I and XXX Corps together formed the British 2nd Army under Maj-Gen Sir MC Dempsey, and the whole force — 1st US Army and 2nd British Army — formed the 21st Army Group under the command of General Montgomery.

In order to secure the flanks and certain of the exits from these beaches, the US 82nd and 101st Airborne Divisions were to land by parachute ahead of the seaborne invasion in the hinterland behind Utah Beach. Similarly, the British 6th Airborne Division were to land east of the River Orne, to the flank of Sword Beach, in order to secure the crossings over the Orne River and the Caen Canal.

All this was to take place on the night of 4/5 June, with the actual landings on the beaches scheduled for an H-Hour which began with 0630hrs on Utah Beach and then, due to tidal variations, varied to 0730 at the other end of the invasion area. But the weather at the beginning of June saw the highest winds and roughest seas experienced in the Channel for 20 years, and the

ABOVE: A SIX-POUNDER (57MM) ANTI-TANK GUN AND ITS TOWING JEEP ABOUT TO LEAVE A DROPPING ZONE. THE 57MM GUN, ALTHOUGH SMALL, FIRED POWERFUL AND ADVANCED ANTI-ARMOR PROJECTILES WHICH COULD DEFEAT EVEN THE TIGER TANK AT MODERATE RANGES AND WHICH PROVIDED FORMIDABLE ANTI-TANK DEFENSE FOR AIRBORNE FORCES. THE JEEP WAS, OF COURSE, THE UNIVERSAL WORK-HORSE.
LEFT: AN AERIAL VIEW OF ONE OF THE LANDING ZONES CLOSE TO THE ORNE CROSSINGS, ILLUSTRATING THE SKILL OF THE GLIDER PILOT REGIMENT IN LANDING CLOSE TOGETHER. NOTICE THAT SOME GLIDERS HAVE OVERSHOT THE MEADOWLAND AND SHED THEIR WINGS WHEN PASSING THROUGH THE BELT OF TREES, AND THAT OTHERS HAVE HAD THEIR REAR SECTIONS REMOVED TO GIVE RAPID ACCESS TO THE CONTENTS.

TWO TITANS OF D-DAY

General Dwight D Eisenhower (1890–1969)

For the first fifty years of his life, Eisenhower's career was the epitome of peace-time soldiering, slow promotion in spite of good performance. After that it took off in a meteoric rise which has never been paralleled in this century, and within two years he had progressed from an unknown lieutenant-colonel to command of the largest invasion force the world has ever seen. His forte was administration, not field command, and he had the gifts of delegation, of tact, and of the ability to weld officers of widely divergent nationalities and personalities into a working organization. Soft-spoken and with immense personal charm, he could, nevertheless, impose discipline with an iron hand when it became necessary.

Eisenhower graduated from West Point in 1915, in the same class as Bradley and Marshall and entered the infantry. In 1918 he trained the first members of the US Tank Corps and by 1920 was a major, a rank he was to remain in for the next 16 years. Between the wars he attended the Command & Staff College, the War College and the Army

Industrial College. In 1933 he became an aide to MacArthur and from 1935 to 1939 was his assistant military advisor in the Philippines. A lieut-colonel by this time, he returned to the USA in 1939 to become Chief of Staff to 3rd Army, and in this capacity came to the notice of Gen Marshall during the 1941 Louisiana Maneuvers. In February 1942 he was named Chief of War Plans Division on Marshall's staff and then Chief of Operations Division. His rise had begun.

In July 1942 he went to England to assume command of all US Forces in Europe, a post which demanded all his tact and administrative skill. In November, promoted to Lt-General, he commanded the US Forces in North Africa; this gave him his first experience of a field command. In January 1944 he was named as Supreme Commander of the Allied Expeditionary Force for the invasion of Europe, a task which was to demand every scrap of his good humor, tact, diplomacy and considerable ability.

Once the invasion was launched, Eisenhower retreated into the background while his army commanders conducted the campaign, but

GENERAL EISENHOWER GIVES A FINAL PEP-TALK TO MEN OF THE 82ND AIRBORNE DIVISION BEFORE TAKING OFF.

nevertheless his was the guidance as to the strategic method. In this he clashed with Montgomery; Eisenhower advocated a broad advance against Germany, whilst Montgomery advocated a narrow thrust. There were good political reasons for the former idea, good military ones for the latter, but in view of the skill which the German Army showed in the Ardennes campaign, it is likely that Montgomery's idea would have failed.

After the German surrender Eisenhower remained in Germany to command the US occupation force but returned to the US to become Chief of Staff in November 1945. He retired in 1948 but returned in 1951 to become Supreme Commander, Allied

Powers Europe. After a year he retired once more to campaign for the Presidency of the USA, which he achieved on the Republican ticket with the greatest majority in US history. After a series of heart attacks he died on 28 March 1969.

Field-Marshal Sir Bernard Law Montgomery (1887–1976)

Opinionated, self-assured, a rigid disciplinarian, a non-smoker and teetotaller, with a sense of the theatrical, for all that, Montgomery deserves his place as one of the outstanding commanders of the Second World War and one of the greatest British generals of history. He never suffered fools for one second longer than necessary, never hesitated to fire an incompetent commander, but was revered by the common soldiers as the man who won battles, and after the long British run of ill-

commanders began to have their doubts about the viability of a landing in such conditions. The principal problem was that some elements of the invasion force were coming from widely-scattered points around the British Isles and were thus beginning their move several days before the actual landings, so that any change in timing could have far-reaching consequences. Moreover it was not possible to postpone the landings on a day-to-day basis past 7 June, since after that date the naval bombardment forces would have to put back to

port to refuel and the tidal conditions would thereafter be wrong for some three weeks.

General Eisenhower kept a careful eye on the weather, while his meteorological experts did everything they could to divine the future. On the morning of 4 June, Eisenhower postponed for 24 hours; on the morning of the 5th the weather showed no sign of improvement, but the forecast for the 6th expressed a hope that things would get better, an interval of fair conditions being indicated. At 0400hrs on 4 June, fortune in 1939−42 this was the thing which counted. He has often been denigrated as 'never willing to take a chance', but the other side of the coin is that he was a firmly orthodox soldier who was not seduced by get-rich-quick schemes of warfare and who never committed his troops to battle without weighing all the options and making sure he had all the men and equipment he thought necessary to win.

Montgomery came from an Anglo-Irish family, attended the Royal Military Academy, and was commissioned into the Royal Warwickshire Regiment in which he served with distinction during the First World War. After various staff appointments he commanded the 1st Bn of his regiment in 1938−39 and on the outbreak of war took the 3rd Division to France. He commanded it skilfully during the collapse of France and the withdrawal through Dunkirk, and on returning to England received command of 5th Corps. Here he built on an existing reputation as a high-quality trainer of troops with his insistence on physical fitness and sound tactical training.

He was marked down to be Eisenhower's deputy for the North African landings, but on the death in an air crash of General Gott, commander-designate of the 8th Army, Montgomery was sent to Egypt to assume his place. He revitalized the Desert Armies, discarded most of the eccentric quasi-organizations which had fragmented the force and sapped morale, reinstated the correct formal organizations, and proceeded to fight the Battle of El Alamein and eject the German Army from Egypt. He then pursued Rommel for the length of Africa and eventually, in conjunction with Eisenhower's forces in Tunisia, completed the clearance of that continent.

He commanded the 8th Army in Sicily and Italy with distinction but was then returned to England to take command of 21st Army Group, the land forces involved in the invasion of Europe. He immediately imposed his views on the planners, to the benefit of the eventual plan, and also made sure that the invasion troops were trained to the standard he felt was desirable. Once ashore he conducted a skilful campaign designed to draw the German armored strength on to the northern sector while the American element made their breakout in the south, a plan which worked admirably.

In August the US 12th Army Group was formed, after which Montgomery was responsible only for the British and Commonwealth forces in the Armies of Liberation. After crossing France and arriving close to the German border the Allied troops were brought to a halt by supply problems; here Montgomery sowed the first seeds of dissent by proposing, with Bradley, a single thrust into Germany. Unfortunately neither commander would agree to be subordinate to the other, and Eisenhower resolved the deadlock by assuming overall command on the ground and maintaining his theory of a broad front thrust. This left Montgomery free to go north through Belgium and Holland in an attempt to outflank Germany, but this plan was severely curtailed by the failure of the airborne attack on Arnhem — possibly the only operation of Montgomery's which failed, and that failure was principally due to elements of command which were in Britain and outside his control.

Montgomery's next testing time came with the German attack in the Ardennes. The spearhead of 8 Panzer divisions split the allied front in two, and Eisenhower placed all the forces north of the split — which included large US elements — under Montgomery. This was an obvious command move, but Montgomery's somewhat acid remarks about US competence did little to endear him to the Americans.

After the Ardennes, 21st Army Group advanced into Germany fighting a text-book series of set-piece battles, until Montgomery finally sat down in a tent on the Luneberg Heath on 8 May, 1945 and accepted the surrender of all the German forces in the West.

In postwar years he became Chief of the Imperial General Staff and Deputy Commander to

GENERAL MONTGOMERY GIVING ORDERS AT PORT-EN-BESSIN, SHORTLY AFTER LANDING ON D-DAY.

Allied Forces Europe; in the former role he made considerable improvements in the living conditions of the soldiers of the British Army, for which he was universally respected, and in the latter post he was a strong protagonist of European self-defense.

Eisenhower took the final and irrevocable decision; D-Day would be 6 June.

As events were to prove, the decision to launch the assault caught the German defenders by surprise, since they were quite sure that no invasion could be mounted in such weather conditions, and their weather service, hampered by the lack of Atlantic Ocean reports, did not foresee the brief improvement.

Shortly after midnight on 6 June the bombing of targets in the invasion area began, and 1136 aircraft of RAF Bomber Command dropped 5853 tons of bombs on ten selected coast defense batteries lining the Bay of the Seine. As dawn broke bombers of the US 8th Air Force took up the task, with 1083 aircraft dropping 1763 tons of bombs on the shore defenses during the half-hour prior to the landings. As they flew away so medium, light and fighter bombers swarmed in at low level to attack individual targets along the coastline and artillery locations further inland.

After the landings, the air forces would continue

AN AMERICAN WACO GLIDER AFTER LANDING, WITH THE TAIL
REMOVED AND TWO SKIDS WHICH HAVE BEEN USED TO DEMOUNT
SOME WHEELED EQUIPMENT, PROBABLY EITHER A 57MM ANTI-
TANK GUN OR A 75MM PACK HOWITZER, BOTH OF WHICH PROVIDED
USEFUL SHORT-RANGE SUPPORT FOR LIGHT WEIGHT.

their efforts, directing their bombing attacks against
communications centers behind the German lines,
while fighter-bombers roamed over the whole area
attacking everything German which offered itself. In
all, during 6 June, the Strategic Air Forces flew 5309
sorties to drop 10,395 tons of bombs, while the Tactical
Air Forces flew another 5276 sorties.

Four and a half hours before H-Hour, the airborne
flank guards began dropping into place. A total of 1662
aircraft and 512 gliders of US 9th Troop Carrier
Command, and 733 aircraft and 355 gliders of 38 and 46
Groups RAF moved the three airborne divisions and
their equipment. The British 6th Airborne Division
were guided by a first drop of 60 'Pathfinder' paratroops carrying radio beacons to guide the following
waves. Many of these men were blown from their
appointed targets by the high winds, but a sufficient
number gained their appointed places to be able to
bring the remainder of the division into the correct
areas. A flight of six gliders with Oxford & Bucking-
hamshire Light Infantry and Royal Engineers crash-
landed yards from their objective, overwhelmed enemy
sentries and secured the vital river and canal crossings.

The parachutists, however, had a less easy task since
the entire area of their drop was garrisoned by two
German infantry divisions, and every village had its
defenders. Most of the troops were in action within
minutes of landing as short and bitter engagements
were fought out between handfuls of men. Eventually
most were able to link up with their companions and
rendezvous at their appointed locations. 7th Battalion
The Parachute Regiment collected at Ranville and then
moved to reinforce the bridgeheads and by 0230 were
fighting furiously on both banks of the River Orne
against German infantry and armor. Their job was to
beat off all opposition and keep the bridges open until
relieved by troops moving up from the beach.

The 3rd Parachute Brigade, faced with a number of
tasks to the east of Caen, were badly dropped. Smoke

and dust from the bombing of a coastal battery at
Merville, at the seaward end of their area, obscured
many of their dropping zones, and the pilots of the aircraft carrying them had insufficient training in their
role. The drop was consequently widely scattered,
many men falling into marshland. The principal task of
this force was the reduction of the powerful Merville
Battery of 15cm guns; this had been previously bombed
but aerial photographs showed that the bombs failed to
pierce the immensely thick concrete protection. It was
therefore felt advisable to make an infantry assault
rather than rely upon bombardment by naval guns.

A force of 1000 heavy bombers unloaded a torrent of
bombs on the battery shortly after midnight — it was
this which caused the 'fog of war' to descend on the
dropping zones — but none of the bombs hit the target.
The Battalion assigned to take Merville were scattered
to the four winds when they dropped, but within a short
time the Battalion Commander had mustered 150 men,
a medium machine gun and some demolition explosives
and set out for the battery. The party split into groups,
made their assault silently, and by 0500 the battery was
in British hands, though at the cost of almost half the
attacking strength.

On the western flank, the 101st Airborne Division
was scattered over an area since estimated at 25 miles in
length and 15 miles wide, and with some small parties
broadcast even further afield. By dawn its organized
strength was some 1100 men instead of the 6600 who
had dropped. 82nd Airborne Division were equally dispersed, only one regiment landing on its allotted zone;
of the remainder of the division only 4 percent were in
the right places. The reason for this violent dispersal
was simply that wind, cloud and anti-aircraft fire all
conspired to drive aircraft from their computed
courses. Navigators simply hoped they were in the right
place at the right time when they gave the signal to
jump, but of the men who jumped relatively few were
able to recognize where they were once on the ground.
The only saving feature of this chaotic affair was that
the Germans could discern no coherent pattern and
could, therefore, take no coherent counter-action until
it was too late.

Typical of the element of chance which reigned was
the ambush of the commander of the German 91st
Division by a scratch party of American parachutists.
They saw a German vehicle approaching, and working
on the policy that anything German was a target, duly
shot it up. As luck would have it, the 91st Division was
the one German division in the area which had been
trained and prepared to deal with airborne attacks, and
was almost the sole mobile reserve in the Utah Beach
area. Thus deprived of its commander at the com-
mencement of the action, the Division was unable to
react to events until far too late.

The first landings from the sea took place on Utah
Beach, where the 8th US Infantry Regiment had the
honor of being the first to hit the beach, 20 landing craft
carrying 600 men in the first wave. Behind them came

the second and subsequent waves, timed to arrive at intervals of a few minutes, calculated to be sufficient to permit the previous wave to have cleared the landing area. Their orders were brief to the point of simplicity: '7 Corps assaults Utah Beach on D-Day at H-Hour and captures Cherbourg with minimum delay.'

As the landing craft made their way across the choppy sea, 276 US aircraft roared overhead to dump over 4000 bombs on the beach defenses, while Landing Craft Rocket launched their noisy salvoes and US warships bombarded with guns of every caliber. Alongside the 20 landing craft swam 28 'Duplex Drive' Sherman tanks, and a swarm of supporting craft fired machine guns, and artillery at the beach, some of it at specific targets, most of them simply 'browning' the area as a morale-booster. Then, as the landing craft closed with the beach, smoke signals stopped the supporting fires, and the ramps went down, the men ran out into the water and towards the pall of smoke and dust which hid the beach from their view. As they splashed through the surf, so the swimming tanks came from the water alongside them, blew off their flotation gear and prepared for their fighting role.

In fact, due to currents and winds, the entire landing was a mile south of the allotted target; the fire from German strongpoints was officially described as 'desultory', and within two hours the leading troops were clear of the beach and headed inland. By 1000 six more battalions had landed without incident and were moving off the beach, by midday three columns were making their way to securing the beach exits, cursing as they waded through flooded areas but suffering nothing more than wetness and inconvenience on their way to link up with the 82nd and 101st Airborne. At the end of D-Day the two infantry regiments who had taken Utah Beach had suffered no more than 12 dead, a scarcely believable figure.

The losses on Omaha

Omaha Beach was a far different story. Across the wide mouth of the Vire and Douve rivers from Utah Beach, some eight miles away, Omaha Beach was pounded by rough surf, and because the landing craft and amphibious tanks were launched far too far out, the losses were enormous even before the landings began.

AMERICAN TROOPS PACK A LANDING CRAFT ON THE RUN-IN TO UTAH BEACH. THE SMOKE ON THE SHORE IS FROM NAVAL GUNFIRE SUPPORT AND APPEARS TO BE THE START OF A SMOKESCREEN TO CONCEAL THE ACTUAL TOUCH-DOWN. NOTE THE TANK ON THE SHORE, PREPARED FOR WADING.

The infantry were shipped into their landing craft no less than 12 miles from the beach, while the commander of the tank landing craft ordered his 32 tanks into rough seas some 6000 yards from the beach. Within minutes 27 tanks were swamped and sank with their crews. Of the remainder, three were unable to launch because of a jam in the ramp, and two, by a combination of brilliant handling and pure luck, actually reached the shore.

The infantry, packed into their frail flat-bottomed craft, bounced and tossed on the waves, were soon seasick, but had to put aside discomfort in order to save themselves as the seas swept over the sides and threatened to swamp them. Bailing furiously with their helmets, they crouched, soaked and cold, as the boats crept towards the shore. Equally disastrous was an attempt to ferry supporting artillery ashore loaded into DUKWs, two-and-a-half ton amphibious trucks. These fair-weather vehicles rapidly sank in the mountainous seas, and three battalions of field artillery together with their 105mm howitzers were dumped into the sea. Under a protecting umbrella of air attacks and naval gunfire the remnants of the invading force closed with the beach, but as they were still half a mile from land all the covering fire stopped. And with scarcely a pause the German defensive fires broke on them as a storm of

AMERICAN PARATROOPS AROUND THE CHURCHYARD IN ST MARCOUF, INLAND FROM UTAH BEACH, ON 8 JUNE. THESE WERE ELEMENTS OF THE AIR DROP EXPANDING TOWARDS THE BEACH TO LINK UP WITH THE SEA-LANDED FORCES.

shells, mortar bombs and bullets began to zero in on the approaching boats. Unknown to the planners, the area had recently been reinforced by the addition of the German 352nd Infantry Division. The aerial attacks had largely been ineffective, and the naval guns were hampered by the configuration of the ground which made observation difficult.

As the exhausted, cold, wet and disorganized troops spilled from their landing craft into the water — for none of the craft reached the beach — they were greeted by a storm of accurate fire, and it was a handful of dazed and dispirited men who finally reached the beach and were able to take shelter in the sand dunes. Half an hour after the landings began some 1000 men were ashore, but they were not fighting the Germans, they were merely concerned with staying alive; weary and exhausted after their nightmare voyage, they almost all needed a respite before they would be in any shape to act as combat troops. What was worse was that many men who had been detailed off for specific tasks — the reduction of this strongpoint, the destruction of that obstacle, the securing of the other feature — were nowhere near their assigned places and therefore were initially at a loss as to what they ought to be doing.

In spite of this confusion, the succeeding waves of men, tanks and engineer equipment began to arrive approximately on schedule, each coming under intense fire as it did so, and within a couple of hours the beach was choked with burning vehicles, wrecked landing craft and wounded and dead men. No exit from the beach had yet been achieved, and the constant inflow of reinforcements threatened to swamp the available ground.

Eventually, as the men on the beach began to assess their situation, as officers began to round up squads and impress their leadership, as engineers began to collect equipment and begin breaching wire and blowing mines, a slow movement began. Exits were blown and fought open, and by afternoon men began moving off the beach. Only 100 tons of the scheduled 24,500 tons of essential supplies managed to land unscathed, but even so, by salvaging what they could from the wreckage on the beach the forward troops were kept supplied and they began to build up momentum. The hard skin of the German defenses yielded, and there were no reserves; once Omaha was left behind it could only get better.

Specialized armor helps out

It will have been noted that there has been as yet no mention of the specialized armored vehicles in the account of Omaha and Utah beaches, other than the few DD tanks. These vehicles had been offered to the Americans by the British, but apart from the DD tanks they were turned down as being unnecessary. By contrast, the British assaulting Gold Beach, ten miles east of Omaha, were led by specialized armor operated by the Westminster Dragoons and the Royal Engineers.

THE BEACHES BECAME A FOCAL POINT FOR AMERICAN
COMMANDERS WORRYING ABOUT THEIR SUPPLY PROBLEMS AND
DISCUSSING THEM WITH THEIR NAVAL COUNTERPARTS. HERE
REAR-ADMIRAL ALAN G KIRK (IN OBVIOUSLY NAVAL UNIFORM),
REAR-ADMIRAL JOHN HALL (CENTER, IN WHAT WOULD PASS FOR A
MILITARY OUTFIT EXCEPT FOR HIS SEA-WETTED TROUSERS) AND
LT-GENERAL OMAR N BRADLEY ARE DISCUSSING PROGRESS ON
UTAH BEACH.

On the far right flank, beyond the arc of fire of the
strongpoints of Le Hamel, it was soon apparent that the
preliminary bombardment had done little to disturb
some of the defensive measures, since only one of the
flail tanks survived the beach minefield and managed to
reach the farther side of the sand. On the left flank,
though, flails performed precisely as promised, clearing
paths through the mines, while Carpet Layers followed
them laying their neat tracks along the cleared strips.
ARKs and fascine tanks followed up, bridging and
filling gaps, craters and ditches as they went. The DD
tanks, due to the bad sea conditions, were brought
inshore and launched directly on to the beach, and
within an hour of the first landings the tanks had swept
the beaches clear, opened four safe paths through the
obstacles and minefields, and delivered the infantry of
the 231st Brigade safely on to their objectives, the
strongpoints which might have threatened them having
been neutralized by Petard tanks. Another hour and
both armor and infantry were well inland.

But within the area commanded by the German
defenses at Le Hamel, the fight was bitter. The Hamp-
shire Regiment, landing here, ran into intense fire
which severely damaged their accompanying armor and
pinned them to the ground. Eventually they were able to
move around and outflank some of the defenses, then
bring up Petard tanks to pound them at short range, but
it was not until the afternoon that they could claim to be
in control of their area and were able to turn their attention to moving away from the beach.

Juno Beach adjoined Sword, and was the responsibility of the Canadians. By the time they landed the rising
tide had reduced the beach to a strip no more than 100
yards deep, and without waiting for their DD tanks to
arrive (most of them, like the Sword Beach tanks,
decided to land dryshod rather than risk swimming in
the choppy water) the infantry of the Royal Winnepeg
Regiment and the Regina Rifles, the Queen's Own
Regiment of Canada and the North Shore Regiment
charged for the sea wall. They suffered casualties from
machine gun fire during this short dash but their
initiative 'bounced' the German defenders out of their
forward positions in a matter of minutes. Flail tanks
and the rest of the specialized armor followed up and
most of the planned exits were opened by 0930 and by
afternoon the leading Canadian elements were well
inland.

On the extreme left flank lay Sword Beach, and the
assault on this did not begin until an hour after the
Americans had struck at Utah and some six hours after
the 6th Airborne had landed, so that there was little

TOP: A VIEW OF ONE OF THE BEACHES TOWARDS THE END OF THE DAY, WITH A STREAM OF TRANSPORT LANDING UNDER THE PROTECTION OF BARRAGE BALLOONS.
ABOVE: BRITISH TROOPS IN LA BRECHE, HAVING JUST LEFT SWORD BEACH ON D-DAY. THE LEFT-HAND VEHICLE IS THE CHURCHILL AVRE, MOUNTING A LARGE-CALIBER MORTAR FOR FIRING DEMOLITION CHARGES AGAINST STRONGPOINTS. ONE WONDERS ABOUT THE THOUGHTS OF THE MAN WHO WAS DETAILED OFF TO LAND ON D-DAY WITH A BICYCLE.

hope or expectation that the Germans were going to be surprised. Indeed the armada which assembled off the beach was in some danger from the coastal batteries around Le Havre, and a flotilla of torpedo-boats essayed an attack from there, to be beaten off after managing to torpedo a Norwegian destroyer.

In spite of the preliminary air attacks and naval gunfire, the defensive fires from the strongpoints around the beach were intense, added to which the onshore wind piled up the high tide and swept many landing craft onto underwater obstacles during the run-in. The DD tanks of the 13/18th Hussars, launched 3 miles out, had a hazardous swim, but by the time they reached the beach the initial landing craft had beached and landed the flails, ARKs and the remainder of the specialized armor. Led by the South Lancashire Regiment, the infantry dashed from their landing craft to creep behind the tanks and up the beach in a storm of shot and shell which left burning landing craft and wrecked tanks along the high-water mark. On their left the East Yorkshire Regiment struggled up the beach and finally gained a foothold clear of the sand and shingle.

By 0930 the armor had cleared seven lanes through

the obstacles and the advance divided, some troops heading for the Caen Canal to relieve the airborne and Commando troops there, others leading the advance towards Caen itself. But a spirited German defense from the commanding Periers Ridge soon stopped the advance in its tracks and the infantry began to dig in around Hermanville.

This small town became a roadblock as the narrow streets were jammed with armor and men, vehicles and supplies; instead of waiting for their accompanying armor, the King's Shropshire Light Infantry elected to advance on their own, but by late afternoon the tanks and self-propelled artillery of the Staffordshire Yeomanry had caught up with them on the road to Caen. Which was just as well, since shortly afterwards they were struck by the first of the German counter-attacks which had been expected all day. Elements of 21 Panzer Division, rushing out from Caen to throw the invaders back into the sea, met the KSLI head-on; the Yeomanry accounted for five of the leading Panzers, whereupon the Germans pulled back into a defensive position on the Lebisey Ridge, against which the KSLI threw themselves in vain.

As the day drew to its close the Germans began to emerge from the cloud of indecision and misinformation which had enveloped them. Thanks to the devastating air attacks behind the invasion area, the dis-location of communications, the blinding of radar, the total Allied air superiority, reports to German head-quarters had been fragmentary and confined to what excited and often panic-stricken men had seen with their own eyes — or thought they had seen — with the result that the 'big picture' totally eluded them.

Although the defenders on each of the invasion beaches had fought resolutely, the absence of an overall view meant that decisions about the movement of reserves were slow in being taken; moreover, due to the centralization of German command functions, every-thing had to be reported back to higher command and up to the Fuhrer himself, far away at his command bunker in East Prussia, before major moves could be made. As a result the I Panzer Corps, west of the Seine, was inviolate, and Rommel was unable to obtain per-mission to move 12 Panzer and the Panzer Lehr Division to contain the American attacks in the West. The only counter-attack force within the area, 21 Panzer was slow in moving off due to lack of com-munication and a total lack of understanding of where the major threat lay. It was not, as we have seen, until late in the afternoon that it finally moved, though when it did so its intervention was decisive and undoubtedly stopped the British from occupying Caen. Moreover, tying 21 Panzer down in front of the British in this way — for, once engaged it could not be disengaged

HITLER'S GENERAL IN FRANCE

Field-Marshal Karl Rudolf Gerd von Rundstedt (1875–1953)

Von Rundstedt has been described as 'the last of the old school of Prussian generals', and although he was in his sixties when the Second World War began, he proved to be as aggressive and adept as any younger commander and skilful in his handling of armored formations.

Born into an aristocratic family near Magdeburg, he became an officer in the Imperial Army and by 1914 was Chief of Staff to an Army Corps. After service on both fronts, he went to Turkey with a military mission which reorganized the Turkish Army. In the inter-war years he was active in developing the highly professional army and was concerned in much of its clandestine rearmament. In October 1938, having reached the age of 63, he retired, somewhat disillusioned about the way the Army was going in the wake of the Fritsch-Blomberg scandals.

During the preparations for war he was recalled to duty and given command of Army Group A for the invasion of Poland. He retained this command for the invasion of France in 1940 and it was his Army Group which broke the French line at Sedan and cut off the British force. In 1941 he was given command of Army Group South for the Russian invasion, attacking the Ukraine. In November he requested permission from Hitler to make a tactical withdrawal of relatively minor importance; upon being refused he relinquished his command.

Reinstated to command in 1942 he was appointed C-in-C West and given the responsibility for the defense of France and the Low Countries. Here he argued with Rommel over the disposition of armored reserves; Rommel wanted them close to the coast where they could be thrown against a landing with minimum delay, while Rundstedt wanted them held back until the shape of the invasion and its objectives were made clear.

Upon the invasion taking place, Rundstedt made a correct appreciation of his position and advocated disengagement and withdrawal to a defensive line on the east of the Seine, in order to save attritional losses. Had he done so, this would have changed the face of the Allied advance in Europe, but, as usual, Hitler refused to countenance giving-up ground, and Rundstedt was replaced by von Kluge in July 1944.

Von Kluge, in turn, fell foul of Hitler and in September Rundstedt was re-appointed C-in-C West, in time to supervise the German withdrawal from France. He directed the Ardennes Offensive in December 1944, though he neither planned it nor took any direct hand in its execution and, indeed, felt it had little chance of success. Upon its failure, he was replaced by Kesselring and finally retired from active military service. Captured by US troops in 1945 he was imprisoned but soon released due to his ill-health. He died in Hanover on 24 February 1953.

without opening the Caen road — prevented it from being used against other areas where it might have been more profitable; against, for example, the tenuous hold of the 6th Airborne Division of the crossings over the Orne.

By the end of the day, therefore, the picture for the Allies was heartening. The British and Canadians firmly held a deep strip of Normandy on the left flank and were attracting most of the German resistance, while away·on the right the Americans were breaking free of the coast and making ready to exploit the lack of resistance in a drive across the Cotentin Peninsula. On the flanks and in the gaps between the beaches, Commandos, Rangers and Airborne troops held on to their gains. On Omaha beach the front line was barely a mile from the sea, but the occupants held on grimly. And the total cost of the day to the Allies added up to 2500 men killed, 1000 of them on Omaha Beach, figures far below the worst-case estimates which many of the planners had expected.

The lessons

To speak of lessons in the context of D-day is rather misleading; lessons imply learning something for use the next time, and D-Day was a one-off. Had it failed, there would certainly have been lessons for the next attempt. In the event it succeeded, so there would be no call to repeat the performance — ever.

But lessons were undoubtedly there, and if, in the future, anyone should need to make an assault upon the shores of Europe, it is reasonable to suppose that the records of D-Day would be brought out and studied. Most of the lessons were in the higher realms of logistics and planning, dealing with such matters as how to arrange the various elements of a division, scattered among a few score of vessels of various shapes and sizes, so that they landed as a fighting entity and not as a mistimed collection of men and equipment; how to provide artillery support from warships and control it to the soldiers' benefit; how to arrange for rations, ammunition, fuel and all the minutae of the soldier's day-to-day existence to arrive in the right place and be distributed to where they were needed with the minimum delay; and how to evacuate wounded across a beach in the face of the stream of incoming men and supplies.

Many of these things had been evolved in the light of the Dieppe experience and other raids, and, of course, from consideration of the American experience in the South Pacific, and while the ordinary soldier took it all for granted, there is no doubt that the higher up the command ladder, the greater was the amount of thought which went into these things.

From the tactical point of view there were several lessons which could be applied to other types of operation. The scattering of the airborne drops drew attention to shortcomings in navigation and the vulnerability of air fleets to the vagaries of wind and weather. The American experience on Omaha Beach taught, yet again, that it is better to take advice than to sacrifice lives in order to learn one's own lesson; had they adopted specialized armor, they could have saved lives, time and effort. (This, though, is one lesson which has never stuck, many armies still being loath to accept advice from another.) British troops learned, also the hard way, that experience in one theater of war does not necessarily carry over to another theater; troops experienced in the Desert and Italy found that the German Army they met in France was a different army to those they had fought in distant fields. There was definitely something about the proximity to their homeland which gave an extra edge to German defensive maneuvers.

In addition, one of the unpalatable lessons which eventually — many years later, so far as the general public were concerned — emerged was the simple fact that the individual Allied soldier was usually inferior to his German counterpart. Whether the reason was training, discipline, indoctrination, ideology, fanaticism — whatever it was, the German had just that little bit more to pull out when the going got really rough. British and American troops, faced with a hard fight, have a tendency to go so far and then say 'That's enough, we've done our best and it didn't work; the hell with it.' Germans, on the other hand, often managed to hang on for that little extra effort which was sufficient to turn the scale in their favor, allowing them to extricate themselves from a sticky position or beat off the last Allied counter-attack. This, plus the frequent reluctance of Allied forces to pursue a fleeing enemy, giving him enough time to regroup, prepare a defensive position and get ready to do battle again, often turned what could have been a knock-out into a win on points.

On a more positive note, the Allied use of tactical air support was well heeded, and seven years later, in Korea, air support was provided using precisely the same command and control arrangements which had been perfected in Normandy and it proved vital to the operations there. Although it would be difficult to trace the thread, there is little doubt that the success of tactical air in 1944 has had its effect on air force organization and on the design and development of aircraft ever since.

But for the future strategian or tactician, the principal lessons from D-Day are to be found in the planning phase, in the organization of deception, in the 'Big Picture', rather than in the movements and operations of troops on the ground. Really, General George Patton had said it all, two years before, during arguments about the "Torch" landings in North Africa. "Never in recorded history," he said, "has the navy put the army ashore at the planned time and place. But if you manage to land me anywhere within fifty miles of Fedala and within a week of D-Day, I'll go in and win!" The secret of success in an invasion lies in putting the troops ashore at the right time and place, in a fit condition to fight; the Allied planners saw to that on 6 June 1944, and the armies took it from there.

CHAPTER EIGHT

THROUGH THE NORMANDY HEDGEROWS

INFANTRY
JUNE – JULY 1944

Overleaf

This painting shows, better than any photograph, the peculiar obstacle
which the Bocage country was to tanks. (*Advance in the Bocage* by T Cuneo, OBE)

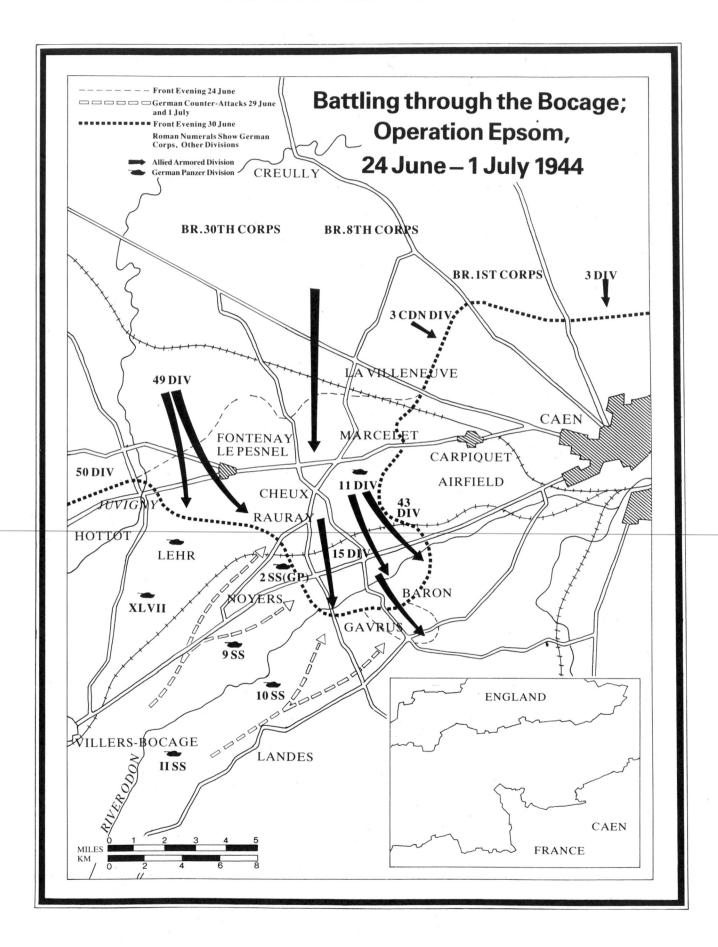

Battling through the Bocage; Operation Epsom, 24 June – 1 July 1944

Front Evening 24 June
German Counter-Attacks 29 June and 1 July
Front Evening 30 June
Roman Numerals Show German Corps, Other Divisions

Allied Armored Division
German Panzer Division

CREULLY

BR. 30TH CORPS

BR. 8TH CORPS

BR. 1ST CORPS

3 DIV

3 CDN DIV

49 DIV

LA VILLENEUVE

CAEN

FONTENAY LE PESNEL

MARCELET

CARPIQUET AIRFIELD

50 DIV

CHEUX

11 DIV

JUVIGNY

RAURAY

43 DIV

HOTTOT

LEHR

15 DIV

XLVII

2 SS(GP)

NOYERS

BARON

GAVRUS

9 SS

10 SS

VILLERS-BOCAGE

LANDES

RIVER ODON

II SS

MILES
0 1 2 3 4 5
KM
0 2 4 6 8

ENGLAND

CAEN

FRANCE

The infantry fight in every battle, as do the artillery, and the armor fights in most battles; it is therefore difficult to single out an 'infantry' battle since it is rare, in modern war, for infantry to operate alone. Operation 'Epsom' has been chosen here, because although it was fought with the assistance of armor and artillery, the ground was such that the entire thing revolved around the infantryman and his ability to make use of the terrain in which he was forced to operate.

For the Allies the war in Normandy fell into three phases, which could be paraphrased in the old military maxim of 'Find, Fix and Strike'. In the Normandy case this became firstly the invasion and lodgement (Find); then the holding and drawing-on of the German counterstroke by the British around Caen (Fix); and finally the break-out by the Americans through the weaker sectors of the German defense (Strike). It was firmly believed that the Allies would, once securely ashore, turn the *Blitzkrieg* weapon against the Germans and storm through France and into Germany behind an invincible armored spearhead. Unfortunately the Allied armor was by no means invincible, and for those who had still not learned, from the Desert campaigns, that unaccompanied armor will always find itself in trouble, there were plenty of German gunners ready to teach them. Above all, the immediate hinterland of the Normandy beaches did not lend itself to dashing tank maneuvers, as a result of which the Normandy holding phase and the early part of the break-out became primarily infantry battles in which the armor gave what assistance it could. The trouble they ran into was 'The Bocage'.

The terrain

The Bocage was the name given to an area comprising a large part of Normandy, south and west of Caen and about fifty miles deep. The northern part is perhaps more intensively cultivated and is divided into an infinity of small fields, each separated from its neighbors by an earth bank some three feet high and surmounted by a thick hedge. A very similar sort of hedge can be seen in Cornwall and parts of Devon. Due to the age of these dividing banks — they are probably two hundred or more years old — they have become consolidated, are as hard as concrete, and the hedges on top have sprouted large bushes and even trees over the years. Between the fields run roads and tracks, sunk between these embanked hedges and often with the trees and bushes arching above and almost touching. The effect, seen from the air, is of a chess-board, with thousands of hedged rectangles, some 100 to 150 yards square. There are occasional streams which break up the symmetry.

The southern part of the bocage, roughly south of a line between Caen and St Lo and stretching for a depth of about thirty miles, is the wilder and less cultivated area. Locally called *la Suisse Normande*, from its claimed resemblance to parts of Switzerland, there are forests, stretches of scrub, few roads, and some sharp but minor hills. The ground rises gently to a plateau about 350m above sea level, and the whole area is dominated by Mont Pincon, 400m high and about 18 miles southwest of Caen.

The problem raised by the bocage was twofold; firstly it was almost impossible to know where the enemy was, and secondly it was almost as impossible to know where your friends were. General Eisenhower was once moved to take a flight across the top of the area to try and orient himself; he wrote afterwards that "even from the vantage point of an altitude of several thousand feet, there was not much to see that could be classed as helpful." It was simply a sea of foliage from the air, with clear spaces in between — and nobody on the ground was going to be stupid enough to stand in one of the clear spaces; so that it became quite impossible to draw any conclusions about friendly or enemy positions.

It was just as bad from the ground, since if you peered over the bank and through the roots of the hedge (if you were lucky enough to find a clear space to see through) the odds were strong that you would find yourself eyeball-to-eyeball with an enemy doing the same thing, or, alternatively, all you would see would be the next hedge a hundred yards further on, across the next field. Once an infantry section moved off, into the sunken tracks and around the first hedgerow, it might as well have been on the moon for all its associated platoon knew about it.

One astonishing thing about the bocage is that although it had been there for centuries, it does not appear to have been appreciated for what it was by the invasion planners. So far as can be ascertained, none of the troops called upon to fight in this country had the slightest idea of its nature before arriving there. The historian of one British armored regiment noted that "it was a far cry from the Dukeries where we had trained" — the Dukeries being a part of Nottinghamshire and largely open rolling farmland — 'good tank country'. General Horrocks, who took command of XXX Corps in the middle of the bocage fighting, wrote, about the troops who had been in the desert campaign and had been brought back to England,

> ". . . they should have been removed to the depths of the country, where the terrain resembled what they might expect in Normandy, and put through some really tough training. This did not happen, and the bocage could hardly have more differed from the open desert and mountainous country of North Africa to which they were used. As a result they suffered unnecessary casualties, particularly in tank commanders, who were used to fighting with their turrets open and were easily picked off by German snipers in the thick hedgerows."

The plan

The overall plan for expanding the lodgement area and making inroads into France was, as already stated, a simple one. The British would attack in the area of Caen with the object of drawing as much of the German

AN AERIAL VIEW OF ONE OF THE MULBERRY HARBOURS, SHOWING
THE GENERAL PRINCIPLES OF OPERATION, FROM THE
BREAKWATERS TO THE FLOATING PIERS AND THE FLEXIBLE
TRACKS WHICH LED IN TO DRY LAND. OUTSIDE THE PICTURE WERE
THE MAJOR LINE OF BLOCKSHIPS AND THE ENORMOUS CONCRETE
CAISSONS WHICH FORMED THE OUTER BREAKWATER AND INSIDE
WHICH CARGO SHIPS COULD MOOR.

armored strength as possible, while the Americans would execute a 'right hook' and break out through the less defended area to the west and south. This, of course, did not mean simply sitting and waiting for the Germans while the Americans tuned up their tanks; it was necessary to keep advancing along the entire front, applying pressure at every point, making ground wherever it could be gained, since sitting and doing nothing soon takes the edge off troops and would have invited a massive German counterstroke. But since the Caen area gave access to good flat going, where armor would be able to make fast progress, it was obvious that this was the greatest threat to the Germans — provided the British made it look as if they were in earnest — and would attract their greatest strength. Moreover, although the Allies failed, at first, to appreciate the fact, the Germans were cognisant of the bocage and recognized it as being excellent country for defense, so they had little fear of an Allied tank attack in that area.

In fact, Montgomery and Bradley were turning the tables on the Germans in a rather neat manner. Guderian and his panzers had, in 1940, made an armored attack through the Ardennes, a piece of country which the Allies considered impassable to armor; now the Allies were going to work the same trick on Rommel, attacking through a piece of country which the Germans considered unsuited to armor and therefore unlikely to be the venue of a concerted attack.

So far as more detailed plans went, on 18 June Montgomery had issued a new directive: 'We must now capture Caen and Cherbourg as the first step in the development of our plans.' The British were to launch a pincer attack on both sides of Caen, while the US forces were to press westward to capture Cherbourg and southward, against the German army, wherever they could. This plan was then amended since it was obvious that the British bridgehead on the east of the Orne was too small to act as a springboard for a full attack. This arm of the pincer would therefore be a relatively minor thrust to extend the bridgehead, while the major effort would go south of Caen. This would be carried out by the VIII Corps, which had now landed in Normandy, with support from XXX Corps, and would begin on 22 June.

But now the weather, which had been giving rise to anxiety ever since the landings, took a turn for the worse. The assembly of the artificial harbors had been slowed due to the choppy seas and wind, and the landing of supplies across the beaches had been well below the forecast figures for the same reasons. During the night of 18/19 June winds sprang up, and by the afternoon were blowing at speeds over 30 knots, and raising six to eight foot waves. It was forty years since such a storm had appeared in the English Channel in June, and with the wind gradually increasing to gale force, it took three days to blow itself out.

The effect on the invasion beachhead was disastrous. The artificial harbors were tossed and wracked, moorings ripped up, boats and amphibians blown ashore. Sections of the Mulberry harbor which were in course of being towed from England to their locations were scattered and sunk. The shuttle of craft bringing supplies was halted, though those en route when the storm broke did their best to make a landfall and deliver their cargoes, some of them being wrecked in the process. When the wind finally died away, some 800 craft were stranded, mostly damaged and many destroyed, and the beaches across the coast of Normandy were piled high with wreckage.

Complete disaster was avoided largely because the breakwaters and blockships sunk out to sea as the initial part of the Mulberry concept had, for the most part, stayed in place, and thus within their boundaries was relatively sheltered water in which a certain amount of unloading of stores could be achieved. The worst to suffer were the Americans, since their artificial harbors were more exposed to the blast of the gale and were severely damaged; the British were more fortunate, though it was a matter of degree, since they had considerable damage.

This setback severely interfered with the planned build-up of stores and men in the beachhead. In the four days prior to the storm, the daily average amount landed was 34,000 men, 6000 vehicles and 25,000 tons of stores; in the four days of the gale these dropped to 10,000 men, 2400 vehicles and 7000 tons. By the time the storm had blown itself out the British Army, already behind schedule when the storm began, was lacking three divisions. The attack had to be postponed until 25 June in order to allow some men and supplies to get forward. Moreover the period of the storm had allowed the Germans four days in which to strengthen their positions and bring in some reserves.

The British troops in Operation 'Epsom', the southern arm of the Caen pincer, consisted of VIII Corps supported by elements of XXX Corps, though VIII Corps was short of troops since all its elements had not landed, due to the storm. It was therefore strengthened by the addition of more armor, to give to a total strength of about 600 tanks, 300 guns and about 60,000 men. In addition it could call on the support of some 400 more guns from I and XXX Corps on its flanks, together with heavy air support.

The attack was to begin by a minor operation by XXX Corps to secure the area around Noyers, to protect the right flank of VIII Corps. The main attack would then begin from the ground held by the Canadian Division between Bronay and Bretteville l'Orgueilleuse, and would force a number of crossings over the Odon and Orne rivers and take the high ground northeast of Bretteville sur Laize, giving it command of the roads approaching Caen from the south. The terrain was, at first, open fields of corn, but as the drive continued, it would find itself getting deeper and deeper into the bocage country. There it was to find that 12 SS Panzer Division and parts of 21 Panzer and Panzer Lehr Divisions had been settling themselves in for three weeks and were completely familiar with the ground. They had strengthened the natural defenses of the bocage by careful application of wire and mines, and

AFTER THE GREAT STORM. A VIEW OF ONE OF THE MULBERRY HARBOURS SHOWING THE DAMAGE WREAKED BY THE WAVES. THE FLEXIBLE TRACKS ARE THE MOST OBVIOUS DAMAGE.

FACE TO FACE IN THE BOCAGE

General Sir Miles Dempsey (1896–1969).

A quiet and unassuming man, Dempsey commanded the 13th British Infantry Brigade in France and Belgium in 1940 and managed to withdraw them skilfully from the collapse. His excellent organizational ability being recognized, in 1941 he was given command of an armored division and was later appointed commander of 13 Corps under Montgomery in the Western Desert. He quickly impressed Montgomery with his tactical skill, and he continued to lead 13 Corps against Sicily and Italy.

His success deserved reward, and he was then appointed to command 2nd British Army for the invasion of Europe. He demonstrated his ability to conduct a slogging battle in the area of Caen and in the Falaise pocket, and once the Germans began retiring he demonstrated his ability to conduct mobile warfare by the speed of his advance on Brussels. In the spring of 1945 he directed the British crossing of the Rhine, and thereafter 2nd Army was in the van of the British advance into Germany, his advanced units being well across the Elbe by the time of the German surrender. As soon as the war in Europe finished, Dempsey was appointed C-in-C Allied Land Forces in South-East Asia.

Lieut-General Courtney Hicks Hodges (1887–1966)

Courtney Hodges was one of those many generals who rarely make headlines but perform a difficult task in a very competent manner. An infantryman of considerable practical skill — he was an expert rifle shot and made his mark in competitive shooting between the wars — he was Chief of Intelligence at the outbreak of war. In 1942 he briefly took charge of Replacement and Training Command but his talents were obviously appreciated by Gen Marshall and he was very quickly moved from this post to take over 10th Corps. In the following year he was promoted Lieut-General and given command of the 3rd Corps, then training in Texas.

In 1944 he was sent to England to become Bradley's deputy and supervised the US preparations for the invasion. When, on 1 August 1944, 12th Army Group was set up and Bradley placed in command, Hodges took over 1st US Army from him and in spite of serious deficiencies in supplies due to the Channel storm, successfully drove out of the beach-head. By October of 1944 the 1st Army had cleared Luxembourg and that part of Belgium not under 21st Army Group and had captured Aachen, the first major German town to be taken. In December his army took the brunt of the German offensive in the Ardennes, but retaliated effectively, and then went on to take the famous Remagen bridge, seize the Roer dams and encircle the Ruhr. Moving from the Ruhr, Hodges then headed for Leipzig and the Elbe, to make contact with the advancing Soviet Army.

they had sited machine guns, mortars and high-velocity anti-tank guns to cover every possible approach.

The attack begins

The attack commenced with an intense artillery bombardment, some 700 field and medium guns backed up by Corps heavy artillery and guns of the warships anchored off the beaches. This, whilst serving very well to disorient the defenders in the first line of German outposts, also advertized the focus of the attack, which enabled the German commanders to bring in whatever reserves they could lay hands on.

At 0730 the infantry began to move forward; they were strung out in a loose line of platoons across the cornfields, farmyards and orchards, walking about 500 yards behind the bursting shells of the artillery's barrage. It had rained during the night, and the morning was overcast, so much so that the promised air support was grounded, but the thundering barrage appeared to be doing all that was necessary to overcome the enemy. Gradually the advancing infantry began to come under sporadic small arms fire as pockets of German outposts who had escaped the shells began to open fire. Most were so shaken by the shelling that their aim was erratic and they were rapidly rounded up and marched to the rear, or despatched by the advancing soldiers. And amongst the soldiers and behind them came the rumbling tanks which were to deal with any heavy opposition.

All went well for the first mile or so; but the ground rose to a small ridge, and there the resistance began to stiffen as more and more machine guns began to fire and snipers began to pick off the advancing men. Now the tanks rolled forward, to take up the burden, but as they crested the ridge, concealed 88mm anti-tank guns opened up with devastating efficiency. The first line of tanks were soon immobile and burning.

Now came a string of small villages, Le Gaule, Mauvieu, Cheux and le Haut du Bosq; battered by the barrage, nevertheless the ruins proved good concealment for the Germans, and the resistance was severe. With the tanks stood off by accurate gunfire the infantry had to close and take these villages house by house, fighting bitterly for every yard. And before the advance had begun to collect itself and gather momentum after the checks for the villages, the 12th SS began counter-attacking. Intensive artillery fire, called for by forward observing officers accompanying the advance, soon stopped these attempts, but from then on there was constant pressure.

Lieut-General Joseph Lawton Collins (1896–1963)

A skilled infantryman, Collins was a hard-driving commander who nevertheless was well-liked by his soldiers, since he was frequently at their side and was always solicitous of their welfare. A thorough and careful planner, he had no hesitation in axing incompetent commanders, and his policy was one of thrusting offensive in order to keep the initiative. His troops nicknamed him 'Lightnin' Joe'.

Collins graduated from West Point in 1918 and commanded an infantry battalion in the Army of Occupation. After the usual round of schools and colleges, he became Chief of Staff of 7th Army Corps in 1941 and then Chief of Staff Hawaii. He first came to notice as commander of the 25th Infantry Division which was suddenly removed from garrisoning the Hawaiian Islands to replace the 1st US Marines on Guadalcanal in January 1943. In fact, by the time they arrived the Japanese had already decided that they ought to cut their losses and evacuate the island, but nevertheless Collins' division had a lively few weeks clearing the western end of the island. He then took command of elements of XIV US Corps in the campaign for New Georgia and demonstrated an undoubted tactical talent.

He was therefore selected to command 7th Army Corps in the invasion of Europe, and his experience in the Pacific proved to be useful in Normandy, since he was quite accustomed to operating without roads and therefore tended to maneuver his troops in directions which frequently took the Germans by surprise, accustomed as they were to the American penchant for being roadbound. His troops took Cherbourg 20 days after landing, led the break-out from Normandy, breached the Siegfried Line, took Cologne, enveloped the Ruhr and eventually made contact with the Soviet Army near Dessau.

General Leo Freiherr Geyr von Schweppenburg (1886–1974)

Geyr entered the German Army in 1904 as a Lieutenant of Dragoons and served with ability though without particular distinction. In the postwar army he gained his Lt-Colonel in 1930 and commanded a cavalry regiment. From 1933 to 1937 he served as Military Attache in London, Brussels and The Hague, reaching general's rank during that time. On 1 September 1939 he was given command of 3 Panzer Division and served in Poland, and in 1940, promoted to General der Panzertruppen, he commanded a motorized corps and, during the invasion of France, was awarded the Knight's Grand Cross, his only major distinction.

In June 1942 he took command of 40 Panzer Corps, and later 58 Panzer Corps. Finally, in February 1944 he took over Panzer Group West, responsible for the defense against invasion. When the invasion occurred, he had difficulty in obtaining permission to use his Panzers, after which his headquarters was destroyed by a British air strike, in which he was wounded. Early in July, together with von Rundstedt, Geyr urged a withdrawal from Caen in the face of the British attacks; for this both he and Rundstedt were sacked by Hitler.

The trouble was that the British 15th Division was advancing on a very narrow front, probably no more than 2500 yards wide at its widest point, while behind them there was a six-mile traffic jam of tanks and reinforcements, and this made a tempting target for the Germans who had decided that they would allow the head of the British column to advance as far as it could and then put in counter-attacks on each flank so as to chop the salient in half. But until the British were in a good position for this, the Germans were content to stand off and use their better positions and command of the ground. The Glasgow Highlanders, who had occupied the village of Cheux, came under intense fire from German mortars on the high ground to the south; 12 officers and 200 men became casualties in the course of the day.

Soon after midday 11th Armoured Division, which

A BRITISH 4.5IN (114MM) MEDIUM GUN IN ACTION CLOSE TO TILLY SUR SEULLES IN SUPPORT OF OPERATION EPSOM. NOTE THAT THE WARTIME CENSOR HAS CAREFULLY PAINTED OUT THE FORMATION BADGES ON THE UNIFORMS OF THE GUNNERS. THE MAN ON THE RIGHT IS AN ARMY CAMERAMAN FILMING THE ACTION.

had been following the infantry, was ordered forward to force a way through to Tourmauville and Gavrus, seizing the bridges there across the Odon. 29th Armoured Brigade moved forward, but were soon stopped by a powerful defense south of Cheux. After some hours of fierce but inconclusive fighting, it became obvious that the river was not going to be reached that day; the tanks were to hold on and the infantry would move through them and take up the spearhead position once more. But the route forward led through Cheux, which by now had been shelled and mortared into ruin, and this became a major bottle-neck, slowing down everything which tried to move through it. As the rain poured down and the daylight faded, so the battle ground to a halt as tired and wet troops on both sides began to find secure positions in which to pass the night as best they could.

At 0500 next morning the attack was renewed; 43rd Division had moved up during the night and taken over the defensive positions, so leaving 15th Division to continue the advance. But at the same time the Germans began making their inevitable counter-attacks, and 43rd Division had their hands full in preserving their hold on Cheux in the face of persistent action by 1 SS Panzer Corps.

The 15th Division fought steadily onwards. Now they were into the bocage and it became a matter of rushing from hedge to hedge, stopping to see what the next field held, seeking out the defensive posts of the Germans, making a plan, and going forward again. Every hedge corner held some formidable surprise, a machine gun post, an anti-tank gun, perhaps no more

TANK AND ANTI-TANK IN THE BOCAGE

GERMAN

The two most formidable tanks on the German side were the King Tiger and the Panther, both of which had been developed after the German Army had met the formidable Soviet T34 and KV tanks. The King Tiger was an improved Tiger, incorporating many refinements developed in the heat of battle. Mounting a powerful 88mm gun and with 15cm of armor on its front, it was practically impervious to any Allied gun. The Panther was lighter and more agile, had a maximum hull thickness of 80mm and mounted a 75mm gun.

The German infantry's antidote to Allied tanks was either the Panzerfaust, a hand-held recoilless gun firing a massive shaped charge and capable of piercing any Allied tank; or the Panzerschreck, a German copy of the American Bazooka firing an 88mm shaped charge rocket which could also defeat 100mm of armor. Both were short-range weapons, but in the Bocage short ranges were the order of the day.

ALLIED

The Sherman, principal Allied battle tank, could only hope to get the better of German armor by maneuvering around to get a flank or rear shot at where the armor was thinnest. Much the same applied to the infantry, since the two Allied infantry anti-tank weapons, the British PIAT and the American Bazooka, could not defeat more than about 75mm of armor and both were very short-range weapons. The M1A1 Bazooka had a transparent flash shield on the front to stop the firer being scorched by the rocket, and a wooden shoulder rest containing the firing batteries which electrically ignited the rocket. The British PIAT was a much shorter weapon which used a steel rod from which the hollow-tailed bomb was launched. Both required operators with nerves of steel to remain quiet until the tank was within 50-75 metres of the weapon before opening fire.

LAYING A GERMAN 120MM MORTAR. THE PECULIAR POSITIONS OF THE MEN ARE DECREED BY THE SIGHTING SYSTEM. THE MAN ON THE RIGHT IS SETTING THE CORRECT ELEVATION ON THE MORTAR. THE LEFT-HAND MAN CLOSEST TO THE MORTAR IS LOOKING THROUGH THE SIGHT AND TRYING TO LAY FOR DIRECTION, WHILE THE MAN BEHIND HIM IS OPERATING THE LEVELLING GEAR TO KEEP THE SIGHT UPRIGHT, TWO TASKS WHICH MUST BE WORKED IN SYMPATHY.

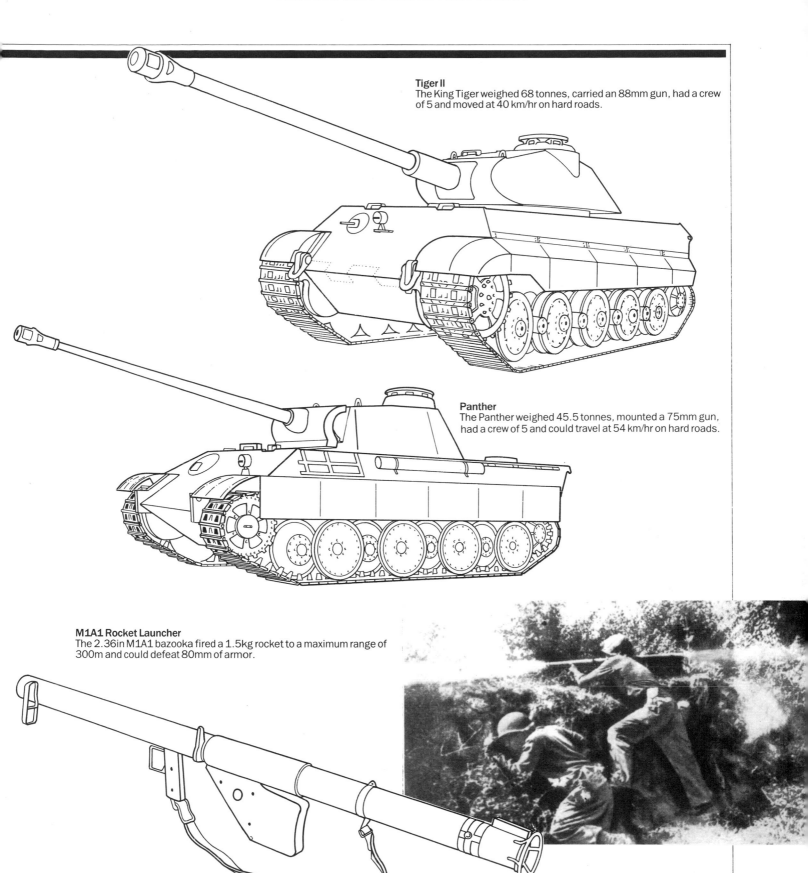

Tiger II
The King Tiger weighed 68 tonnes, carried an 88mm gun, had a crew of 5 and moved at 40 km/hr on hard roads.

Panther
The Panther weighed 45.5 tonnes, mounted a 75mm gun, had a crew of 5 and could travel at 54 km/hr on hard roads.

M1A1 Rocket Launcher
The 2.36in M1A1 bazooka fired a 1.5kg rocket to a maximum range of 300m and could defeat 80mm of armor.

than a single determined German soldier with a panzer-faust, but hidden away in the green maze and with stout earth banks to protect them, even individual soldiers could put up a defense out of all proportion to their size.

The advancing infantry relied firstly upon their own portable firepower — light machine guns, rifles and grenades, with the occasional use of mortars where a target could be defined. But for the most part the fighting was at too close range for mortars to be useful.

TOP: A PATROL IN THE BOCAGE COUNTRY SOUTH OF CAUMONT, ADVANCING ON DE FONTAINE. NOTE THE SUPPORT TANK IN THE BACKGROUND.
ABOVE: A SHERMAN TANK FITTED WITH THE CULLIN HEDGEROW DEVICE, SANDBAGS TO GIVE EXTRA PROTECTION AGAINST PANZERFAUSTS, AND A GROUP OF INFANTRY ALONG FOR THE RIDE TO THE NEXT OBSTACLE.

The PIAT — that remarkable anti-tank weapon used by the British — performed as a close support gun, being more often fired at machine gun posts than at tanks, though in this close country the PIAT came into its own as an anti-tank weapon since it became possible to get in telling shots at very short range whenever a German tank appeared.

Among the most useful auxiliaries for the British was the 79th Armoured Division's collection of peculiar armor. The flail tank proved useful for smashing down hedges and the flame-throwing 'Crocodile' for removing dogged groups of defenders. But the earth banks proved a deathtrap for tanks; as the tank clambered slowly up and over the bank, so it exposed its thin belly to the enemy, and even the smallest anti-armor weapon was capable of putting its projectile through this easy target.

Eventually, in the late afternoon, the 2nd Argyll & Sutherland Highlanders managed to capture a bridge over the Odon river, near Tourmauville, crossed it and formed a small bridgehead on the far bank. Soon afterwards tanks of 11th Armoured Division were able to come up, cross the river and fan out to the southeast, to the foot of a minor eminence which soon became known to the British as Hill 112. Following the tanks came the 159th Infantry Brigade and then the remainder of 29th Armoured Brigade.

Hill 112

On the following morning 29th Armoured Brigade moved from the bridgehead to attack Hill 112. But here the Germans were in strength and intended to make a stand, and concealed anti-tank guns and artillery soon stopped the advance. In the face of this, orders were given for the British force to consolidate its position, hold on, and wait until the 15th and 43rd Divisions had tidied up the area between Cheux and the river Odon, after which a major attack would be mounted.

The British advance now formed a major salient protruding into the German area, and there was a danger that a vigorous counter-attack might cut it off. It appeared that German reinforcements were moving towards the threat, and even in the face of air attack; actually the poor weather prevented fighter support from airfields in England, but there were a good number of aircraft working out of airstrips inside the beachhead by this time and they were able to get in some excellent work against German ground operations. Nevertheless, the Germans were still moving forward, taking the risk and covering themselves with strong anti-aircraft defenses wherever possible.

The salient was now strengthened by the addition of the 3rd Guards Brigade, and with their protection the 15th Division now began a drive to the south in order to clear the ground between Grainville and Rauray. This ran into strong opposition from Germans dug in along the railway embankment and 15th Division made no further progress that day. The Argylls, having captured the first bridge over the Odon, had then moved along

BREN CARRIERS OF THE RIFLE BRIGADE IN A SUNKEN ROAD SOUTH OF LE BERY BOCAGE, 2 AUGUST 1944. THIS SHOWS THE SORT OF PROTECTION EVEN A RELATIVELY MAJOR ROAD COULD PROVIDE.

the river bank to the west and had captured the village of Gavrus and its bridges, but they were now isolated there since a German counterstroke had severed the road between them and le Valtru. It is indicative of the type of country that the Argylls took five hours to cover the distance between Tourmauville (the first bridge) and Gavrus, which was slightly over a mile.

Meanwhile the 29th Armoured Brigade had managed to attack and take the northern end of the plateau which was Hill 112; in the process they captured a German SS officer who was carrying plans for a forthcoming counter-attack, which enabled 15th Division to prepare for it and beat it off when it came. Unfortunately this piece of advance information was not relayed up the chain of command to General Dempsey; he regarded the defeat of the counter-attack as no more than a minor affair, not realizing that it was, at that time, the last shot in the German commander's locker. Dempsey was concerned about the potential threat to the salient, since by now elements of I SS and II SS Panzer Corps and 9 and 10 SS Panzer Divisions had been identified around the British perimeter, and on the following day he pulled 11th Armoured back from the bridgehead to prepare for an attack. This removed the principal strength from the bridgehead, and the Germans, seizing the opportunity in their usual manner, attacked and regained Hill 112.

Hill 112 now became the focus of both sides, and according to those who fought there eventually resembled something from the Flanders battlefield of 1916-17; mud, corpses, and constant gunfire. By this time both sides had been hard at each other's throats for

five days and neither had sufficient edge to make a decisive move, so that the battle eddied around Hill 112 without reaching a decision. To Montgomery it was obvious that 112 was not going to be taken without a major and bloody assault; and, frankly, it wasn't worth that. And so Operation Epsom came to an end.

Epsom was one of those operations which both failed and succeeded. The original intention — to 'pincer' around Caen — failed. On the other hand, by bringing on four major German formations and stopping them, Epsom drew the sting from the German counter-attack which might, had it been given a clear run, have broken through the beach-head and gained the sea, to the discomfiture of the invasion. In that respect Epsom was a major success, but unfortunately Montgomery had announced that he would take Caen, the newspapers expected Caen, and anything less was an anti-climax. Nevertheless, the threat to Caen had made Rommel divert armor from the American sector and send it to counter the bridgehead over the Odon; it has since been calculated that at the height of the battle there were about 140 tanks facing the US forces across the front and no less than 725 facing the British bridgeheads.

The price paid for this was a heavy one; VIII Corps lost 4020 men, and of that total 2331 were from 15th Division, while 11th Armoured and 43rd Division suffered 1256 casualties. More significantly, these figures, when compared with the figures of actual front-line troops in the divisions, meant that something over 50 percent of the infantry engaged in Epsom had been wounded or killed. This was a rate of attrition which the British Army was in no position to support, and it was this, as much as anything else, which led Montgomery to close the operation down.

Three days after Epsom ended, the US First Army

TOP: A PATROL OF THE GREEN HOWARDS REGIMENT MOVING PAST A SHATTERED HALF-TRACK, THE REMAINS OF AN ATTEMPTED VEHICULAR RECONNAISSANCE, ON 4 AUGUST.

ABOVE: GERMAN TROOPS LOADING THEIR 120MM MORTAR. THIS WEAPON WAS COPIED FROM A CAPTURED SOVIET DESIGN AND BECAME THE PRINCIPAL GERMAN CLOSE-DEFENSE WEAPON OF THE LATTER PART OF THE WAR. IT FIRED A 16KG HIGH EXPLOSIVE BOMB TO A RANGE OF 6KM AND COULD DO THIS 15 TIMES A MINUTE WITH A WELL-TRAINED CREW.

Montgomery, was for the US First Army to pivot on Caumont and sweep round to form a north-south line extending down to Fougeres, some 40 miles away. This would clear a sizeable area to allow General Patton's Third Army to form up and become operational, after which the great advance on Paris would commence. Bradley ordered VIII Corps to lead off on 3 July, take La Haye du Puits and continue to Coutances; VII Corps would begin operations on 4 July, advancing to Periers, and finally XIX Corps would, once Periers was secured, advance to St Lo. With all these moves completed, 1st US Army would be deployed on a line Coutances-Caumont, ready to move against Avranches, the gateway to Brittany.

Overcoming the obstacles

The VIII Corps under Gen Middleton duly moved off on 3 July, intending to chase the Germans 20 miles and stop at Coutances. They then fell into the bocage and took five days and 5000 casualties to get four miles to La Haye du Puits. Every hedge line became an obstacle, every field a killing ground, and infantry, moving forward feet at a time, were the only force which could have any effect. The Americans, incensed at seeing their mechanical and weaponry superiority negated by something as primitive as a hedgerow, gave some thought to methods of beating the obstacles, and the solution soon appeared.

The 'Culin Hedgerow Device' or 'Sherman Prong' was devised by Technical Sergeant Culin of the US Army; it consisted of steel blades resembling ploughshares, welded to the front of a Sherman tank so that the tank could charge the hedge bank and, by burying

began its contribution to the Battle of the Hedgerows. The American army had already become acquainted with the bocage during its operations to extend the beachhead and advance on Cherbourg, but what it had so far seen was relatively small beer compared to what now lay in front of it. The general plan, issued by

ORDER OF BATTLE

ALLIED	AXIS
2nd British Army: (Commander: Gen Dempsey)	**Army Group B (Commander: Fld-Marshal Rommel)**

1st Brit Corps
   Guards Armd Div
   7th Armd Div
   3rd Brit AGRA
	V Pz Army
	   86 Corps
	   1SS Pz Corps
	   2 SS Pz Corps
	   47 Pz Corps

8th Brit Corps
   8th Brit AGRA
	VII Army (Commander: Hausser)
	   2 Parachute Corps
	      3 Para Div
	      352 Inf Div
	   84 Corps

2nd Canadian Corps
   2nd Cdn Inf Div
   3rd Cdn Inf Div
   2nd Cdn Armd Bde
   2nd Cdn AGRA
	XIX Army

51st Highland Div 11th Armd Div 49th Div	**Panzer Group West (Commander: Gen von Schweppenberg)**

1st US Army: (Commander: Gen Bradley)	1 SS Pz Corps
	   1 SS Pz Div Liebstandarte Adolf Hitler
	   2 Pz Div
	   9 SS Pz Div
	   272 Inf Div

5th US Corps (Commander: Gerow)
   2nd Armd Div
   1st Inf Div
   2nd Inf Div
   29th Inf Div
	2 SS Pz Div
	9 SS Pz Div
	10 SS Pz Div
	12 SS Pz Div
	21 Pz Div
	Pz Lehr Div

7th US Corps (Commander: Lt-Gen Collins) 4th Inf Div	17 SS Pz Gren Div
9th Inf Div 79th Inf Div 90th Inf Div	6 Parachute Regt
7th US Corps (Commander: Middleton)	77 Inf Div

19th US Corps (Commander: Corlett)
   29th Inf Div (from 5 Corps)
   20th Inf Div
   35th Inf Div
	91 Inf Div

	243 Inf Div
	265 Inf Div
	709 Inf Div

the blades in the earth, uproot a section of hedge and make a sufficient gap to allow it to drive through without exposing its undersurface. By scouring the beaches and removing the remains of German steel obstacles, sufficient material was obtained to allow these simple devices to be made and welded on to the tanks by the Divisional workshops, and from then on the progress through the hedges became very slightly faster. Nevertheless, even though the tanks could get through the hedges, there were still many formidable German weapons waiting for them; at one stage of the battle it was estimated that 100 Allied tanks per day were being put out of action.

VIII Corps continued its advance, but with an ever-slowing momentum. It took a further seven days and another 5000 casualties before it covered three more miles and reached Lessay, at which point the Corps was virtually useless, having suffered something over 80 percent casualties in its infantry element.

VII Corps began its attack in the Carentan sector on 4 July, but its area was restricted by marshland on either flank and there was only sufficient space for a single division at the head of the advance. The first day saw an advance of 400 yards through mud and water, taking six

prisoners for the loss of 1400 men. The second day saw a slightly better advance, and a second division was added to the spearhead. But after 11 days and 8000 casualties they had still not reached Periers, ten miles from their start line.

Finally XIX Corps moved off on 7 July, expecting to do little better than their predecessors, but in fact struck a weak spot in the German defenses. They crossed the Vire river and Vire-Taute Canal, securing a bridgehead. Seeing this indication of success, General Bradley moved 3rd Armoured Division through the bridgehead with orders to move south and outflank St Lo. But the tanks soon bogged down in the bocage and swampland, and before long the infantry were complaining that all the available routes were blocked by armor.

By this time the Germans had become alarmed at the prospect of this American Corps thrusting forward, be it ever so slowly, and rushed the Panzer Lehr Division to the scene with orders to counter-attack. This they did, but in their turn they fell foul of the bocage; now the boot was on the other foot, the Americans were forming the defensive positions in the hedgerows and the Panzers were shot to pieces, losing a third of their tanks on the first day's drive.

General Bradley was by now disturbed at the enormous casualty rate and the slow progress First Army was making. He decided to change his tactics; instead of a general advance on a broad front, he would concentrate all his strength into a narrow thrust which would steamroller a way out of the bocage, assisted by enormous air bombardment. Bradley therefore modified his aims, and instead of continuing the advance, as planned, to reach the Coutances to Caumont road, he ordered his force to make for the high ground overlooking a closer objective, the Lessay — Periers — St Lo road. Here he would anchor his line, re-organize, punch his way into St Lo and then set up a massive air bombardment to start Operation Cobra and see Patton on his way.

St Lo was by this time a heap of smoking rubble, since it had been bombed constantly since before D-Day. But it controlled the roads, and for this reason was of value to both sides. The German II Parachute Corps defended the remains of the town, and Bradley ordered a frontal attack by the US XIX Corps. But before St Lo could be entered it was necessary to clear a commanding height, Hill 192, some four miles to the east. This was to be done by the 2nd Division of US V Corps which would attack at the same time as XIX Corps. As usual, the hill was a maze of hedges and defensive positions, and a previous attack in June, also by the 2nd Division, had been driven off with 1200

THE LESS SALUBRIOUS ASPECT OF WARFARE; A SHERMAN PASSING A DEAD HORSE DURING ITS ADVANCE TO THE BOCAGE COUNTRY. THE SHERMAN HAD BECOME THE UNIVERSAL ALLIED TANK, BUT THE FIGHTING IN NORMANDY SOON SHOWED THAT IT WAS OUTCLASSED BY THE GERMAN TIGER AND PANTHER TANKS. HURRIED UP-GUNNING INCREASED ITS EFFECTIVE RANGE BUT LITTLE COULD BE DONE ABOUT ITS WEAK ARMOR PROTECTION, WHICH ALLOWED A TIGER TO DESTROY IT AT RANGES BEYOND THAT OF ITS 76MM GUN.

casualties. This time, no doubt profiting from what they had learned, they did better, gaining a hundred yards here, a hundred yards there, using their Corps artillery to blast the infantry onto their objectives. The hill was taken in half a day, and the Americans began organizing for the inevitable counter-attack.

The battle for St Lo took eight days; during the night of 17/18 July the remaining German troops slipped out of the town and back to the safety of their own lines, leaving a handful of outposts to delay the occupation as much as possible. At midday on the 18th the first US troops moved into the town, fighting past the outposts to do so, and at last they were clear of the bocage.

Twelve divisions had fought for 17 days and had sustained 40,000 casualties to gain seven miles. But at the end of it the 1st US Army had secured its baseline and Bradley could begin planning the breakout which would unleash General Patton and the Third US Army.

The lessons

The principal lesson learned by the Allies in the month following D-Day was simply that the German soldier was a formidable enemy, no matter where you met him; on a one-for-one basis he was generally better than any Allied soldier, and given the slightest advantage in terrain or position, he could make an impression out of all proportion to his numbers. Most of the Allied troops involved in the invasion had little or no experience of the German fighting with his back to the wall; those who had fought him in the desert had respect for him, but they were inclined to think that by this stage of the war, and given the Allied superiority in equipment, there would be little left for them to learn. They soon found their mistake.

The US Army was prone, as can be seen from the description of the battle for St Lo, to make advances on a broad front, with the intention of reinforcing success wherever it came. This is as sound a method as any, one supposes, but depends entirely upon the commander's ability to make lightning decisions and move his troops around rapidly. At this stage of the invasion the American command simply did not have the ability to react fast enough, nor were its troops sufficiently skilled or motivated to move quickly even if orders were given in good time. When Bradley decided to concentrate his attack into a narrow but violent thrust, he did rather better than with his broad front, but without any doubt the nature of the country was the decisive factor, and even a concentrated drive was liable to come rapidly to rest when confronted with the bocage.

As we have noted above, the bocage came as an unpleasant surprise to almost all the Allied troops, from commanders to private soldiers. This was a failure of intelligence which had serious repercussions. It caused an immense strain to fall on the infantry, with the result that their casualty figures were out of all proportion, but the fact remains that only infantry were capable of taking that wretched country, yard by yard, field by field.

CHAPTER NINE

" ..THAT GODDAM THIRD ARMY AND THAT SON-OF-A-BITCH PATTON.."

MOBILE WARFARE
JULY 1944 — MARCH 1945

Overleaf

A somewhat idealized portrait of General George S Patton, backed up
by a Sherman tank, the backbone of his Third Army.
(*Gleam of Command* by A LaMontagne. Courtesy American Heroes in Print Ltd/Robert N Anderson)

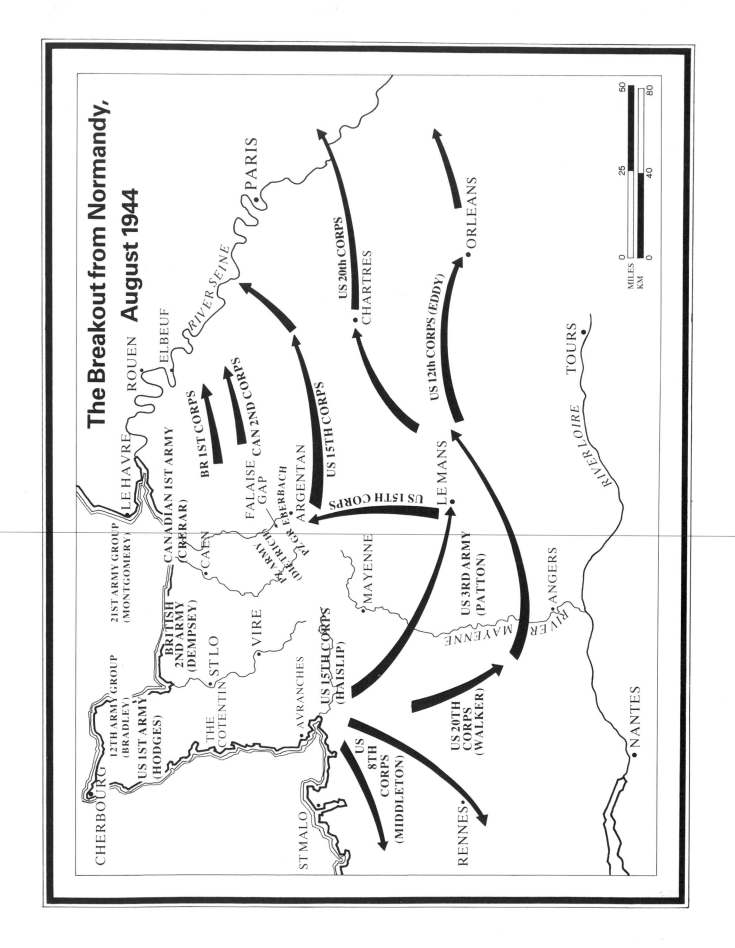

The Breakout from Normandy, August 1944

CHERBOURG

LE HAVRE

ROUEN

ELBEUF

PARIS

RIVER SEINE

21ST ARMY GROUP
(MONTGOMERY)

CANADIAN 1ST ARMY
(CRERAR)

BR 1ST CORPS

CAN 2ND CORPS

FALAISE
GAP

CAEN

FIFTH
PANZER
ARMY
(DIETRICH)

EBERBACH

ARGENTAN

US 15TH CORPS

12TH ARMY GROUP
(BRADLEY)

US 1ST ARMY
(HODGES)

BRITISH
2ND ARMY
(DEMPSEY)

THE
COTENTIN

ST LO

VIRE

US 15TH CORPS

US 20th CORPS

CHARTRES

US 12th CORPS (EDDY)

ORLEANS

LE MANS

MAYENNE

AVRANCHES

US 15TH CORPS
(HAISLIP)

US 8TH
CORPS
(MIDDLETON)

US 3RD ARMY
(PATTON)

RIVER MAYENNE

ANGERS

RIVER LOIRE

TOURS

ST MALO

US 20TH
CORPS
(WALKER)

RENNES

NANTES

MILES
KM

0
0

25
40

50
80

If the German Army sowed the doctrine of *Blitzkrieg* in Poland in 1939, they most assuredly reaped the result in France and Germany in 1944–45 as the US Third Army under General George S Patton stormed across France, cleared the Palatinate and reached Pilsen before being brought to a stop by the war's ending. Patton had an indisputable genius for handling armor in mobile warfare, and this campaign gave him every opportunity for displaying it; unfortunately, it has to be admitted that he had no comparable genius for positional warfare, and, again, this campaign had moments which proved it. He was also politically naive and no sort of strategist, but these shortcomings were less obvious in France, and in some ways they were to his benefit; a man with a longer view might well have balked at some of the moves which Patton made and which produced striking success. Even so, whilst he often failed to see the political and economic consequences, he was no fool when it came to forecasting military possibilities, and his foresight in this respect saved the Allied cause from near-disaster in the Ardennes.

The background

The strategy of operation Overlord is discussed elsewhere; so far as it concerned the US Third Army, the general plan was that General Montgomery and the British 21st Army Group would hold an area around Caen, in the north of the beachhead, attracting as much German armored strength as possible so as to reduce the resistance in the southeastern area of the landings and thus allowing the American forces to spread westward. This would enable them to cut off the Cotentin Peninsula and capture the port of Cherbourg which could then be brought into use as an Allied supply base. Once this was done, with Montgomery still fixing the German armored strength around Caen, the American force would break out from the beachhead and strike across France.

Third Army's place in all this was to be the striking force, and its movements were kept secret for a considerable period in order to confuse the Germans. Third had spent two and a half years in the USA being trained, firstly by General Krueger and latterly by General Hodges. Early in 1944 its staffs sailed for England, to be greeted with the news that they were now to be commanded by General Patton; scarcely had they assimilated this than they were told that many of them would be found other jobs, because Patton was bringing his own senior staff, who had served with him in 2 Armd Div in North Africa and Sicily. This was something of an innovation for the US Army, though common enough practice in the British, that an incoming general should bring his own staff to supplant the incumbents. But as Patton once said to Eisenhower, "I don't want a brilliant staff, I just want a loyal one," and putting in his own men was one way of ensuring this.

Whilst the bulk of Third Army was being shipped across the Atlantic and given its last licks of training, Patton now had to lend his name to a deception plan, 'Operation Fortitude'. Briefly, this was the creation of a phantom invasion force in Southeast England, created by the erection of dummy camps and the operation of skeleton radio networks, which gave German intelligence the impression that a mighty force of 50 divisions was poised to invade the Pas de Calais, and that the landings in Normandy were merely a feint. Allied with this radio deception, carefully planned rumors were allowed to leak that this force was under Patton's command, and eventually the German planners were convinced of the presence of *Armeegruppe Patton*.

Third Army was, meanwhile keeping a 'low profile'; its presence was scarcely acknowledged, and its part in subsequent operations kept very quiet. As Patton himself said, in a speech to one of the formations in the spring of 1944,

> "... I am not supposed to be commanding this army; I am not even supposed to be in England. Let the first bastards to find out be the Goddam Germans. Some day I want them to raise on their hind legs and howl Jesus Christ, it's that Goddam Third Army and that son-of-a-bitch Patton ..."

He was to get his wish.

The plan

Patton arrived in Normandy on 9 July, 1944 to make a personal reconnaissance. Since he was supposed to be commanding Armeegruppe Patton still, his presence in France had to be kept quiet. With his well-known tall figure, accompanied by his bull-terrier, in General Bradley's headquarters near Isigny, a place well stocked with pressmen, this was something of a problem. It was neatly solved by Bradley's intelligence officer, Colonel Monk Dickson, who rounded up all the journalists and addressed them briefly: "Gentlemen, I don't know whether any of you have seen what you took to be General Patton around here with his dog? You were mistaken. Good morning gentleman." The journalists entered into the spirit of the deception and Patton's presence was never even hinted at.

Meanwhile his headquarters had crossed the Channel and had set up shop in an orchard near Briquebec, in the Contentin Peninsula, and after conferring with Bradley, Hodges, Collins and Montgomery, Patton went there to begin his planning. His first move was to plan an amphibious landing.

Montgomery, after attracting all the German armor he could, mounted 'Operation Goodwood' with the intention of threatening Falaise and drawing even more German armor away from the rest of the front. Two days later this ground to a halt in a combination of powerful German resistance and highly unseasonable rainfall. The US First Army were fighting a very slow and expensive battle through the hedgerows, taking the country yard by yard. The result was a general slowing down of the battle, and Eisenhower was looking for some way of putting movement into the war. His first idea was that the Third Army should outflank the Germans by making a seaborne landing in the area well west of Cherbourg.

The planning was passed to Patton, and he soon came up with a proposal to land one armored and two infantry divisions close to Morlaix and advance through Dinan, thereafter swinging north to take the Germans facing US First Army in their rear. Once this was done, First and Third armies could then take off eastward in the general direction of Chartres. It all sounded very simple and impressive, and some postwar commentators have suggested that had Patton been given permission to mount this operation much of First Army's hedgerow problems would have been solved and the advance across France would have taken place much sooner. The principal objections came from the naval staffs; they pointed out that the area selected by Patton was heavily defended, promised insuperable navigational problems, and was far too close to several German U-Boat bases from which rapid and fatal counter-strokes could have been launched. The air staffs also pointed out that Morlaix was at the extreme limit of fighter cover and thus air support would have been extremely difficult.

The Morlaix landing, however, was soon forgotten when Bradley developed a plan for 'Operation Cobra', which he unfolded before Eisenhower on 11 July. This proposed that US VII Corps, supported by a massive air bombardment, should break through on a narrow front in the center of First Army's area and drive to Coutances with a mass of armor. This would be followed by a second thrust to Avranches, at the base of the Cotentin Peninsula. Avranches was a bottleneck, but whoever held it controlled the rest of Brittany, and with this gained, Bradley proposed to pour Third Army through to take the whole of Brittany, set up a supply port in Quiberon Bay and then turn eastwards for Alencon.

Patton's view of 'Cobra' was rather different to that of Bradley and the SHAEF staffs. SHAEF was primarily attracted by the prospect of setting up the Quiberon Bay facility to act as a supply base capable of supporting 100 divisions. Patton, a more practical soldier, was more concerned with the prospect of moving east and taking on the German Army. A simple man, he was never easily seduced by theories about areas of influence, economic gains and control of territory; he never lost sight of the fundamental strategic truth that the object of military operations is to destroy the enemy's forces on the ground. Once that is done the other benefits automatically accrue.

Patton's reading of 'Cobra' was, therefore, first to head for Quiberon Bay with the intention of cutting off the base of the Brest peninsula and isolating the German forces there; once that was done they could be 'rolled up' at leisure, since they would have been isolated from the main battle and virtually sterilized. At the same time 6th Armored Division would head for Brest, clearing much of central Brittany and, again, isolating a large body of German forces to be cleared out in due course. Finally a special 'Task Force A' would seize the main railway line, capturing the bridges before they could be destroyed, so as to ensure a working supply route for the future. With all this completed, Third Army would then, leaving the bottled-up Germans to be dealt with by others, turn eastwards and charge en masse through the rear of the German Army, doing as much damage as possible.

Preparing the ground

'Cobra' was scheduled for 24 July, but at the last moment the weather turned bad and air support, upon which the initial breakout depended, was almost impossible. At the last minute the air attack was cancelled, but much of the attacking force was airborne by that time and failed to hear of the cancellation. Fighter bombers attacked their targets successfully, but the heavy bombers, due to poor visibility and high winds, dumped several hundreds of tons of bombs haphazardly across the front, much of which landed in the US areas. The attack was re-scheduled for 25 July, when better weather was forecast; once more the ground troops stood by to advance, once more the air forces mounted their attack, once more, by bad planning and inaccurate bombing, US troops were killed by the hundred.

A BRITISH CROCODILE FLAME TANK PROVIDING SUPPORT FOR US TROOPS ATTACKING THE FORTRESS OF BREST. THE US SERVICE OF SUPPLY HAD REFUSED THE BRITISH SPECIALIZED ARMOR, BUT US COMMANDERS SOON REALIZED WHAT THEY WERE MISSING AND MANAGED TO 'BORROW' PARTICULAR TYPES OF ARMOR WHEN THEY WERE NEEDED.

Nevertheless the advance began; although the German Panzer Lehr Division, facing the advance, had been badly battered by the bombardment, the divisions on its flanks had been less affected and were soon putting up a stiff resistance. By nightfall the American advance had made about 2000 yards, and on the following morning Collins sent in two mobile divisions. The first, advancing east towards Marigny met little opposition, but the other, going for Coutances, was soon fighting desperately.

It was now time to make the move towards Avranches, and Bradley sent Patton forward to act as his deputy commander on this front, which came as something of a shock to First Army who had never experienced Patton's brand of leadership before. Under Patton two armored divisions set off southward; the German forces facing them moved sideways in order to avoid the frontal blow and also to position themselves to take the Americans in the flank as they passed, but inadvertently they side-stepped into the path of VII Corps and were cut to pieces. By 30 July Avranches was secured and Patton was ready for his breakout; he had VII US Corps at Avranches, XV and XX US Corps behind them, and in the rear was XII Corps HQ busily marshalling the last elements of Third Army as they left the beachhead and moved up to where Patton awaited them.

To round out the preliminaries there was a re-shuffle of the US commanders; General Hodges took over First US Army, General Bradley became commander of 12th Army Group, and on 1 August the US Third Army officially became operational as part of that group. The status of Third Army was not made public; "In the interests of cover and deception there will be no announcement of this for some time" ordered Eisenhower. Georgie Patton and his army were going to be a big surprise for the German high command.

The advance
Under the orders of VIII Corps, as they stood on 31 July, General Wood, commanding 4th Armored Division, was to advance and take Rennes. At one minute past midnight on 1 August, Patton took over command and he immediately ordered Wood to continue beyond Rennes and take Quiberon, so sealing off the Brittany peninsula. Wood needed no urging, and by evening his troops were at the gates of Rennes, facing a vigorous defense from the German garrison. That night General Koenig, commanding the 91st Infantry Division, arrived outside Rennes with more troops and, being senior, assumed command from Woods, allowing the latter to refuel his tanks, bypass Rennes, and head for Quiberon.

The 6th Armored Division, under General Grow, had been ordered to take Dinan, but Patton now appeared and ordered him to go instead for Brest, bypassing any resistance he encountered on the way. Patton had made a bet with Montgomery that Patton's troops would have Brest 'by Saturday night', and that

THE REMAINS OF A PANZER IV TANK AFTER BEING HIT AT SHORT RANGE. IN SPITE OF THE OVERAWING THREAT OF THE TIGER AND PANTHER THE PANZER IV WAS STILL THE BACKBONE OF THE GERMAN ARMORED FORCE. BY 1944 IT HAD BEEN PROGRESSIVELY IMPROVED UNTIL IT HAD 80MM OF ARMOR AND A POWERFUL 75MM GUN. OVER 8000 WERE BUILT AND IT REMAINED IN FULL PRODUCTION UNTIL MARCH 1945 IN SPITE OF ALLIED AIR ATTACKS ON GERMAN FACTORIES.

was five days and 200 miles away. By the evening of 2 August Grow was outside Dinan, having covered 35 miles that day. But Dinan was strongly held, so Grow decided to leave it to 79th Infantry Division, who were following him up, to deal with while he bypassed and went ahead for Brest. But after advancing another 30 miles he was halted by a furious General Middleton, who ordered Grow to turn about and return to Dinan to capture it as part of a Corps plan of attack against St Malo.

The next morning, as Grow and his staff were mulling over their new orders and how to go about turning round an entire Armored Division, Patton appeared like a thunderbolt. "What the hell are you doing here? I told you to go to Brest!" he shouted. Grow produced his written orders from Middleton; Patton read the order, stuffed the offending paper in his pocket, and said "I'll see Middleton; you go where I told you to go." But the day's delay had proved fatal; it was all the time the German Army had needed to get reinforcements into Brest and prepare their defenses. With a highly professional and tough German paratroop commander, General Hermann Ramcke in command of 40,000 troops, several Saturdays came and went before the US flag flew above Brest.

While these moves had been taking place there had been a rapid change in the strategic picture. Because of withdrawals of troops to reinforce the battles around Caen, and the withdrawals to garrison the ports, the German forces were now very thin on the ground in the rest of Brittany. Moreover the French Forces of the Interior were coming to life, and it was considered that with their help a single US Corps could now clear the Brittany area. Bradley therefore made sweeping changes in his plan; he ordered Hodges and First Army to advance towards Mayenne and Domfront, and, cancelling Patton's previous orders, Third Army were now to secure the Brittany ports 'using minimum forces' and, with the bulk of the army, set off eastward and clear the countryside south to the line of the River Loire. They were then to hold themselves in preparation for further action to the east and southeast.

Once again, Patton envisaged his own version of this plan. His eye was firmly on the German forces who were to the east of the River Seine, and he was of the opinion that a very rapid dash due east, followed by a sharp left turn and an equally rapid move north would encircle them. And so as soon as Bradley had given him his marching orders, Patton sent XV Corps off with orders to get to the Mayenne river, between Mayenne and Chateau-Gontier, while XX Corps headed south for the Loire. These two rivers marked the limit of his first 'bound', and after both Corps had arrived on this line they would then make a second 'bound' towards Le Mans. His third step would depend upon what the German reaction would be to his first two, but he warned the commander of XV Corps not to be surprised if he was to be ordered to move north.

The German Army, however, was not waiting around to see what Patton was going to do; they had their own ideas. On 2 August radio intelligence picked up a message from Hitler's headquarters to von Kluge, German Commander in the West; he was instructed to ignore the American break-out, collect four Panzer divisions, add some infantry divisions, and aim this force at Avranches in a counter-attack. Bradley's task now was to spoil this attack, but to do it in a manner which would not reveal to the Germans that their coded radio traffic was being intercepted and decoded. Next came a reply from von Kluge to Hitler, pointing out that the proposed attack would "lay open my whole attacking force to be cut off in the west." This brought an equally quick reply from Hitler that the attack must be carried out, and Eisenhower ordered Montgomery to be

prepared to move down from the north while Bradley's 12th Army Group prepared to move from the south, so encircling the Germans in exactly the manner which von Kluge feared.

On 7 August, at dawn, the Panzers struck with enough momentum to carry them nearly seven miles through the American positions before massive artillery fire and air strikes halted them. By nightfall von Kluge signalled Hitler that the advance had been stopped and half his tanks destroyed, and that he intended to withdraw in view of a possible British advance from the north. Hitler, as usual, absolutely refused to countenance any withdrawal: "I command that the attack be prosecuted daringly and recklessly towards the sea, regardless of risk . . ." He then ordered three more Panzer divisions from the Caen area to move down to reinforce von Kluge and help get his attack rolling once more. But before they could begin their move, the Allies struck.

The drive for Falaise

The first move was from the north, with the Canadian Army attacking towards Falaise. In spite of 1000 bombers blasting away before them, the Canadians were halted eight miles from their objective, the three Panzer divisions which should have gone to von Kluge being the principal obstacle.

On 8 August Bradley and Eisenhower decided that it was time to spring the trap; Patton was ordered to turn XV Corps north from Le Mans and 'advance on the axis Alencon-Sees to the line of the Army Group boundary.' This boundary was a line drawn between Sees and Carrouges, south of Argentan. Hodges was ordered to thrust up towards Flers, on Patton's left, the general intention being for these two forces to arrive on the boundary line and serve as the anvil against which the hammer of the British and Canadian advance would crush the Germans. Whilst this may have been a sound enough plan for Bradley, it did not satisfy Patton, and he modified the orders, instructing XV Corps to advance to the boundary but to be prepared to continue moving northward until they met the Canadians or the British coming the other way, so closing the net around the German forces.

What happened after that has been the source of argument and contention ever since. Patton's XV Corps moved northward, but were delayed when the French 2nd Armoured Division, which had been attached to XV Corps, strayed on to the wrong road and thus blocked the American advance on Argentan. By the time this had been sorted out, as usual the delay had given the Germans valuable time in which to organize their defense, and the subsequent American advance made little progress.

In the north the Canadian and Polish armored divisions planned an attack which was compromised when a Canadian officer, with the plans in his pocket, was captured. The German defenses were hurriedly re-aligned and the Canadian advance stopped in its

ORDER OF BATTLE	
ALLIED	**AXIS**
3rd US Army (Commander: Maj-Gen Patton)	1 Ger Army: (Commander: Gen von Rundstedt)
12th Corps (Commander: Eddy) 15th Corps (Commander: Haislip) 20th Corps (Commander: Walker)	5 Pz Army (Commander: Gen von Manteuffel) 3 Pz Bdes 1 Pz Div (24 tks) 1 Pz Gren Div

THREE SOMEWHAT APPREHENSIVE AMERICAN SOLDIERS LOOK
OVER AN ABANDONED PANTHER TANK OUTSIDE THE FRENCH
CATHEDRAL OF CHARTRES. THE PANTHER WAS THE GERMAN
RESPONSE TO THE SOVIET T-34 TANK, AND WITH UP TO 110MM OF
ARMOR AND A POTENT 75MM GUN IT WAS ALMOST AS FEARED AS
THE MORE FAMOUS TIGER. ALMOST 6000 WERE BUILT BETWEEN
JANUARY 1943 AND APRIL 1945 AND IT FORMED THE BASIS FOR THE
JAGDPANTHER TANK DESTROYER ARMED WITH AN 88MM GUN.

tracks. An attempt to unstick it with an air attack had
the usual result; the aviators misread their maps, killed
over 60 Canadian and Polish troops and wounded
another 250.

By the end of the day on 14 August the Canadian and
Polish forces were being firmly held three miles from
Falaise, while in the south Patton had decided to move
across the boundary line and was headed for Falaise as
fast as he could go. But at this point he was halted by
Bradley; all troops in the vicinity of Argentan were to be
pulled back, all further movement north was to stop,
and XV Corps was to 'concentrate preparatory to
operations in another direction'.

Just what made Bradley issue this order has never
been made clear, and it is this order which lies at the
heart of the controversy about the closing of the Falaise
Gap. Bradley's stated reason for giving it was that had
XV Corps been allowed to continue northwards they
might have bumped the Canadian Army coming south
and caused what he called 'a calamitous battle between
friends'. This can only be considered as a thin excuse;
armies have staffs who are skilled at arranging this sort

of encounter; they have radios with which they can
communicate; they have observation aircraft which can
report on the positions of the forces on the ground. It
has also been alleged that Montgomery deliberately
withheld permission for XV Corps to cross the boundary, but the records show that he actually urged them
to advance further, to take Chambois and Trun, and he
was too firmly set on destroying the German forces to
sit pedantically on a matter of a corps boundary. He
doubtless overlooked the formality of issuing permission, but at the same time Bradley and Eisenhower
should have been alert to it and formally asked for permission. But in any event, Patton was already over the
line and going well when Bradley stopped him.

Eventually the Falaise Gap was closed when
Canadian and Polish troops battered their way south
and met the Americans near Chambois on 19 August.
Over 10,000 German troops were killed and 50,000
taken prisoner in the pocket, while the loss to the
German Army in guns and transport was enormous.
But by that time Patton and the Third Army had moved
on. On 17 August Bradley had ordered him east to the
River Seine, there to secure a crossing.

Patton leads the charge

Patton's XII Corps, under Maj Gen Cook, led the way
and by the 19th they were at Orleans and Chartres. The
liberation of Orleans, with its association with Joan of
Arc, caught the journalists' fancy, and it was then
decided that the news that the Third Army was loose,
under Patton's command, would be released to the

COMMANDERS IN THE MOBILE WAR

Major-General George S Patton (1885–1945)

'**G**eorgie' Patton was flamboyant, opinionated, reckless of authority and avid for publicity; having said that, one must also add that he was without doubt the most brilliant commander of mobile armored forces that the Allied armies produced during the Second World War, and if a balance has to be struck it must be admitted that his abilities as a fighting soldier more than compensated for his shortcomings as a diplomat.

Patton came from a well-to-do military family, graduated from West Point in 1909 and made his mark in the Mexican Expedition under General Pershing. A cavalryman, he went to France in a staff post, pestered Pershing for active command, and became the first member of the nascent US Tank Corps, eventually leading his tanks with typical Patton panache in the St Mihiel and Meuse-Argonne battles. Seeing no future in the emasculated postwar tank corps he returned to the cavalry, but kept up his interest in mechanized warfare. In 1940, within sight of retirement, he was given command of 2nd Armored Division and then I Armored Corps, and in 1942 inaugurated the Desert Training Center. In 1942 he was selected to command ground forces in the US invasion of North Africa. After the defeat at the Kasserine Pass he took over US 2nd Corps and revitalized it, leading it very ably for the remainder of the Tunisian campaign.

In 1943 he led 7th US Army into Sicily with great success but was then withdrawn to Britain in the wake of a scandal caused by his excitedly slapping a shell-shocked soldier in a field hospital. Taking over the 'Armeegruppe Patton' he then assumed command of 3rd US Army. At the end of the war he took over the Military Government of Bavaria, but his undiplomatic tongue soon had him in political hot water over the question of employing ex-Nazi officials, and he was given the command of the 15th US Army, an organization which by then was no more than a small staff charged with writing the official history of the European campaign. On 9 December 1945, setting out on a day's duck-hunting expedition, he was involved in a traffic accident, suffered a broken neck, and died on 21 December. He is buried with his 3rd Army soldiers in Luxembourg.

Maj-Gen Omar N Bradley (1893–1981)

Omar Bradley was every inch the professional soldier, a highly-skilled infantryman with a sound grasp of tactics and a high awareness of the possible. A quiet and withdrawn man, he was the very opposite of Patton and yet the two worked well together — probably because he posed no danger to Patton's love of the limelight. Careful of his troops, he was a popular general, and probably one of the best all-round soldiers the US Army has produced.

Bradley came from Missouri and graduated from West Point in 1915, entering the infantry. Between the wars he did the usual progression of Infantry School, Command & General Staff College and War College, and at the outbreak of the war he was commanding the Infantry School at Fort Benning. He was then given command of the 82nd Infantry Division and later the 28th. He accompanied the American invasion of North Africa as Eisenhower's observer, but when Patton was given command of 2nd Corps and sent to redress the Kasserine setback, he asked for Bradley as his deputy. When Patton moved on, Bradley took command of 2nd Corps and led it with quiet efficiency throughout the rest of the Tunisian campaign.

He continued to command 2nd Corps as part of Patton's 7th Army in the Sicily campaign, and **GENERALS BRADLEY (LEFT), EISENHOWER (CENTER) AND PATTON REVIEWING EVENTS IN THE MIDDLE OF BASTOGNE.**

captured Messina after five weeks of operations. In view of his combat record, Bradley was then selected to command the US troops in the Normandy invasion, and he returned to Britain to assume command of 1st US Army. He led this army in fine style, and to him must be given the credit for organizing the American breakout from the beachhead. On 1 August 1944 he was given command of 12th Army Group, consisting of the US 1st, 3rd, 9th and 15th Armies, and this became the force which swept across France and liberated Paris. In the winter of 1944–45 he successfully withstood the final German throw in the Ardennes, after which his troops crossed the Rhine at Remagen, drove across Germany and met the Soviet Army at the Elbe.

In postwar years he headed the Veterans Administration, then in 1948 became Chief of Staff. From 1949 to 1953 he was Chairman of the Joint Chiefs of Staff, being promoted General of the Army in 1950.

Field-Marshal Gunther von Kluge (1882–1944)

Von Kluge was an energetic and

ambitious soldier, somewhat intolerant of the shortcomings of others, but a skilled practitioner with a sound tactical sense, ample initiative and capable of lightning decisions in the heat of battle. He enjoyed soldiering and was often to be found well forward among his troops, though he was never on particularly good terms with the soldiers.

In the immediate pre-war years von Kluge had many differences of opinion with Guderian over the employment of armor, not having very much faith in Guderian's views (he once complained that all Guderian's operations "Hung by a thread"), and yet during the invasions of Poland in 1939 and France in 1940 he commanded the Fourth Army with skill and dash, making full use of the armor under his command. For the invasion of Russia he was given command of Army Group Center, and distinguished himself in the long defensive battles of 1942–43.

When von Rundstedt fell from favor, von Kluge was sent to France to replace him as C-in-C West, and five days later the Allied invasion struck. Expected to 'hold on everywhere' he was poorly served by High Command in respect of strategic guidance, but he did his best to implement Hitler's orders, mounting an unsuccessful counterattack against Bradley's 1st Army. He saw the possibility of his troops being trapped at Falaise, said as much to Hitler and demanded permission to withdraw them, for which he was relieved of his command. Already under suspicion for his lack of

enthusiasm for the National Socialist ethic, he was further suspected as a possible conspirator in the July Bomb Plot, though he actually had no part in it. Appreciating that surrender was the only logical course, and with suspicion closing in around him, he took poison on 18 August 1944.

General Hasso von Manteuffel (1897–   )

Von Manteuffel entered the German Army as a Lieutenant of Hussars in 1916. Remaining in the army after the war, he became interested in the possibilities of armor and spent some time at the Panzer Training School. He filled a number of relatively minor posts until late in 1941 when he was appointed to command a Panzer Grenadier Regiment. In July 1942 he took over 7 Panzer Brigade, and in February 1943 was promoted to Major General and given command of the Division 'von Manteuffel' on the Russian front. He soon moved on to command 7 Panzer Division and then the elite 'Gross-Deutschland' Panzer Grenadier Division.

Throughout all these moves he had progressively demonstrated his considerable ability as a commander of armored troops, and many experts regard him as one of the finest Panzer commanders of the war. In September 1944 he became General der Panzertruppen and took command of 5th Panzer Army, in which capacity he faced Patton on the German border. In February 1945 he moved to command 3rd Panzer Army, and retained this post until the war ended.

world. The occasion was marred by Maj Gen Cook being taken ill and hospitalized; Cook was a thruster, and Patton was to feel his loss.

Leaving Chartres behind, the 79th Armored Division moved ahead once more and reached the Seine at Mantes-la-Jolie, some 30 miles northwest of Paris. A foot patrol found a small weir over which they were able to cross the river, and by the afternoon of 20 August a pontoon bridge had been thrown across and a bridgehead established. Leaving this for future use by First Army, Patton now swung his force eastward and aimed for the eastern side of Paris, crossing the Seine at Fontainbleu, Montereau and Sens.

In this latter town the arrival of the American Army was so unexpected that the advance troops rounded up German officers taking a Sunday afternoon stroll in their dress uniforms. Having made their initial crossings, some delay was caused by the need to construct bridges heavy enough to carry the armored vehicles, but by 25 August there were four major bridgeheads across the Seine to the east of Paris and one to the west. On that day General Dietrich von Cholitz, commander of the Paris garrison, surrendered the city, with all its bridges intact, to the US First Army.

In the west, the German Army, in spite of the terrible price it had paid at Falaise, was still a formidable fighting force, and it was making an orderly withdrawal towards the Seine at Rouen, pursued by the British and Canadian armies, which were having to fight for every step of the journey. If the Seine crossing around Rouen could be taken by an Allied force, then once again a large German force would be surrounded and ripe for destruction. Patton was therefore ordered to turn XV Corps west and drive along the left (southern) bank of the Seine west of Paris, to Louviers, whilst XIX Corps advanced against Elbeuf. This move was so obvious that the Germans had anticipated it, and it took XV Corps five days to cover the 20 miles to Louviers, while XIX had similar problems in getting to Elbeuf.

In those five days most of the retreating German forces managed to fall back on Rouen, cross the river and get away. Had Patton been allowed to cross the river and move along the northern bank he would have met less opposition and would have been in a position to catch the Germans as they came out of the bridgeheads. According to General Speidel, CoS of German Army Group B, this would have totally destroyed the German forces. As it was, some 50,000 escaped across the river to fight another day.

With the crossings of the Seine intact, Third Army could look with some satisfaction on their advance from Normandy. In 26 days they had advanced 400 miles, had accounted for over 100,000 German troops, 500 tanks and 700 pieces of artillery, and had achieved this for casualties of about 16,000, less than 13 percent of the total Allied casualties since the invasion. But there was no time to rest on their laurels. On 26 August the advance began again, Patton now being ordered to follow the general line of the principal eastward roads to the area of Metz and Strasbourg on the German border, the area which Patton called 'The Nancy Gap'.

The Nancy Gap has been the traditional gateway to France since time began and has seen invaders of every shape and size pass through. As a result it has been fortified in one way or another since the time of the Roman legions, and by the dawn of the 20th Century the fortifications were among the most powerful in the world. The strong defenses built under the French failed against the Prussians in 1870, who thereby gained the area as part of Germany and set about making the defenses even stronger. When Metz and Strasburg passed back into French hands in 1918 they again overhauled the fortresses, and when the Germans took them again in 1940 they underwent more strengthening. It was into this hornet's nest that the Third Army were now headed.

Patton's plan was relatively simple; first to clear to the River Marne, then to the Moselle, then to the Saar and finally reach the Rhine. The rivers were about 30 miles apart and thus gave a natural sequence of bounds. Once arrived at the Rhine, bridgeheads would be established and the subsequent actions would then be decided. But on 20 August things began to go wrong.

On that day it became obvious to Patton that he had little or no organized German resistance in front of him, and that so long as Third Army kept up the pressure there was no way they could be stopped before the Rhine. He ordered Walker's XX Corps and Eddy's XII Corps to cross the Meuse at Commercy and Verdun before the Germans could blow the bridges there, and then go as fast as possible for the next boundary, the Moselle. The two corps set off in high spirits, but shortly afterwards came the first hint of trouble; Patton's supply column, back in Orleans, reported that the day's air-lift of 140,000 gallons of gasoline had failed to arrive. It transpired that there was a plan afoot to drop paratroops ahead of First Army, and for this reason the supply aircraft which should have delivered Patton's fuel had been withdrawn. Hardly had he assimilated this news than a message came from Eddy that he was stalled at Saint Dizier, thirty miles short of the Meuse, because he was running short of fuel.

The fuel problem

Patton ordered him to push on until his tanks ran dry, then get out and walk the rest if he had to, but take the Meuse crossings. By draining fuel from non-essential vehicles to feed the armor, Eddy managed to reach the river and make a crossing at Saint Mihiel.

Next day, instead of going forward to lead the drive to the Moselle as he had intended, Patton instead went to Bradley's headquarters to plead for fuel. "Damn it, Brad," he cried, "just give me 400,000 gallons of gas and I'll put you inside Germany in two days!" But as Bradley later said, "George might as well have asked for the moon". There was no gasoline. The Allies had outrun their supply lines.

The principal cause was the absence of port facilities.

Only Cherbourg had so far been liberated, and the greater part of the Allied supply requirement was still being manhandled across the invasion beaches. Once ashore, the next problem was to move the supplies — fuel, rations, ammunition — to where they were needed, in the front line. Original Allied forecasts had assumed that the Seine would be reached on D + 90, after which there would be a period for consolidation and for the build-up of a supply base. In fact the Seine had been crossed on D + 74 and there had been no pause for stocktaking. The French railway system was so badly damaged by Allied air attacks, intended to prevent German reinforcements moving forward, that it was in no condition to move large quantities of supplies. And the last straw was an agreement to provide Paris with 1500 tons of supplies daily, most of which appears to have gone straight on to the black market; certainly in late 1944 the air was full of stories of Patton's tanks being stalled while his gasoline was being sold on the back streets of Paris.

One way of breaking this deadlock was the institution of the 'Red Ball System'; two road routes from the Normandy beaches to a dump area north of Paris were signposted 'RED BALL UP' 'RED BALL DOWN'. Along the UP route went convoys of trucks, day and night, ferrying supplies forward; on the DOWN route the same trucks roared back empty to fetch more supplies. Both routes were prohibited to other traffic and patrolled by military police and rescue crews who removed any broken-down truck before it could cause delay. In this way over 7000 tons of supplies moved up every day, but at a terrible cost. Units were stripped of their transport to feed the Red Ball Route, thus immobilizing them, and far too much of the precious gasoline was burned up in carrying the rest forward.

One way and another, though, the Third Army managed to keep moving. Captured fuel dumps went into Patton's tanks and were not reported back to 12 Army Group HQ as they should have been; raids were made on neighboring formations not of Third Army; French towns were systematically combed for fuel. But to no avail; the daily requirement of 400,000 gallons was met by 300,000, then by 150,000 then, finally, by no more than 32,000. Patton was going to have to stop.

The problem was, of course, compounded by the fact that Patton's was not the only army on the move; there was also Hodges' First Army and Montgomery's 21st Army Group to be supplied via the Red Ball Route. It was now that the argument between the single thrust and the broad thrust began to have some point; in brief the 'single thrust' argument claimed that it would be better to concentrate the Allied might into a single powerful fist which would smash through the German defenses and drive right to Berlin. The 'broad front' argument said that a single thrust was asking to be chopped off and that a more efficient, if slower, advance would be made by all the armies working in concert. Practical soldiers, like Patton and Montgomery, were certain that the single thrust was the answer; the only question was which force was to do the thrusting, and there they disagreed — naturally enough. Patton wanted to go through the Nancy Gap and swing up into the Ruhr, while Montgomery wanted to strike from Belgium and swing down to the Ruhr.

Eisenhower was firmly against both of them, and the principal protagonist of the broad front theory; and since he was the Allied Commander in Chief, that settled the argument. But in the face of the gasoline shortage he had to lay down some firm rules about who was going to move and who was not. On 2 September, at an Army Commanders' conference, he decreed that the First US and Second British armies operating around Mons would complete their planned moves, after which the front would fall static until a sufficient base of supplies had been built up. Once this was done, First and Third US Armies would attack the German 'West Wall' defenses, while the British 21st Army

TROOPS OF THE THIRD ARMY, ACCOMPANIED BY A 'TANKDOZER' PASSING THROUGH THE SIEGFRIED LINE DEFENSES. THIS SECTION IS A BELT OF 'DRAGON'S TEETH' CONCRETE TANK OBSTACLES, AND IT CAN BE SEEN THAT WHERE THE ROAD PASSES THROUGH THE BELT THERE ARE RETRACTABLE STEEL OBSTACLES FOR CLOSING THE ROAD. THE SIEGFRIED LINE WAS NEVER AS COMPLICATED AS THE MAGINOT LINE AND WAS NOT A FORMIDABLE OBSTACLE.

Group would advance into Belgium. Patton protested, and pointed in vain to 'Ultra' decryptions which showed quite plainly that German defenses were in disarray and that a firm push would undoubtedly break through and into Germany with little opposition. But Eisenhower's mind was made up and the broad front policy ruled.

There is no doubt that Eisenhower was wrong in every particular in this instance. Had Patton been given his head — or Montgomery for that matter — there is every likelihood that the war would have been shortened by six months. Two-thirds of all the Allied casualties in Europe occurred after this vital conference, and had Germany been invaded by a strong mobile armored force in October 1944, the map of Europe might today show considerable differences.

Be that as it may, on 4 September, with supplies having been built up, Patton was given permission to renew his advance to the Saar river. But the 12-day pause had given the Germans all the time they needed to organize their defenses, and the opportunity had been lost to make any spectacular drive. Von Rundstedt had been appointed Commander in Chief West by Hitler and had appointed General Westphal, a brilliant soldier, as his Chief of Staff. Their orders were to hold the British at arm's length, command the Low Countries, and in time mount a counter-attack towards Reims and Paris.

Facing Patton was General von Knobelsdorff, a Panzer veteran of Russia, who had rounded up sufficient troops to establish a seven-division defensive front backed by a Panzer brigade. Moreover Patton's forces were now leaving the rolling farmland which had characterized the terrain all the way from the beachheads and were now entering hilly, wooded country with deep ravines and sunken roads, difficult enough for foot soldiers and almost impossible to clear by armored forces. And neither Patton, nor General Walker of XX Corps, appear to have had the slightest inkling of what lay waiting for them in the fortifications of Metz.

Snarl-up at Metz

The US Army had never, ever, been called upon to attack fortifications as the Europeans knew them; the US engineer manuals described fortification, but what they really meant was 'field fortification', makeshift works put up by a field army to give sufficient protection to keep off minor raids and patrols. Moreover the US soldier of 1944 probably assumed that modern aircraft, armor and artillery had rendered fortification obsolete.

What confronted Patton was series of *festen,* best described as a piece of terrain into which a massive granite and concrete labyrinth had been sunk, bristling with concealed artillery, machine guns, flamethrowers, mortars and every other kind of weapon. Every weapon was protected by concrete or armor or both; there were subterranean command posts, hospitals, power plants, barracks, kitchens, telephone exchanges and repair shops. The whole area was surrounded by barbed wire, deep ditches, unclimbable fences and mines. Inside the area the various strongpoints were separated above the ground by wire and mines, traps and obstacles, and each strongpoint was covered by the fire of at least two others. The underground tunnels connecting each component were also mined, so that if, by some fluke, an enemy managed to occupy part of the *feste*, he did not automatically gain access to all of it.

Eight of these strongpoints had been built around Metz, others around Thionville to the north, all carefully sited to prevent any crossing of the Moselle. During most of the war they had been far from any fighting and had been used as schools of military instruction, supply depots and administrative units, but now they were swept and dusted and put into fighting order.

In order to get Third Army moving once more the first job was to distribute gasoline to the hundreds of vehicles stranded around the area between Verdun and Reims, to get them moving and concentrate them. It was not until 6 September that the advance could get under way; and it is a token of Patton's speed of movement that the SHAEF map section were unable to provide him with maps, since his advance had outstripped their map printing schedule. All that Third Army had to go on were a quantity of Michelin tourist maps rounded up from the shops of Paris. Hampered by a stiff rearguard action from 17 SS Panzer Division, the Third Army forces moved towards the Moselle to find that all the bridges had been blown.

However, reconnaissance troops reported four or five areas which appeared fordable, but when the advance units tried to reach them they ran into trouble. Every approach to the river in this area is down a narrow ravine, and every ravine was mined and covered by German artillery. It took some severe fighting to get the first US troops to the river bank, and once they were there they had to wait for the engineers to struggle through the backed-up traffic in the ravines in order to bring up the bridging equipment. 5th Infantry Division was ordered to make a crossing at Dornot, but 7th Armored got there first, and the result was a traffic jam of monster proportions as two divisions struggled to get free of each other. And in the middle of it all, sleet began to fall.

What these two divisions did not know was that across the river were two of the Metz forts, Sommy and Ste Blaize, sited years before simply and solely to deny any crossing at Dornot. And at daybreak on 8 September these two forts began pouring fire into the seething mass of men and vehicles on the river bank.

By afternoon, two companies of infantry had managed to get across the river in assault boats and set out to capture Fort Ste Blaize. God knows what they expected, but when they finally left the shelter of a wood they found themselves confronted by five rows of barbed wire, a 4m high steel fence, and a dry ditch 15m wide and 5m deep. A captured prisoner informed them that the fort contained 1500 SS men, and this decided the Operations Officer that the task was beyond the capability of two companies of infantry.

He pulled back and called for artillery fire which landed on top of him, causing several casualties. It also provoked fire from the fort and the arrival of German infantry who began attacking on two sides. The only course open was a quick retreat back to the bridgehead. The 5th Infantry requested permission to abandon the attempt, but they were told to stay; their attempts might not yield much result but they were taking pressure off another bridgehead being put across at Arnaville. The Dornot bridgehead held until the night of 10 September when it was withdrawn, with only two officers uninjured and 200 casualties.

The Arnaville bridgehead was successful, even though it was under constant fire from several forts, and 2nd Infantry Division, advancing to the north were also held up by a ring of forts. The Americans applied their usual solution and called up Thunderbolt P47 fighter-bombers with 500lb armor-piercing bombs; they did no discernable damage to the forts at all. After several more attempts to move had been blocked, 5th Infantry were withdrawn and replaced by the 90th Infantry Division. They tried advancing in a different direction but merely ran into a fresh cluster of forts and were stopped dead.

PLAN OF FORT DRIANT

Fort Driant was typical of the Metz works attacked by the Third Army. Built in 1899 by the Germans, it was the key to the western defenses of Metz. Built on a plateau to the southwest of the city it was intended to hinder any enemy advance from the south along the Moselle Valley. It was to have been garrisoned by about 2000 men. Originally called 'Feste Kronprinz' it was re-named when the French took it over in 1918. The fort is roughly triangular, about 1km long and from 300 to 500m deep. The area is protected by a wide barbed wire fence, and the main fort additionally isolated by a deep ditch. Across the top of

the fort were four gun batteries, two each of three 100mm guns and two of three 15cm howitzers. There were also five concrete barracks, numbers of infantry shelters and armored infantry posts, pillboxes and concreted trenches, all connected by underground passages so that the occupants could move from one place to another without exposing themselves. In addition there was a detached three-gun battery at the south-east corner which covered the slopes across which an attack would have to come.

Driant was besieged by the US 5th Infantry Division from 27 September to 13 October 1944, when the Americans withdrew, unable to take the fort. It had, after all, been designed by experts for the very task, of repulsing an enemy from the southwest.

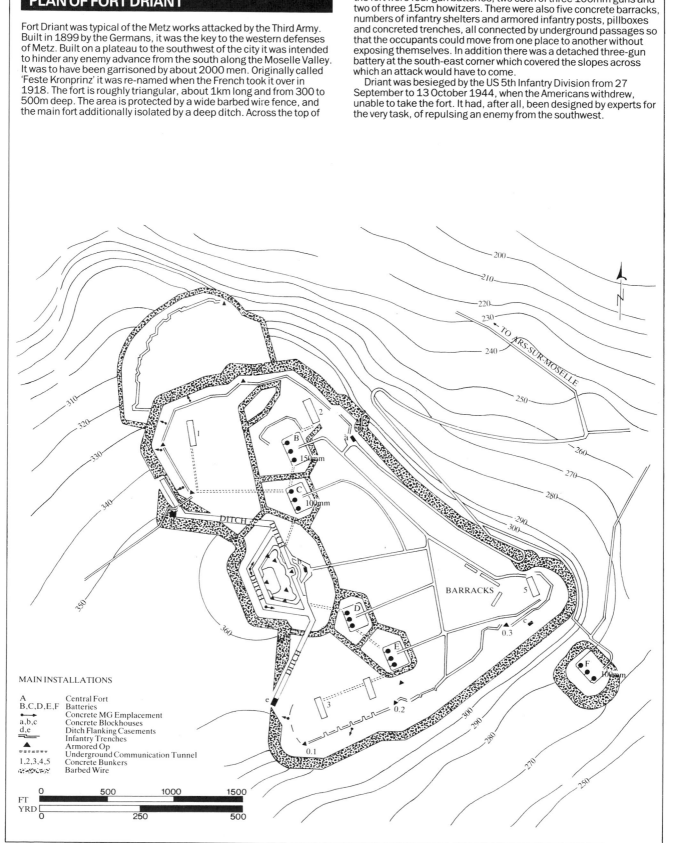

MAIN INSTALLATIONS

A	Central Fort
B,C,D,E,F	Batteries
●▶	Concrete MG Emplacement
a,b,c	Concrete Blockhouses
d,e	Ditch Flanking Casements
┄┄┄	Infantry Trenches
▲	Armored Op
┄┄┄┄	Underground Communication Tunnel
1,2,3,4,5	Concrete Bunkers
ᴥᴥᴥᴥ	Barbed Wire

FT   0   500   1000   1500
YRD   0   250   500

167

By the end of September the Allied line was in trouble. The weather had broken, rivers were flooded, tracks and roads turned into bogs, and the effects were soon felt in the supply line. Third Army was restricted to patrol activity, and most of the effort went to the north of the Allied front where the British and Canadians were attempting to clear the Scheldt river and open the port of Antwerp to relieve the supply problem. Third Army continued to batter against the Metz forts without success, until in early November it was decided to try and sweep around Metz and leave the forts to starve. Indeed, the orders for advance on 9 November actually contained the words 'the destruction and capture of the Metz garrison without the investiture or siege of the Metz forts.'

The 90th Infantry Division was to move around the north side of Metz, while the 10th Armored Division would sweep around the south, to meet 5th Infantry who would break out of their Arnaville bridgehead. 90th Infantry thus discovered that Thionville was heavily fortified too, and one fort had to be taken by costly frontal assault before bridging could be completed and the force could cross the Moselle. The encirclement was duly made and US troops then advanced into the city of Metz, gradually securing it since the Garrison Commander refused to surrender. But the forts were left alone, to surrender in their own time, and the last did not capitulate until 9 December when it had run out of food.

The noticeable thing about the hold-up around Metz was Patton's absence from the scene. Normally a man who was in the thick of the action, and a man who, like all good officers, was unerring in appearing at any bottleneck or disaster, he kept well clear of Metz, leaving it to Walton Walker to sort out. It is hard to resist the conclusion that in this particular battle Patton knew he was out of his element. Not that he was idle; he spent the time profitably, chasing up his supplies and making sure Third Army were well supplied with winter clothing and equipment, rations and mail, checking on his workshop facilities and rear echelons. And, of course, preparing plans for his next move once Metz was secured.

Advance on a broad front

The next move, coordinated by Eisenhower, was to be a general advance; First Army would attack from Aachen and secure a bridgehead across the Rhine near Cologne. Ninth Army would move northward to meet Montgomery's 21st Army Group south of Nijmegen and then swing east across the top of the Ruhr while First went across the bottom and then north until the whole Ruhr was encircled. Third Army was to play a secondary role while all this went on, crossing the Rhine somewhere between Worms and Mainz 'when logistic conditions permit'. But the weather was foul and the whole operation was postponed indefinitely until it improved sufficiently to allow the preliminary bombardments and air strikes.

The operation eventually began on 8 November and the Third Army moved over the Moselle. Almost immediately the weather broke once more and in appalling conditions they struggled forward until, early in December, they had closed up to the West Wall defenses on the German border. Aided by information from a talkative prisoner they then sat down to prepare for an attack on 19 December. But it was forestalled by the German counter-attack against VIII Corps in the Ardennes, which became known as the 'Battle of the Bulge'.

Col Oscar Koch, Patton's intelligence officer, had foreseen this German move; for some time he had been amassing information about what appeared to be an unusual build-up of German forces in front of VIII Corps, to Patton's north. He drew Patton's attention to this, and as a result he and Patton devised a number of contingency plans. When the German attack took place, on 16 December, Bradley's reaction was to take 10th Armored Division from Patton and 7th Armored Division from Simpson's 9th Army to reinforce VIII Corps. Patton was less than pleased to see his projected Saar offensive emasculated by the removal of one division, but he soon realized that Oscar Koch's predictions had come true and sent the division on its way within an hour.

Next day things looked grim; no less than fourteen

AN ANGRY GENERAL PATTON RETURNS TO HIS JEEP AFTER CHASTISING THE COMMANDER OF AN M26 PERSHING HEAVY TANK FOR CARRYING TOO MANY PROTECTIVE SANDBAGS. THE DESIRE FOR ADDED PROTECTION FREQUENTLY LED TO THIRD ARMY TANKS BREAKING DOWN UNDER THE ADDITIONAL WEIGHT AND ADDING TO THE LOGISTIC PROBLEMS.

German divisions had been identified opposite VIII Corps and the German thrust had driven over 50 miles, almost reaching Dinant. American units were dragging cooks, clerks and drivers into action, and countless small-unit actions were being fought as individual groups of US troops, bypassed by the Panzers, fought it out with the follow-up infantry. Thanks to Koch's precision, Patton was ready to move his entire force if necessary, and when Eisenhower asked him for assistance he was able to perform a minor military miracle, withdrawing his army from contact, turning it through a right-angle and moving it off northward so that within 48 hours of receiving his orders he had two divisions engaging the enemy and a third following up. Within a week he was to move 250,000 men and 133,000 vehicles over 50 miles in freezing weather over ice-bound roads and in a major snowstorm. It was one of the most remarkable feats of command and organization in military history, but unfortunately one which is only appreciated by the experts who know how difficult such a maneuver is.

On Christmas Day 1944 General Gaffey's Combat Command B of 4th Armored Division broke through the encircling Germans to relieve Bastogne; this was the turning point. On the following day the weather began to improve, Allied air forces were able to make an appearance in force for the first time since the battle began, and the Germans began to withdraw. Patton now urged Eisenhower to allow him to strike northward, across the base of the 'Bulge', in conjunction with Hodges' First Army striking south, so as to repeat the Falaise Gap entrapment. But Eisenhower disagreed; this would upset his 'Broad Front' strategy; instead, First and Third would indeed attack from north and south but not at the base. They would drive into the 'Bulge' about halfway along its length, to meet at Houffalize. This was duly done, against stiff opposition, and the armies met at the appointed place on 16 January. Although the maneuver was successful, it had not gathered in the quantity of troops and equipment which would have resulted had Patton's idea been adopted, and a large slice of the German Army survived, to regroup in Germany and prepare for more battle.

Patton now looked forward to resuming his Saar offensive, but this did not fit in with Eisenhower's plans; Third Army was to sit on the defensive, to permit the maximum supplies to go to First and Ninth Armies who were headed for the Ruhr. This course of action did not appeal to Patton; he had a well-trained army at the top of its form, and to allow it to sit around would soon take the edge from its morale. So Patton examined his front carefully to see what he could find in the way of an excuse for some action. He soon appeared before Bradley asking for permission to mount a minor operation in the Eifel Mountains 'so as to prevent the enemy withdrawing troops for use against other sectors'. This seemed a quite reasonable maneuver, and Bradley approved an operation to 'pierce the Siegfried defenses

THIRD ARMY INFANTRY DASH INTO WERNBERG, SUPPORTED BY A SHERMAN TANK OF THE 11TH ARMORED DIVISION AND UNDER THE COVER OF SMOKE PROVIDED BY A BURNING BUILDING. NOTE THE SPARE AMMUNITION AND OTHER ACQUISITIONS PILED ON THE BACK OF THE TANK AND SECURED BY A TARPAULIN.

north of the Moselle and advance quietly to the Kyll', this being a small river some 12 miles inside the German border. There he was to stop and set up a bridgehead for future use.

Although the other Allied operations to the north ran into problems, principally from the weather, Third Army moved ahead very smoothly and by 22 February they had taken a sizeable piece of the Siegfried Line defenses between Bitberg and Prum and established a bridgehead over the Sauer river near Trier. On hearing of this Bradley telephoned Patton and suggested that he should now go on the defensive. Patton replied that he was the oldest and most experienced soldier in the US forces in Europe and if Bradley wanted him on the defensive he could damned well relieve him. Bradley did not pursue the argument.

Patton goes his own way

Patton now fell back on a favorite maneuver, the 'reconnaissance in force.' This is a perfectly valid military practice, but as performed by Patton had a new twist. He would send out a patrol with orders to reconnoiter some objective. The patrol, instead of merely reconnoitering and reporting back, would radio in 'we have reached village X and it is unoccupied'; or 'We have reached village X and have come under fire'. Either way, Patton would look surprised and say 'Good Gracious, we must do something to assist those poor fellows', and would then send a supporting force either to fill the vacuum or relieve the hard-pressed reconnaissance troops. And thus the American line had made a small advance; this, of course, meant that a little salient had been formed, and it was therefore vital to move the

line forward on the flanks. So Patton's static line was always inching forward, and by the end of February he was well past the Kyll river.

On 2 March Bradley sent orders for Third Army to drive through the Eifel Mountains for Koblenz while First Army were moving against Cologne. In spite of the mountainous country and narrow roads, 4th Armored Division moved ahead fast and within two days had advanced 35 miles and cut off a large number of German troops. Organized resistance west of the Rhine collapsed. First Army found an undamaged bridge at Remagen, which they seized, and Bradley now sent Patton into the Palatinate, a roughly triangular area of southern Germany bounded by the Rhine and Moselle rivers. At the base of this triangle lay the US Seventh Army, fighting against the West Wall defenses, and if Patton was now to swing southwards into the Palatinate he could cut off a large number of German troops as well as relieving the pressure on Seventh Army.

On 13 March, Patton took off from his start line on the Moselle with nine divisions. The move of XX Corps from Trier attracted a counter-attack from a German mountain division, which led to some stiff fighting but which pulled German strength away from XII Corps who were thus able to get four bridges across the Moselle and put 14 battalions of infantry across the river. 4th Armored now moved into the lead and within two days were on the line of the River Nahe, halfway across the Palatinate.

Patton now reasoned that if the Germans had anything at all left with which to fight, the Nahe was where they would make their effort, and he halted his advance and brought up all his artillery. Just as he had assumed, the German counterattack came, and it was blown to

shreds by artillery fire and then rolled back by XII Corps. By this time XX Corps had overcome its opposition and came up alongside XII Corps, and together they rolled over the rest of the Palatinate to strike the Rhine between Mainz and Mannheim. As predicted the West Wall defenses crumbled under the threat from their rear and the US Seventh Army came through; by 21 March German resistance in the Palatinate was ended, with the loss of over 70,000 prisoners.

Patton had, all this time, been working to his own private plans; and now he had his forces on the Rhine precisely where he had foreseen months before. He had a special naval squad with amphibian carriers rehearsing back at Tours, in France, and with General Eddy of XII Corps he had picked out a possible crossing point from the map several weeks before. He now sent for the naval squad, while Maj Gen Conklin, his Chief Engineer, moved up all the bridging equipment he could muster. Assuming the Germans would be expecting an attempt to cross in the vicinity of Mainz, Patton set up an artillery barrage and smoke screen while XX and XII Corps drove south along the bank of the Rhine. Under cover of the smoke 5th and 90th Divisions dropped out of the line of march, turned east and dashed for the river at Oppenheim, 15 miles from Mainz.

The Amphibians were brought up, rubber boats removed from trucks, and at 2200hrs, with no air cover, no artillery bombardment and no commotion, the 23rd Infantry Regiment slipped across the Rhine. By dawn they had six battalions across for negligible losses, accompanied by some amphibious tanks, and the bridgehead was secured. Conklin's engineers now moved in and began laying a pontoon bridge across the Rhine as fast as they could go.

Patton was delighted. The crossing of the Rhine was the Holy Grail of the Allied advance at that time, and great preparations were being made by 21st Army Group and First Army to make powerful crossings in their zones. Now Patton telephoned Bradley, who was eating breakfast in his HQ, and said "Brad, don't tell anyone, but I'm across!" "Well I'm damned," said Bradley; "You mean across the Rhine?" "I sure am," said Patton. "I sneaked a division over last night. There are so few Krauts around they don't know it yet, so don't make any announcement. We'll keep it secret and see how it goes."

You do not keep secrets of that sort from the German Army for long, and during the day some 150 air strikes were mounted against Conklin's pontoon bridge, though without doing serious damage. In the evening Patton again rang Bradley: "Brad, for God's sake tell the world we're across. We knocked down 33 Krauts today when they came for our bridge. I want the world to know that Third Army made it before Monty starts across!".

Next morning Patton went to Oppenheim to inspect progress. After satisfying himself over the bridge and its defenses, he led his party across the bridge. Halfway over, he stopped. "Time for a short halt" he said; then turned to the edge of the bridge, unbuttoned his breeches and urinated into the Rhine. "I've been looking forward to this for a long time" he said, and then walked on across the Rhine and into the heartland of Germany.

The lessons

In a campaign as long as Patton's crossing of France, one can doubtless extract a wide variety of lessons on

THE M4A3 SHERMAN TANK

Designed in 1941, the M4 Sherman tank became the most important Allied tank of the war. The design was aimed at a vehicle capable of mass-production, using a welded hull and cast turret, and armed with a 75mm turret gun capable of all-round fire; this replaced the earlier M3 design which had a 75mm gun only capable of fire over a limited arc. Several design features were suggested by a British Military Mission, based on experience in combat in the Western Desert.

Production began in early 1942 and 11 different plants manufactured a total of 48,600 before the war ended. The Sherman appeared in a number of variations, and the M4A3 was the standard American Army vehicle. It differed from other designs by using a specially-designed Ford V-8 engine; the M4A4, used by the British Army, had a General Motors engine, while the M4A2 used a diesel engine and was largely supplied to Russia. Some 11,000 M4A3 were built, armed with 75mm and 76mm guns or 105mm howitzers.

Although there were logistic and training advantages in having a standard tank, the fact was that the Sherman stayed in production too long and by 1944 should have been replaced. But nothing was ready, and the Sherman remained as the Allies' principal battle tank even though it was overmatched by most of the German armor it met. The Sherman is still in use by several countries today, little changed from its wartime specification.

A Third Army Sherman tank, with sandbags, logs and spare wheels acting as additional protection.

A SHERMAN TANK FITTED WITH A MULTIPLE ROCKET LAUNCHER.
KNOWN AS 'CALLIOPE', THIS FIRED SIXTY 4.5IN ROCKETS, SINGLY
OR IN A SALVO, AND WAS POPULAR AS A BOMBARDMENT WEAPON
OR AS A PROTECTION FOR RIVER CROSSINGS. NOTE THE SIMPLE
CONSTRUCTION; ELEVATION WAS GIVEN BY ATTACHING A LINK
BETWEEN THE BARREL OF THE TANK GUN AND THE LAUNCHER.

relatively minor points. But taking the campaign as a whole, it can be seen that two salient points stand out. Firstly, supply; the sinews of war are the supply lines, and unless supply is properly organized disaster is never far away. Had the supply situation been better, Patton need never have been stalled for the lack of gasoline and he would undoubtedly have been in Germany several weeks or even months sooner. This, though, does not count against Patton, since the provision of supplies was out of his hands. He could, and did, plead eloquently and pound the table, but to little avail. The organization for supply was faulty and that was the sum and substance of the matter.

Secondly, one can draw the conclusion that when a commander has a flair for mobile warfare, it is better to give him his head, even at the expense of curtailing action in other sectors, than to put a bridle on him. Generals who can 'read the battle' are few and far between, and Patton was one of them. He had a gift for seeing through the overlying detail to the heart of a tactical situation, and he had a gift for divining what the enemy was likely to do, and a general in that class deserves to be given the benefit of any doubt.

Patton offered Eisenhower many opportunities to take action which, had they been properly exploited, might well have shortened the war and put a different political face on postwar Europe. In August 1944 he was halted at Argentan instead of being allowed to close the Falaise Gap, thereby allowing several thousand German troops to escape to fight again. Had he cleared the northern bank of the Seine instead of the southern, he could have removed what remained of the Falaise escapees. Had he not been held back by Eisenhower's rationing of fuel he could have crossed the Rhine and broken a hole in the German defenses. Had he been allowed to chop off the German salient in the Battle of the Bulge at the point he wanted, several more thousand German troops would have been removed from the board. And, outside our timespan, had he been given his head and reached Prague ahead of the Soviets, who knows what the consequences might have been for the Czechs?

This is not to say that Patton was omniscient; far from it. He had put up some monumental follies prior to the invasion — the famous slapping of a sick soldier in Sicily was but one of his more prominent idiocies. He was far from adroit at positional warfare, as he showed at Metz. He was a showman who resented other showmen who might take some of the limelight — which is why he detested Montgomery. But for all that he was a fighting soldier, and probably the best exponent of mobile armored warfare on the Allied side. He was one of the few Allied generals who could say, with the Duke of Wellington, 'I don't think it would have been done had I not been there.'

OPERATION VERITABLE WESTERN EUROPE

ARTILLERY
FEBRUARY 1945

Overleaf

The Reichswald battles during Operation Veritable were bitterly
contested but they did open up the way to the Rhine, which Montgomery approached with caution
with a massive assault planned in detail. (*Crossing thc Rhine at Xanten* by T. Cuneo, OBE. Courtesy
Royal Tank Regiment)

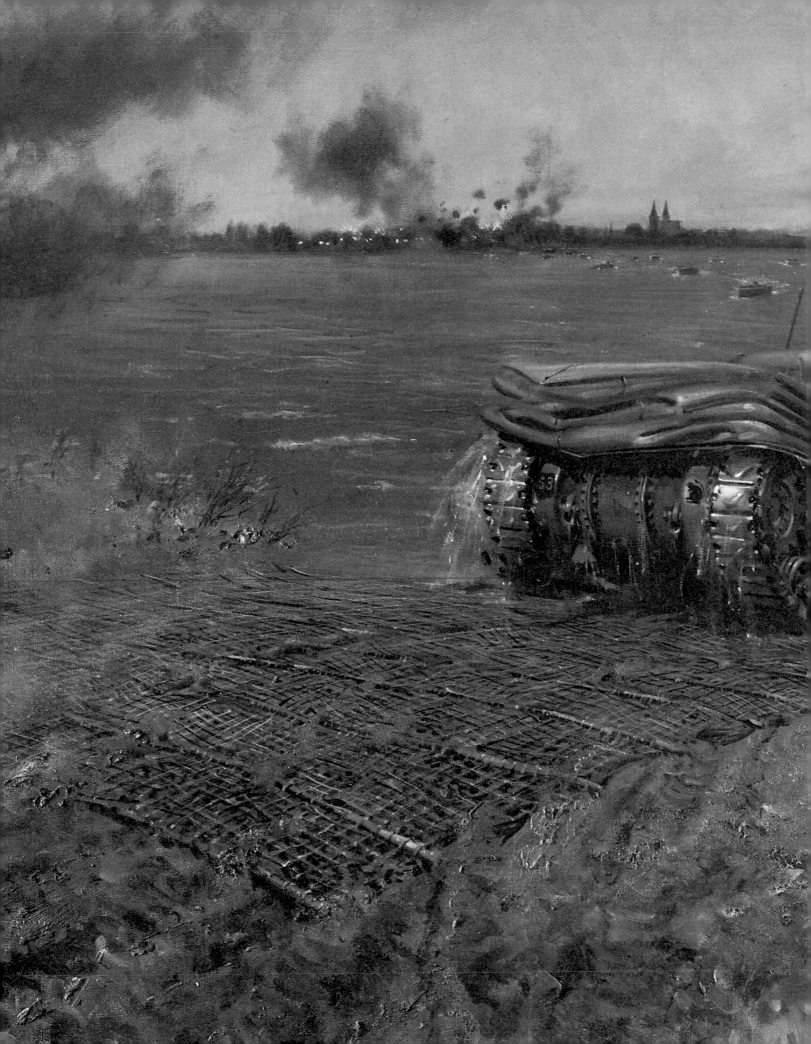

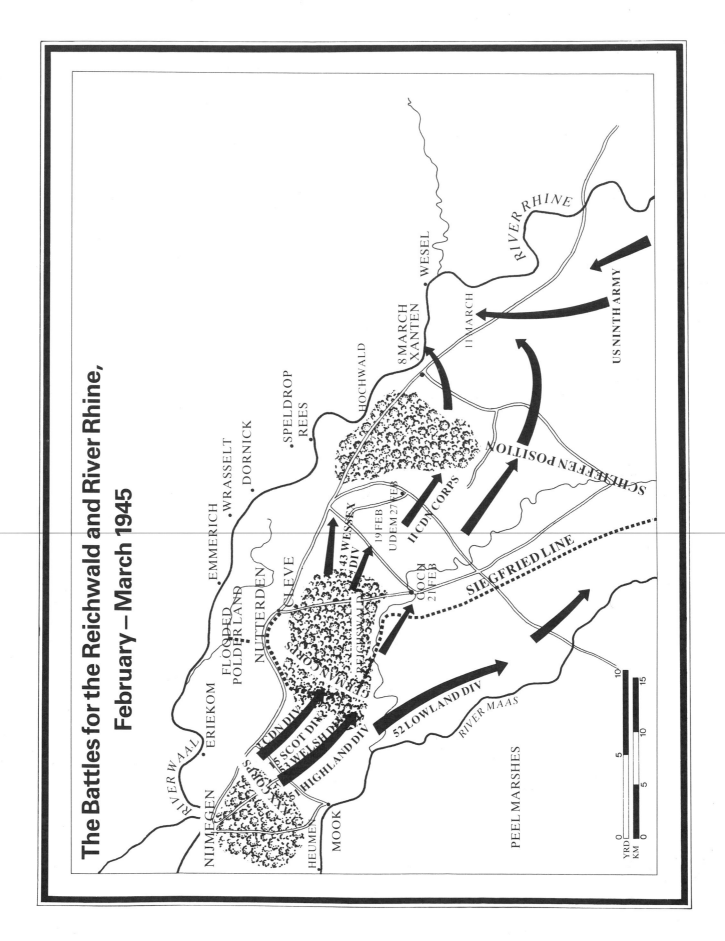

The Battles for the Reichwald and River Rhine, February – March 1945

RIVER RHINE

WESEL

US NINTH ARMY

8 MARCH
XANTEN

11 MARCH

HOCHWALD

SPELDROP
REES

SCHLIEFFEN POSITION

DORNICK

WRASSELT

EMMERICH

II CDN CORPS

43 WESSEX
DIV

19 FEB
UDEM 27 FEB

CLEVE

SIEGFRIED LINE

NUTTERDEN

FLOODED
POLDER LAND

GOCH
21 FEB

ERIEKOM

RIVER WAAL

NIJMEGEN

GERMAN CORPS

REICHSWALD

XXX CORPS

I CDN DIV

15 SCOT DIV

53 WELSH DIV

51 HIGHLAND DIV

52 LOWLAND DIV

RIVER MAAS

MOOK

HEUMEN

PEEL MARSHES

YRD 0   5   10
KM 0   5   10   15

As with infantry, so it is difficult to select a battle in which nothing but artillery has been used to effect the result; in every battle it is the combined efforts of the 'teeth arms' which produce the final answer and apportioning credit between them can be a very sensitive matter. Operation 'Veritable' has been selected, after much thought, since it represents what was probably the zenith of British artillery organization. Never again is the world likely to see such concentrations of artillery, if only for the fact that they would invite instant missile strikes if they were ever tried on a modern battlefield. Moreover the technology of war has moved in such a direction that the devastation once caused by a thousand pieces of artillery can now be duplicated by a single nuclear bomb. So 'Veritable' is of interest less from its tactical aspects than for its technical ones.

Even the most critical of analysts will generally admit, when pressed, that they can find little wrong with the operations of the Royal Regiment of Artillery during World War Two. Montgomery himself, not given to lavish praise, singled the artillery out for mention in his final despatch, whilst, most recently, the historian Mr Corelli Barnett, in a letter to the *Sunday Telegraph* on 17 August, 1986 dealing with the Western Desert campaign was moved to say '. . . the Eighth Army as a whole (the Royal Artillery excepted) was the military equivalent of British Leyland in terms of professionalism and sluggishness . . .'. Winston Churchill might be thought critical when he (reputedly) said 'Renown awaits the commander who restores artillery to its pre-eminence on the battlefield' but in fact he was saying nothing the artillery did not know already and was attempting to drive the facts of life into the heads of senior commanders at a time when dispersion and fragmentation were the fashion.

The background

Although the British artillery organization had undergone some upheavals in the first months of the war, shifting from a somewhat unrealistic system of organization foisted on them in peacetime into something more capable of providing the support the army required, by 1944 they had tuned and refined it until it was probably the finest artillery system in the world. Not the largest; the Soviets took that prize easily, with the Americans close behind, but neither of them had the carefully constructed system of interlocking components nor the ability to control the guns which the British had perfected.

The basic building block of the Royal Artillery, insofar as the field army was concerned, was the battery of field guns, which in 1944 meant eight 25-pounder guns. These weapons were capable of firing their 25lb shell at high or low angles of fire, so replicating a gun or a howitzer as necessary, and they had a maximum range of 13,400 yards which out-ranged their equivalent in the US or German armies though with a lighter projectile. The battery was split into two troops, which could act

independently or together as required, and three batteries formed a regiment, which was normally the direct support of a brigade. Three regiments formed the support for a division, and this 'rule of three' matched the infantry components; the three regiments supported the three brigades of the division, and the three batteries of the brigade's regiment each looked after one battalion.

ORDER OF BATTLE

ALLIED

21st Army Gp

1st Canadian Army (Commander: Gen Crerar)

2nd Cdn Corps (Commander: Simonds)

   11th (Brit) Armd Div
   4th (Cdn) Armd Div

30th Corps (Commander: Lt-Gen Horrocks)

   Guards Armd Div
   2nd Cdn Div
   3rd Cdn Div
   15th (Scottish) Inf Div
   51st (Highland) Div
   53rd (Welsh) Div
   43rd (Wessex) Div (Reserve)
   Elements 79th Armd Div (attached)

Gun strength:	1050 guns & howitzers
	12 × 32bbl rocket projectors
	114 40mm LAA guns
	80 4.2in mortars
	60 75mm (Sherman tank) guns
	24 17pr anti-tank used as field
	188 Vickers machine guns

Ammunition —	preliminary bombardments — 91,330 shells, 1596 tons
	Pepper-Pots — 145,000 shells, 520 tons
	Barrage — 160,338 shells, 2793 tons
	Concentrations — 54,329 shells, 1044 tons
	Machine guns — 2 million rounds
	Total ammunition expended — 5953 tons

Casualties: 15,634 K/M/W

GERMAN

Army Group 'G' (Commander: Gen von Blaskowitz)

1 Parachute Army (Commander: Gen von Schlemm)

2 Parachute Corps

   190 Inf Div
   7 Parachute Div
   8 Parachute Div

86 Corps (Commander: von Luttwitz)

   84 Inf Division
   180 Inf Div
   Elements 2 Parachute Div

17 Panzer Corps

47 Panzer Corps

Reserve: 116 Panzer, 15 Panzer Grenadier Divs

Gun strength: 68 Field; 36 Med; 31 Heavy AA; 12 other. Total 147

Casualties 22,000 K/M/W, 22,000 POW

A BRITISH 3.7IN ANTI-AIRCRAFT GUN FIRING IN THE GROUND SUPPORT ROLE. USED IN THIS WAY IT COULD SEND ITS 12.7KG SHELL TO A MAXIMUM RANGE OF 18,800M, AND THE AUTOMATIC LOADING MECHANISM GAVE IT A RATE OF FIRE OF 25 ROUNDS PER MINUTE SHOULD THIS EVER BE REQUIRED. WHY WAS IT NEVER USED AS AN ANTI-TANK WEAPON LIKE THE GERMAN 88MM GUN? BECAUSE THE BRITISH ARMY NEVER HAD ENOUGH OF THEM.

However, it would be wrong to think, as many laymen do, that this was the sum total of the artillery's organization and that the divisional regiments did more or less as the division pleased. They certainly obeyed the requests of the divisional commander; but the rule in the artillery is that the guns are to be controlled from the highest possible level, and as each level of command was reached, so there was an artillery commander, working with his formation commander. Thus the divisional HQ held the Brigadier RA; he commanded the divisional artillery but, in his turn, was under orders from the Corps Commander RA at corps HQ, who in turn referred upwards to the Commander RA of Army HQ.

The commanders at Corps and Army level had artillery of their own in the form of regiments of medium (4.5in and 5.5in guns), heavy (155mm guns, 7.2in and 8in howitzers) and superheavy (240mm howitzers and 8in guns) which would be allocated to their various levels in accordance with whatever they felt was required for a particular operation. And above all this came the 'AGRA' — Army Group RA — commanded (naturally) by the 'CAGRA', which disposed of all these artillery reserves and, on occasion, commanded some of them operationally.

All these levels were connected by the artillery's own radio network which extended, in relays, down from the CAGRA to the lonely forward observer sitting in a slit trench alongside the infantry platoon commander, and this allowed a flow of information from the front to the rear which very often produced better intelligence than the rest of the army's networks. Moreover, and this is perhaps the most vital point, the system allowed a single observer anywhere on the front to call down the fire of his own regiment, of his divisional artillery, of the corps artillery or even, in extreme cases, of the entire army artillery on to a target. The speed of response to such a call — which was signalled by special codewords — became a point of pride within every gunner regiment, since the observer never called for higher formations unless he had good reason.

A field regiment of three batteries could produce fire on the ground from such a call within one minute; the response time, naturally, slowed as the participation grew, since the observer's request had to be relayed by his regimental HQ to Division and then disseminated by division to the other two regiments, and so on up the line (though most artillery batteries had 'acquired' spare radios, listened surreptitiously to the regimental network, and were very often preparing for a target before the official order reached them). But in good conditions the entire army artillery could be turned on to a single target within ten or fifteen minutes.

Added to this formal organization, came a somewhat less formal one which, nevertheless, was stitched into the network very efficiently when required. This was composed of what the soldiers elegantly referred to as the 'odds and sods' of artillery which might or might not be available. For example, in Italy and Northwest Europe, by 1944 the Allies had air superiority and there were several regiments of 3.7in anti-aircraft guns which had little to do in their basic air defense role. Many were therefore co-opted into the field army organization, since a 3.7in gun had a very useful long-range bombardment capability. Heavy mortars and anti-tank guns were also a gunner responsibility at that time, and if there were spare units, they could be brought into the overall plan.

The plan

By the beginning of 1945 the Allied armies had fought their way through France, Belgium and Holland, had beaten off Hitler's last throw at the Battle of the Bulge, and were preparing to take their final step and cross the River Rhine into the German heartland. Confronting them was the Siegfried Line, Hitler's answer to the Maginot Line, which barred the way to the Rhine. As a preliminary to crossing the river it would be necessary to clear the ground on the Allied side, and this meant a head-on collision with the defenses.

By this time too the Allied commanders were feeling the manpower pinch; even the Americans were short of infantry replacements, and the British had already been forced to disband divisions and use their component parts to reinforce other formations. The Allied generals had by now realized that elegant tactics were all very well in their place but they tended to be heavy in casualties, and that the German (and the Japanese) soldier was not to be displaced by slippy footwork; he had to be punched, and artillery was the fist.

The overall plan for the run up to the Rhine had been put together by Eisenhower at a meeting in Brussels in October 1944; in broad terms, 12th and 21st Army Groups would destroy the Germans west of the Rhine and then cross to clear the area of the Ruhr and advance through the North German Plain. Having been handed this, Montgomery commanding 21st Army Group, gave the 1st Canadian Army the task of planning an offensive south-east from the Nijmegen area into the area between the Rhine and Maas rivers. But before much could be done the Battle of the Bulge erupted and put the plan back; it also re-distributed the forces somewhat, 12th Army Group now being further south than had been originally envisaged.

The final plan was unchanged so far as the 1st Canadian Army was concerned, but the other element now became Operation Grenade, carried out by the 9th US Army who would advance northwards, crossing the Roer river and then swinging north-east to meet the oncoming Canadians and so pinch the German defenses between them.

Geographic, tactical and climatic difficulties appeared at every turn. As to the geography, the area to be cleared was a strip of land between the Rhine and Meuse rivers — known, in this region, as the Waal and Maas. At Nijmegen, the starting point of the attack, the

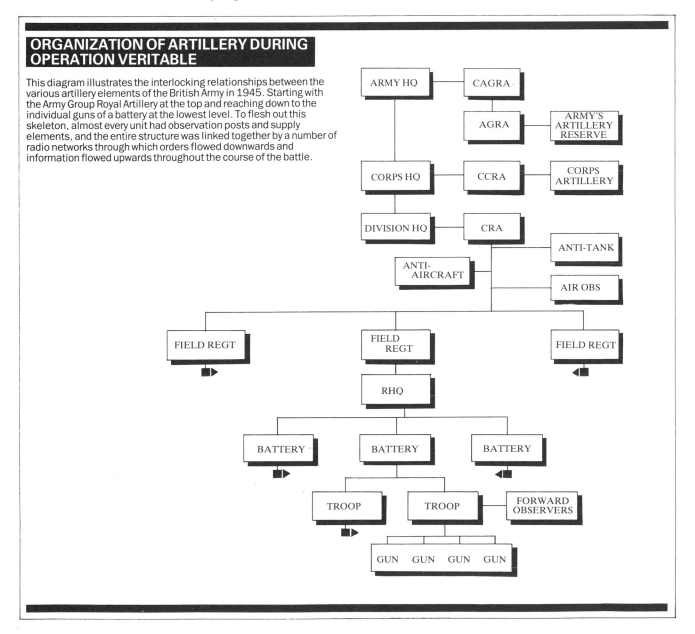

ORGANIZATION OF ARTILLERY DURING OPERATION VERITABLE

This diagram illustrates the interlocking relationships between the various artillery elements of the British Army in 1945. Starting with the Army Group Royal Artillery at the top and reaching down to the individual guns of a battery at the lowest level. To flesh out this skeleton, almost every unit had observation posts and supply elements, and the entire structure was linked together by a number of radio networks through which orders flowed downwards and information flowed upwards throughout the course of the battle.

A PANTHER STALKING ITS PREY. THE SPARE TRACK LINKS HUNG AROUND THE SIDES ALSO ACT AS AUXILIARY PROTECTION AGAINST LIGHT HAND-HELD WEAPONS SUCH AS THE BAZOOKA AND PIAT, AND THE ENTIRE TANK HAS BEEN COATED WITH 'ZIMMERIT', AN ANTI-MAGNETIC PASTE PREVENTING MAGNETIC MINES AND GRENADES STICKING TO THE ARMOR LONG ENOUGH TO DO DAMAGE

two rivers were about six miles apart, but as the attack moved south-west, so the rivers diverged, until towards the Ruhr the distance was between forty and fifty miles. This led to a tactical problem; the classic maneuver is to start on a wide front and funnel troops into a narrow one to concentrate the force into a spearhead with local superiority, so punching through the opposition. Here the reverse obtained; the troops would start out tightly bunched and then be spread thinner and thinner as they advanced.

More geographic problems arose when the terrain was considered. The area between the rivers was partly low-lying 'polder' or recovered farmland, which could be easily flooded and had been by the Germans, so that the Allied advance was denied what might have been good clear areas for armor to operate. There was, too, the enormous area of the 'Reichswald' state forest, some fifty square miles divided by rides and fire-breaks which gave excellent fields of fire to machine guns but which were generally too narrow to support traffic.

The climatic problems had been made worse by the delay imposed because of the necessity of fighting the Battle of the Bulge. The plan had originally called for an attack in December, when the ground would be frozen hard and would give firm going for armor, solid gun platforms, good roads for resupply and dry, if cold, feet for the infantry. But by the time the attack was finally mounted, early in February, an early thaw had set in which, combined with several days of heavy rain, had turned the area into a sea of mud which grew worse with each day.

And finally, of course, there were the defenses and the troops manning them. There were three principal defensive lines; the first rested its northern flank on the flooded polder at Wyler and ran south-south-east to rest its southern end on the Maas just downstream of its confluence with the River Niers, so that the whole line ran along the western face of the Reichswald. The second line, which was anticipated to be the most formidable, was the northern section of the vaunted Siegfried Line, coming up behind the Maas from the area of Venlo and generally following the line of the Dutch border to Goch. From Goch it swung west to Hekkens and then north across the center of the Reichswald to Frasselt, followed the highway to Donsbrucken and finally cut across the flooded area.

Although viewed with misgivings by the planners, in fact it was no more formidable than the other lines, since in this area it was not the highly sophisticated concrete and steel fortifications found further south, but had been more of a notional defense line until the approach of the Allies had called it into use.

The third defensive line was some miles further back, running from Rees, on the Waal opposite a relatively unflooded stretch of ground, down to Geldern. All these lines were composed of multiple rows of trenches, minefields, belts of barbed wire, a variety of strong-points which ranged from purpose-built pillboxes and bunkers to farmhouses strengthened with sandbags, and anti-tank ditches, obstacles and traps; the whole generously covered by machine guns and mortars. In addition the principal villages and towns had also been converted into independent strongpoints, ringed by defensive lines, so that they could each be the focus of a hard-fought defense irrespective of what might be the state of the main defensive lines.

Manning these defenses there was General Schlemm's First Parachute Army, comprising II Parachute Corps, LXXVI Infantry Corps, and elements of 7th Parachute Division. These forces were supplemented by the XLVII Panzer Corps who were in the process of reinforcing the area, and 116 Panzer and 15 Panzergrenadier Divisions as reserves. Early in February another parachute regiment had been moved into the area, and there were two battalions of medically-downgraded personnel holding the rear line; one was usually referred to by the Germans as the 'Stomach' Battalion, the other as the 'Ear' Battalion, and legend has it that the 'Stomach' were put into the line because the 'Ear' were unlikely to hear any opening barrage and might not know they were being attacked. To support these various formations there were about 36 self-propelled guns, no tanks, and just over 100 wheeled artillery pieces.

To take this difficult target, the Canadian 1st Army produced 340,000 men and just over 1000 guns, comprising II Canadian Corps and XXX British Corps. General Crerar, commanding the Canadian Army and what was now called Operation Veritable, decided on three distinct phases in the operation. Firstly the clearance of the Reichswald to a line beyond the second

German defensive line and running roughly between Cleve and Gennep; secondly a push past Goch to a line about halfway to the third German defensive line; and finally to breach this third line and reach his objective, a line between Gildern and Xanten.

The battle opens with formidable artillery support

A considerable amount of air support was made available to soften up the defenses; the whole of the 2nd Tactical Air Force was to be on call, but in addition a number of heavy bomber squadrons were put at the disposal of General Crerar. The question was where and when to use them; there were only two useful roads running through the area, which joined at Cleve and ran from there to Nijmegen as a single route. It was obvious that possession of this route was vital to the Allies, but it was equally obvious that the Germans were going to use these roads to bring up reserves, and the question thus became whether or not to interdict. The two vital points were Cleve and Goch and the matter came to a head when Crerar asked General Horrocks, commanding XXX Corps, whether he wanted Cleve 'taken out'.

Horrocks, afterwards, always recalled this as one of the worst decisions he was ever called upon to take, since he knew that 'taking out' mean the utter destruction of a beautiful town and the death of a large number of civilians; on the other hand, failure to 'take out' Cleve would leave the road open for German reinforcements to rush forward and counter his attack. So he

BELOW: A BRITISH 25-POUNDER FIELD GUN, BACKBONE OF THE DIVISIONAL ARTILLERY WITH A MAXIMUM RANGE OF 12,250M. NOTE THE AMMUNITION TRAILER, CAMOUFLAGED, IN THE FOREGROUND.
BOTTOM LEFT: THE 40MM BOFORS ANTI-AIRCRAFT GUN BEING LOADED WITH ITS FOUR-ROUND CLIP.
BOTTOM RIGHT: LOWERING THE BARREL ON TO THE 8IN HEAVY GUN, WHICH WAS TRANSPORTED IN TWO SECTIONS, CARRIAGE AND BARREL, AND ASSEMBLED ON SITE BY MEANS OF A CRANE.

OPPONENTS IN THE REICHSWALD

Lieut-General Sir Brian Horrocks (1895–1985)

LT GEN HORROCKS, SHORTLY AFTER TAKING OVER AS COMMANDER OF BRITISH 30 CORPS IN NORMANDY.

Known throughout the British Army as 'Jorrocks', General Horrocks was a colorful and competent officer who made his reputation principally as commander of 30 Corps in Northwest Europe; Montgomery, no mean judge of performance, considered him to be one of the best commanders of the war.

Horrocks first went to war in 1914 as a subaltern in the Middlesex Regiment, survived six weeks combat and spent the remainder of the war as a prisoner. Between the wars he served in regimental and staff posts, and in 1940 was an Instructor at the Royal Military Academy. From here he went to France commanding the 2nd Middlesex Regiment throughout Belgium and the Dunkirk evacuation.

He was, to some extent, a protege of Montgomery's, being appointed by him to command 13 Corps in the Western Desert in 1942. Here he fought at Alam Halfa and Alamein and continued the pursuit of Rommel to Tunisia, where he was severely wounded by an air attack, being forced to return to England to recuperate. Once fit, he was immediately recalled by Montgomery to take over 30 Corps in Normandy and continued to command it through Belgium and Holland and into Germany. He was involved in the ill-fated Arnhem operation, which failed through no fault of his, but the Reichswald was undoubtedly his greatest set-piece battle.

General Henry DG Crerar (1888–1965)

Crerar was appointed Chief of the Canadian General Staff in 1940 and sent to London to organize the training of Canadian troops as they arrived in Britain. In 1941 he resigned his post and accepted a drop in rank in order to command in the field, becoming Commander of 1st Canadian Corps, leading them in Sicily and capturing Catania. In 1943 he returned to Britain and took command of 1st Canadian Army, taking part in the invasion in June 1944. His army was involved at Caen and Falaise in 1944, then took Le Havre, Boulogne, Calais and finally, with 8 British divisions attached, cleared the mouth of the Scheldt estuary. His forces later broke through the Siegfried Line in Operation Veritable and entered Germany.

GENERAL CRERAR, COMMANDING THE 1ST CANADIAN ARMY AND OVERALL COMMANDER OF OPERATION VERITABLE.

General Johannes von Blaskowitz (1884–1945)

Blaskowitz was a quietly competent officer who had a reputation for speaking his mind. He commanded the 8th Army in the Polish Campaign and afterwards became commander of the Army of Occupation in Poland. In this post he attempted to run things in military fashion and twice complained to Hitler about the SS treatment of the population in general and the Jews in particular, though without effect. He held commands in Russia in 1942 and 1943, and in 1944 he was given Army Group G, composed of 7th and 15th Armies, holding the area between the Alps and the Loire River in France.

Under the pressure of the Allied advance, Army Group G found itself guarding the Rhine and its original composition was altered by the addition of a number of units, among them Schlemm's 1st Parachute Army. After the breakthrough by Horrocks, Blaskowitz' forces gradually retreated into Germany and became inextricably mixed with other groups. Blaskowitz was sent to command operations in the Netherlands and in May 1945 he surrendered to the Canadians and committed suicide before Nuremburg.

---

reluctantly agreed to have Cleve bombed, but stipulated incendiaries; the RAF, in their inscrutable wisdom, substituted high explosive and dumped 1384 tons of bombs on to the town, destroying it utterly and also making such a mess of the roads that when the time came the British and Canadian troops were unable to get through the wreckage for several hours.

The artillery support provided for the battle was formidable; probably the most powerful concentration of gun power ever employed by the Western Allies during the course of the war. A total of 576 25-pounders each with 700 rounds, 320 medium with 350 rounds, 76 heavy with 150 rounds, 6 super-heavy with 140 rounds and 72 3.7in heavy AA guns firing in the ground role took their places for the opening bombardment. In addition to this, Veritable saw the first application of a new idea, the 'Pepper-Pot Barrage'. It should be noted that the ammunition figures above refer to the ammunition which was with each gun when the battle began; they were to be resupplied throughout the battle thereafter.

For some time there had been argument between gunners and others as to what aspect of shelling had the greatest effect on the recipient. Was it the weight of shells dumped on him, or was it the quantity — or, as the current phrase had it, the number of bangs? One 100lb shell was effective, but was it four times as effective as one 25lb shell? Or would four 25lb shells, giving four distinct explosions, make the defender four times as apprehensive as the single explosion of the 100lb shell?

Operational Research suggested that it was the number of bangs which had the effect on morale, and therefore the Pepper-Pot Barrage was devised to increase the number of explosions. In this, every other weapon within range which might otherwise be un- or under-employed during the opening phase of the attack would be encouraged to add its quota of missiles to the bombardment, firing into areas of known enemy occupation. So for Veritable, the 'formal' bombardment by the 1050 guns just enumerated was backed up by the fire of 188 Vickers machine guns, 80 4.2in mortars, 114 40mm Bofors light anti-aircraft guns, 60 stationary Sherman tanks using their 75mm turret guns

as artillery, 24 17-pounder anti-tank guns firing high explosive shells and last, but very far from least, 12 32-barrel rocket launchers. This gave a grand total of 850 additional weapons in the pepper-pot. (According to one officer who was there the effect was enhanced by the troop officers standing behind the guns and discharging their revolvers into the air at an angle of 45°, but I do not think we need take this observation too seriously.)

The rocket launchers used in this bombardment were a relatively new addition to the Allied artillery strength. A 3in rocket with a high explosive head had been developed in Britain in 1938 as an air defense weapon and had been widely employed in Britain. In 1944 work had begun on utilizing this rocket as a ground support weapon by taking the motor and grafting on to it a 5in 29lb high explosive warhead fitted with an impact fuze. A one-ton trailer was fitted with 32 'barrels', which were merely an open frame with 32 spiral launching rails. The eventual result was a weapon which could

THE LAND MATTRESS ROCKET SYSTEM

THE LAND MATTRESS WAS A BOMBARDMENT ROCKET CONSTRUCTED BY GRAFTING A 3IN AIRCRAFT ROCKET MOTOR ON TO A 5IN 29LB NAVAL ROCKET WARHEAD AND FITTING AN IMPACT FUZE. THE LIGHTWEIGHT LAUNCHER WAS MOUNTED ON A ONE-TONNE TRAILER AND WAS LITTLE MORE THAN A SET OF HELICAL RAILS, WHICH GAVE THE ROCKETS A DEGREE OF SPIN AS THEY FLEW, WHICH HELPED ACCURACY. THE AMOUNT OF ELEVATION GIVEN BY THE LAUNCHER WAS LIMITED AND RANGE WAS CONTROLLED PARTLY BY ELEVATION AND PARTLY BY FITTING AERODYNAMIC SPOILERS TO THE WARHEAD TO DEGRADE THE FLIGHT. THE ROCKET HAD A MAXIMUM RANGE OF 7315M AND A BATTERY OF LAUNCHERS COULD SATURATE AN AREA SOME 800M SQUARE IN A MATTER OF SECONDS.

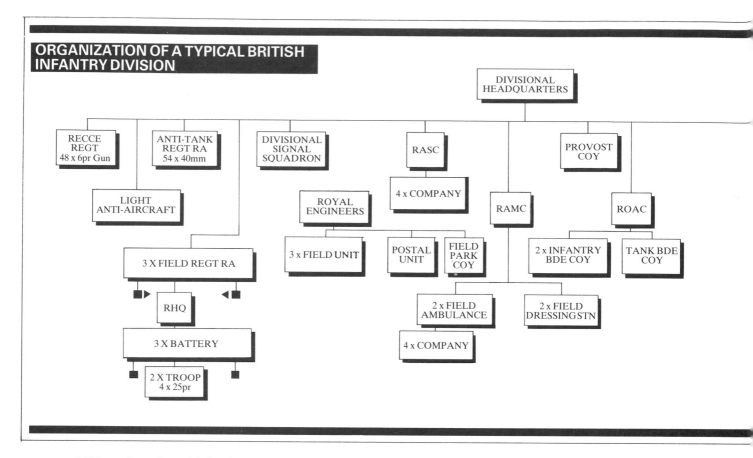

ORGANIZATION OF A TYPICAL BRITISH INFANTRY DIVISION

range to 8000 yards and could fire its 32 rockets in a volley taking about two seconds. Its accuracy was far from precise, but as an 'area weapon' it dumped the same weight of explosive as a regiment of medium guns from a lightweight trailer which could be towed by a single jeep.

The 'Land Mattress' as the field rocket was codenamed, had first been used by the Canadian Army in the clearing of Walcheren Island; there was some official reluctance to allow the weapon to be used at such an early stage in its development, a reluctance compounded by the fact that the impact fuze was officially described as 'grossly unsafe', but the Canadians overcame these objections and, manning the new weapon with rapidly re-trained ex-anti-aircraft gunners, found that it was a formidable bombardment device which terrified the enemy. And so Land Mattress joined the Pepper-Pot.

The assembly, emplacement and concealment of this vast collection of artillery in such a small area was a daunting task, made more difficult by traffic congestion, weather conditions, and the need to conceal the build-up from the German observation posts. Moreover the positioning of the guns was a small matter compared to the enormous task of bringing up and dumping half a million shells, a weight of about 11,000 tons. For it had been decided that surprise and fancy footwork had no place here; it was obvious to both sides what had to be done and where, and as General Horrocks said "There was no room for manoeuvre and no scope for cleverness; I had to blast my way through three defensive systems, the centre of which was the Siegfried Line". So the attack would be preceded by an enormous bombardment, followed by the classic rolling barrage to carry the infantry on to their objectives.

The bombardment was designed with three purposes; to neutralize all known German guns and mortars, to destroy all known headquarters and communications, and to neutralize localities in the infantry's line of advance. In addition the more prominent defensive works were singled out for special attention from the 8in guns and 240mm howitzers of the Super-Heavy Road Regiments. These would have their observers well forward and would take on these individual strongpoints by observed fire. This demanded daylight, and, as it happened, this demand fitted in well with other aspects of the plan. It was thus decided to make H-Hour 1030hrs on 8 February, 1945, and the preliminary bombardment would begin at 0500hrs.

Duly at 0500 the 1050 guns opened fire with a thundering crash which could be heard for many miles. Their object was to subject every known enemy location, HQ, defense post or communications line to at least six tons of high explosive. At the same time the multitude of weapons in the Pepper-Pot opened fire and drenched the defenders in the first line so as to prevent them making any kind of movement, be it reconnaissance, supply, reinforcement.

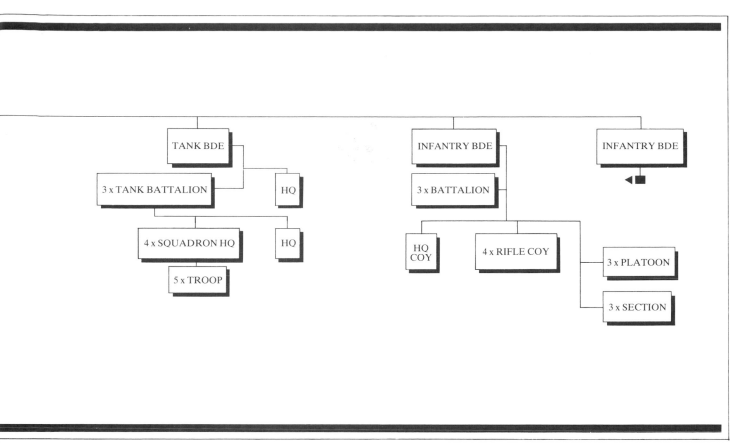

The barrage continues

Switching from target to target the bombardment kept going, building up in intensity, until 0730hrs when every gun stopped and a sudden silence reigned. Then came a gently popping and banging as a few selected guns fired a thick smoke screen in front of the German first line. Now, a smoke screen 13,500 yards long is a remarkable sight, especially if you have just sat through two and a half hours of constant bombardment, because it usually portends a forthcoming attack, and the natural reaction of the Germans was to get to their fire positions, open fire with their machine guns, and call for their defensive artillery in order to catch the attack before it got too close.

Which is precisely what the Allied troops were waiting for; not one infantrymen had moved — indeed most of them were nowhere near their start lines. As the smokescreen wafted and swirled across the silent battlefield, the sound of German firing began to build up as the defenders went about their prepared defensive plans. And behind the Allied lines were teams of sound-ranging experts, flash-spotting experts, ground radar

A COMMANDER'S VIEW OF THE EFFECT OF A CHURCHILL CROCODILE FLAME GUN, DIRECTED AGAINST A HOUSE ON THE ROAD TO CLEVE. WITH A COMBINATION OF HEAVY BOMBARDMENT FROM THE AIR AND LAND THE BEAUTIFUL OLD TOWN OF CLEVE WAS ALMOST TOTALLY DESTROYED.

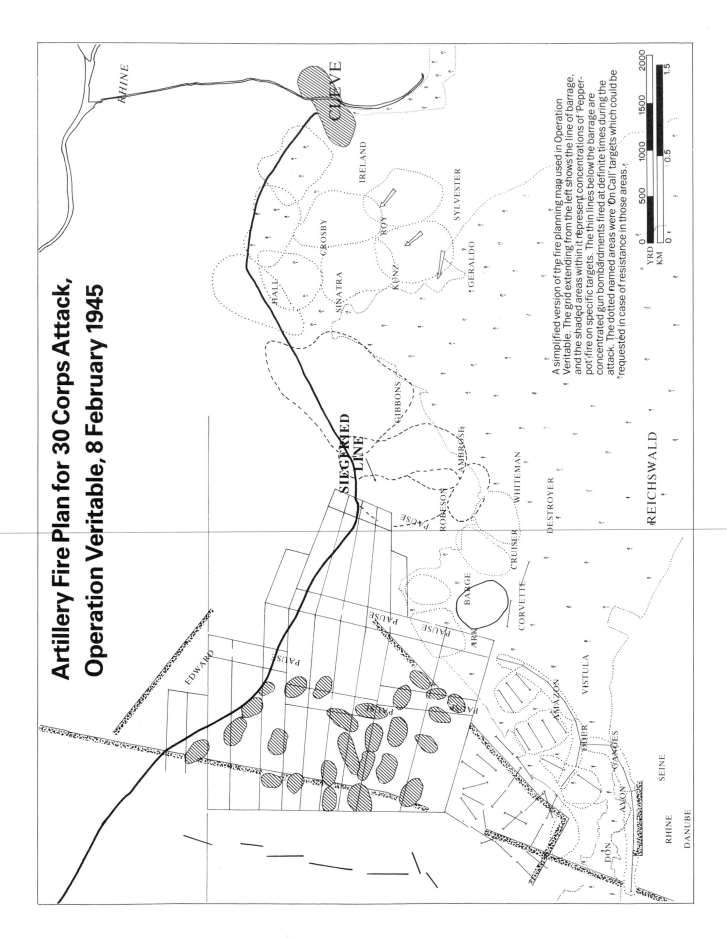

Artillery Fire Plan for 30 Corps Attack, Operation Veritable, 8 February 1945

A simplified version of the fire planning map used in Operation Veritable. The grid extending from the left shows the line of barrage, and the shaded areas within it represent concentrations of 'Pepperpot' fire on specific targets. The thin lines below the barrage are concentrated gun bombardments fired at definite times during the attack. The dotted named areas were 'On Call' targets which could be requested in case of resistance in those areas.

sets, mortar-locating radar sets and sundry other observation systems, noting down everything which fired. Their observations were rapidly converted into information on fresh targets for the guns, and at 0730 the bombardment began once again, with those defensive posts which had revealed their positions now included in the list of targets. At 0800hrs the Pepper-Pot chimed in once more, and kept up its work until 1015hrs.

At 0920 the bombardment slackened very slightly as some of the guns turned to firing the first line of the corps barrage, engaging it with a mixture of high explosive and smoke shells. This was fired at a slow rate and continued for 70 minutes. As the time grew closer to H-Hour so more and more guns switched from their bombardment tasks to the barrage line, until by 1030hrs over 500 guns were firing on a line about 4000 yards wide and 500 yards deep, and behind this dense screen the assault formed up.

The infantry move forward

At 1030hrs the barrage made its first lift; this meant that the guns firing on the rearmost line stopped, re-laid, and began firing ahead of the front of the 500-yard belt; they would then be followed by the next line stopping and leapfrogging, and the whole operation was timed so that the 500-yard belt of shells advanced at a rate of 300 yards every 12 minutes. As the line closest to the infantry stopped, so selected guns would fire rounds of yellow smoke into the barrage to indicate to the infantry that they could begin moving up, since the rear edge of the barrage was now free of high explosive shells. And as the first of these yellow markers blossomed, so moved the 53rd (Welsh) Division, the 15th (Scottish) Division, and the 2nd Canadian Division. The 51st (Highland) Division were attacking to the south and elected not to use a barrage but to rely upon a series of precisely-timed concentrations of fire on specified targets to blast them into their objective. But whether they walked behind a barrage or a concentration, they walked behind an impressive weight of bursting high explosive.

The result had some points of resemblance with the great barrages of the First World War; the shellfire kept the defenders out of action, but the result of the bursting high explosive on the thawing and rain-soaked ground was to churn it into a landscape of mud in which the foot soldiers slipped and cursed their way forward, wheeled vehicles simply got stuck and tanks found hard going, some tanks even managing to become mired. Fortunately, the 79th Armoured Division — which we have previously met in these pages — was providing the support with its 'funnies', and these were almost entirely based on wide-tracked Churchill tanks which were virtually immune to mud. But apart from the mud, there was very little else to hold up the soldiers as they advanced behind the barrage.

As the advance arrived close to the first German defensive line, so the barrage came to a halt and

WHAT WAS LEFT OF CLEVE WHEN THE ROYAL AIR FORCE HAD FINISHED WITH IT. THIS PHOTOGRAPH APPEARS TO HAVE BEEN TAKEN SOME DAYS AFTER THE RAID AND AFTER THE ARMY HAD CLEARED SOME ROADWAYS THROUGH THE RUINS. MOVEMENT IN THE TOWN WAS IMPOSSIBLE IMMEDIATELY AFTER THE BOMBING.

continued to pound down upon the same spot for half an hour, giving the defenses a thorough treatment. At the end of the pause, the yellow smoke shells signalled the advance once more, the curtain of explosive rolled forward, and the flame-throwing tanks, supported by flail tanks to deal with any mines which had escaped the shellfire and bridging tanks to deal with the anti-tank ditches, surged forward to break through belts of wire which remained.

Now, it was revealed, some of the German mortar and artillery units had been endowed with more self-restraint than others and had not fallen into the dummy smoke-screen trap. These, which had so far escaped registration by Allied observers, now opened fire on their defensive tasks, seeking to catch the advancing infantry as they closed with the defensive line. But even this had been foreseen, and a number of heavy artillery regiments had been waiting for just this moment. As each German battery opened fire, so it was carefully registered by sound-ranging or flash-spotting techniques and counter-bombardment began as soon as their coordinates were sent to the gun batteries.

The barrage rolled and thundered on its ponderous way, steamrollering everything it found, until it reached the area of Frasselt and the Siegfried Line at about 1600hrs. Here, after another half-hour pause to thoroughly hammer this line and soften it up for the tanks, the barrage finally stopped. From this point on, support would be provided by concentrations of fire on to defensive localities, all pre-planned and given names or numbers, and called for by the advancing troops as and when they needed them, since the advance had now gone as far as could be reasonably expected in conformity with a timetable.

One of the defects of the barrages and fire-plans of the First World War was that they had had to be meticulously planned to carry the infantry all the way to their objective; and once the infantry set off, there was no further communication with them nor any hope of their being able to alter the fire plan. If they got out of step with the barrage, as they often did, then the battle went wrong. But in 1944, with radio communication, it was possible to amend a fire plan at short notice if the infantry lagged or found their advance could be made more quickly.

Nevertheless, the barrage had rolled them forward for something like 6km, and it was unreasonable to expect that the advance and the fireplan could be kept in synchrony for much longer. It was, therefore, much safer to allow the infantry and armor to move at whatever speed the situation dictated, merely saying to them 'Here are the places we think you may need artillery fire; if you do, say the code-word and it will arrive.'

In all, something like 6000 tons of shells had been fired during the day, and every unit had taken its objectives with little trouble. German artillery, except for a brief spasm of activity as the advance reached the first line, had never been troublesome, even though it had, at times, been quite severe until the counter-bombarding heavy guns set to work.

The value of research

One of the unusual features of Operation Veritable was that close on the heels of the advancing British and Canadian troops went an Operational Research team, to assess the effect of the artillery fire, hoping, perhaps, to find some evidence which would settle the weight-v-bang argument. In the immediate path of the barrage the defenses had 55 guns of various types, and examination showed that 28 of these had been destroyed and the remainder had been withdrawn during the battle. More revealing was the interrogation of prisoners.

They confirmed that within a short time of the start of the preliminary bombardment not a single telephone wire remained serviceable; no orders were received; officers were unable to get to their troops. And the final confirmation of the value of the artillery fire came when the casualties were studied; on the first day of Veritable the attackers captured 1115 prisoners for the loss of 349

THE CELEBRATED GERMAN 88MM ANTI-AIRCRAFT GUN EMPLACED IN THE ANTI-TANK ROLE. AN EXPOSED POSITION LIKE THIS IS STRICTLY AN EMERGENCY AFFAIR, BUT THE 88 WAS VERY FAST INTO ACTION AND OUT OF IT, AND A DETERMINED CREW COULD GIVE A PURSUER SOME NASTY SURPRISES. IN A GROSS PANIC, THE GUN COULD BE FIRED FROM ITS WHEELS WITH NO ILL-EFFECTS, AND THIS BECAME A USEFUL PRACTICE DURING AN ADVANCE.

CORPS SUPPORT ARTILLERY

THE BRITISH 7.2IN (183MM) HOWITZER, SEEN IN THE FIRING POSITION WITH ITS 200LB SHELL ON THE LOADING TRAY. THE 7.2IN WAS THE LARGEST BRITISH ARTILLERY PIECE TO SEE EXTENSIVE SERVICE; LARGER WEAPONS, SUCH AS THE 9.2IN AND 12IN HOWITZERS, HAD BEEN ABANDONED SINCE THEIR DESIGN DATED FROM THE FIRST WORLD WAR AND THEY WERE INCAPABLE OF BEING MOVED RAPIDLY ENOUGH FOR MODERN CONDITIONS. THE 7.2 CALIBER WAS SELECTED IN 1940 AS A MEANS OF UTILIZING OLD 8IN WEAPONS BY RE-BARRELLING THEM, AND THESE WERE ON TWO-WHEELED CARRIAGES WHICH WERE INCAPABLE OF ABSORBING THE IMMENSE RECOIL THRUST. THEY WERE EMPLACED WITH ENORMOUS WOODEN WEDGES BEHIND THE WHEELS, UP WHICH THE MOUNTING RECOILED, AND IF THE POSITIONING WAS FAULTY THE HOWITZER JUMPED CLEAN OVER THE TOP AND HAD TO BE MANHANDLED BACK INTO PLACE. THE WEAPON SHOWN HERE WAS THE MARK 6, A COMPLETELY NEW BARREL MOUNTED ON TO THE AMERICAN 155MM Z GUN CARRIAGE, NUMBERS OF WHICH WERE OBTAINED VIA LEND-LEASE. IT HAD BETTER MOBILITY AND A MAXIMUM RANGE OF 17,900M. THE 7.2IN HOWITZERS WITH 21ST ARMY GROUP FIRED A TOTAL OF 159,898 SHELLS DURING THE NW EUROPE CAMPAIGN.

men, a ratio of 3.2 to 1. When it is considered that the attack is usually expected to lose heavily when going against prepared positions of this type, these figures seemed to justify the expenditure of ammunition.

The question at the heart of the argument was 'Is this weight of fire justified?' The artillery had covered the area with something like 2500 shells per square kilometer per hour, a rate which demanded an enormous concentration of equipment, ammunition and manpower. Might not the same effect be obtained with a lesser weight? Careful analysis suggested that there was, indeed, an upper limit to artillery saturation of something in the order of 100 tons per kilometer per hour, above which nothing was gained. The word 'overkill' had not, then, been coined, but the suggestion was there all the same. By this stage of the war, however, there were to be few opportunities left to make such analyses, but there were suggestions that the Pepper-Pot system was as effective a way of delivering suppressive fire as the more formal type of artillery and needed a lesser weight of ammunition to obtain the same results.

A noticeable feature of Veritable was that there were no cases of the enemy being demoralized by the force of the artillery fire, even though, as we know, some of the units in the German line of battle were scarcely at the peak of physical condition. Prior to Veritable, back in November 1944, the British 43rd (Wessex) Division had mounted a small attack on Geilenkirchen. One of the objectives was the village of Bauchem, which was to be assaulted by the 5th Battalion of the Dorset Regiment.

Bauchem was defended by about 150 men in entrenched positions around the village, and they were bombarded for ten minutes by artillery, delivering 49 tons of shells in that time. Then, without a pause, mortars opened fire for three hours, dumping 44 tons of bombs, plus the addition of a small Pepper-Pot from 20mm, 40mm and 75mm guns — another 19 tons of ammunition — and finally the artillery weighed in again for a further half hour, delivering 73 tons. The whole bombardment added up to 185 tons of projectiles falling in three and three-quarter hours, averaging 1.8 tons on every 100-yard square in the defended area. When the attack went in there was absolutely no resistance by the defenders; the Dorsets reported that when they reached the German positions, the enemy were 'absolutely yellow-coloured' from shock, and prisoners said that they were completely overwhelmed by a

A STURMGEWEHR ASSAULT GUN EMERGES FROM AN AMBUSH POSITION ALONGSIDE A COUNTRY ROAD. THESE ASSAULT GUNS WERE MADE IN GREAT NUMBERS, SINCE THEY WERE CHEAPER AND QUICKER TO BUILD THAN TANKS AND THEY COULD CARRY A HEAVIER GUN THAN A COMPARABLE SIZE OF TANK. THIS 'STUG' COULD FUNCTION AS A DIRECT SUPPORT GUN FOR ADVANCING INFANTRY OR, AS HERE, IT COULD BE EMPLACED IN AN AMBUSH POSITION AS A TANK DESTROYER. THE LONG 75MM GUN WAS A VERY ACCURATE AND POWERFUL ANTI-ARMOR WEAPON, AND IT COULD ALSO FIRE HIGH EXPLOSIVE AND SMOKE SHELLS TO GIVE BASIC TACTICAL SUPPORT FOR GROUND TROOPS.

feeling of helplessness. The assaulting troops suffered only three casualties in this action, while the defenders had a casualty rate of about 14 percent. It was possibly the only recorded case in Northwest Europe of complete demoralization from artillery fire.

The subsequent course of Veritable followed the plan but without the ease of the first day; the key to the whole affair was a high point called Nutterden, and with this secured it would be possible to allow Canadian troops in amphibious vehicles to move through the flooded polder to outflank the German positions. The 15th Scottish took the feature in a close race with the German 7 Parachute Division, but thereafter the advance slowed simply because of traffic congestion in the mud and filth of the forest area. Cleve, hammered to the ground, held up the advance for a critical period, which allowed the Germans to make some moves to regroup and consolidate, and from then on Veritable

became a vicious slogging match, eventually won when 43rd Wessex Division broke out of Cleve on 12 February and made for Goch, fighting every inch of the way. Goch fell on 21 February to mark the end of Veritable, but the interest for us has been solely the first day and the action of the artillery in, as Horrocks said, 'blasting a way through'.

The lessons

Very few lessons, other than the tentative conclusions about weight of fire which the Operational Research teams broached, came out of Veritable for the artillery. It was, as I said at the beginning, the zenith of the Royal Artillery's system which had been developed throughout the course of the war, and there was very little left for them to learn. Such minor matters as ammunition supply and dumping were open to criticism, but this was more a comment upon the extremely restricted area from which they had to operate than a criticism of the system.

The organization which provided the artillery support for Veritable, and one or two subsequent operations in Germany such as the Rhine Crossing, no longer exists; it could exist, if there was the artillery equipment to warrant it, though its form would be somewhat different due to modern communications and data transmission systems. But modern warfare is unlikely to demand such concentrations of artillery, if only because there are other weapons which can produce the necessary effect without the huge infrastructure demanded in 1944.

INDEX